Nina Vale

Divine Duality
Understanding the God and Goddess in Wicca

Copyright © 2024 By L. A. Santos
All rights reserved.
No part of this book may be reproduced in any form or by any means without written permission from the copyright holder.
Cover image © Booklas.com
Review by Marco Avelar
Graphic design by Tania Navarro
Layout by Paulo Xavier
All rights reserved to:
L. A. Santos
Category: Religion/Wicca/ Witchcraft

Summary

Prologue 5
Chapter 1 Natural Religion 7
Chapter 2 Ancient Traditions 11
Chapter 3 Divine Polarity 16
Chapter 4 The Threefold Law 21
Chapter 5 The Wheel of Life 26
Chapter 6 The Five Elements 31
Chapter 7 Elemental Kingdom 37
Chapter 8 Vital Energy 42
Chapter 9 Sacred Space 48
Chapter 10 Personal Altar 53
Chapter 11 Sacred Tools 58
Chapter 12 Ritual Garments 63
Chapter 13 Triple Goddess 68
Chapter 14 Horned God 73
Chapter 15 Divine Pantheons 78
Chapter 16 Spirit Guardians 84
Chapter 17 Protective Circle 89
Chapter 18 Power of Colors 94
Chapter 19 Magical Herbs 99
Chapter 20 Precious Stones 104
Chapter 21 Natural Meditation 110
Chapter 22 Creative Visualization 116
Chapter 23 Sacred Chants 121

Chapter 24 Ritual Dances	126
Chapter 25 Waxing Moon	131
Chapter 26 Full Moon	137
Chapter 27 Waning Moon	142
Chapter 28 New Moon	147
Chapter 29 Harvest Festivals	152
Chapter 30 Light Festivals	157
Chapter 31 Life Festivals	160
Chapter 32 Transformation Festivals	166
Chapter 33 Candle Magic	171
Chapter 34 Knot Magic	176
Chapter 35 Mirror Magic	181
Chapter 36 Sigil Magic	187
Chapter 37 Sacred Ogham	192
Chapter 38 Ancient Runes	197
Chapter 39 Black Mirror	202
Chapter 40 Oracular Herbology	207
Chapter 41 Wiccan Totemism	212
Chapter 42 Lunar Magic	218
Chapter 43 Solar Magic	223
Chapter 44 Ancestral Magic	228
Chapter 45 Power Rituals	234
Chapter 46 Inner Circles	240
Chapter 47 Personal Initiation	246
Chapter 48 Wiccan Priesthood	251
Chapter 49 Spiritual Legacy	257
Epilogue	263

Prologue

Within every human being pulses an ancient connection to nature and the cosmos, a link that has been forgotten, yet never erased. This book is not merely an invitation; it is a calling. A calling for you to awaken your dormant essence, to embrace the energies of the Earth, the sky, and all that exists between them. There is a world beyond the visible, a web that intertwines everything that breathes and moves. On this path, which unfolds before your eyes, every leaf, every stone, every river reveals secrets long held—a timeless wisdom that beats and vibrates.

The elements are living forces, entities that speak not through words but through a subtle touch on your soul, asking to be honored. In Wicca, this force is not distant; it pulses in all things natural, in the firm ground beneath you and in the waters that purify you. The call of Wicca is a call back to the deepest roots of existence, where every act you take reverberates and transforms the world around you. If you hear this call, you will sense that the journey this book offers is meant for you—and for you alone.

Throughout these pages, you will not find rigid rules or doctrines that limit the spirit. On the contrary, you will find the freedom to live and feel deeply, embracing the changes that the universe brings. This book is a guide, a guardian of rituals that honor the Earth and the cycles of the year. It invites you to walk with renewed purpose, to understand that your impact on the world is not mere chance, but part of a cosmic dance. Here, each word will lead you deeper, awakening a different perception of the everyday and a harmony that can only be found when living in tune with the universe.

Imagine a circle, traced with the intention and respect that the universe demands. This circle is your sanctuary, a space where the veil between worlds is thin, where the spiritual and the physical meet. As you read this book, you are stepping into this sacred space, prepared to receive what the divine wishes to share with you. The primordial energies of the elements—Earth, Air, Fire, Water, and Spirit—await recognition and honor from you, so that together they may transform your reality into a reflection of universal harmony.

As you dive into the teachings of this book, you will find yourself on a path of growth and self-discovery. The secrets of natural forces, the cycles of life, and the energies of each season will reveal themselves not only as external phenomena but as parts of yourself. With each page, you will come to understand that wisdom is not distant but at the very heart of nature and that you are part of this divine totality. The universe is a mirror, and as you explore this book, you will perceive that the reflection it reveals is your own.

As you embark on this reading, feel the calling to open your perception and allow this ancient knowledge to manifest within you. Allow yourself to be transformed, to understand that divine duality—the balance between masculine and feminine, light and shadow—is a living, pulsating truth. The cosmic dance of opposites and complements does not happen outside you; it is your very being. Every word here is a key to unlock your hidden potential, guiding you to a state of union with the whole.

Thus, this book is a portal. A portal to a more authentic way of being, to a life aligned with the sacred that permeates each moment. By opening these pages, you choose to answer the call. Prepare yourself, for this journey will lead you to the core of your being, where the material and spiritual worlds meet, and where sacred knowledge awaits you. This book is not just a read; it is an awakening.

Chapter 1
Natural Religion

In the stillness of a forest at dawn, with the first light slipping between ancient trees and the delicate rustle of life beginning to stir, one might sense the presence of something timeless, something deeply sacred. For those who follow the Wiccan path, this moment, this connection to nature, is not merely an appreciation for beauty—it is a fundamental part of their belief, a devotion to a religion that sees the natural world as a reflection of the divine. Wicca, a nature-based spiritual tradition, recognizes the earth as a living, breathing entity, and this reverence underpins every ritual, every invocation, and every moment of quiet contemplation.

In a world that rushes forward with the pulse of technology and endless data, the allure of Wicca lies in its simplicity, its rootedness in ancient rhythms, and its insistence on honoring the cycles of nature. Unlike many structured religions, Wicca does not mandate rigid doctrines or distant deities. Instead, it offers a way of being—a path to walk in harmony with nature, to see divinity in every leaf, every river, and every star.

This path is one of personal responsibility and spiritual exploration. There are no grand cathedrals, no prophets to dictate commandments; rather, there are forests, stones, sacred waters, and the moon's light to guide the way. For Wiccans, the natural world is the ultimate temple, and each individual is both the seeker and the sacred.

To understand Wicca is to understand its roots in ancient pagan traditions, where communities lived in concert with the land, depending on its bounty and respecting its power. These early societies acknowledged that the earth and sky, the sun and moon, held mysteries beyond human comprehension, mysteries that could only be honored through reverence and ritual. Modern Wicca draws upon this heritage, embracing the natural cycles of life, death, and rebirth as fundamental truths. Each cycle, each turning of the seasons, mirrors the journey of the human spirit—a reminder that we, too, are bound to the earth and to each other.

In Wicca, nature itself is divine, and every element of the natural world holds spiritual significance. The elements—earth, air, fire, water, and spirit—each represent a fundamental aspect of existence, reflecting both the physical and the mystical. Wiccan practitioners work with these elements, seeking balance and understanding, honoring the interconnected web of life that binds all beings. The earth is more than soil and stone; it is a grounding force, a source of sustenance and stability. The air, ethereal and invisible, carries inspiration and the breath of life. Fire, powerful and transformative, symbolizes passion and the spark of creativity. Water, with its gentle flow and profound depth, embodies emotion and intuition. And spirit, the intangible force that unites all things, is the essence of life itself.

Through ritual, Wiccans celebrate these elements and the cycles of nature. The phases of the moon, the solstices, and the equinoxes become sacred times of reflection and renewal. These rituals are both personal and communal acts, moments to pause and realign with the natural world. A Wiccan ritual may be as simple as lighting a candle in gratitude for the day's blessings, or as elaborate as a seasonal gathering where the community honors the turning of the Wheel of the Year. Each act, each word spoken, is a reminder of the sacredness of life and the divine presence in all things.

In recent decades, Wicca has found a place in the hearts of those seeking an alternative to conventional religion, those disillusioned by dogma or seeking a personal, experiential connection with the divine. This growing interest in Wicca is more than a trend; it is a reflection of a profound spiritual hunger, a yearning for a way of being that is connected, mindful, and respectful of the earth. As environmental crises and social upheavals challenge modern societies, Wicca offers a path that is both ancient and refreshingly modern, a way to live in harmony with nature and to seek spiritual fulfillment in a world that often feels chaotic and disconnected.

The Wiccan path is open and adaptable, welcoming those who wish to walk it in their own way. There are no strict rules or fixed doctrines; instead, Wicca emphasizes individual experience and personal growth. The Wiccan Rede, a guiding principle for practitioners, is simply, "An it harm none, do what ye will." This phrase captures the essence of Wiccan ethics: a commitment to harm none, to live with integrity, and to respect the free will of all beings. It is a reminder that true power lies not in control or dominance, but in harmony and compassion.

This principle of "harm none" extends beyond human relationships to encompass all of life. Wicca teaches that all beings are interconnected, and that our actions have consequences, not just for ourselves but for the world around us. This understanding is the foundation of the Threefold Law, a belief that whatever energy one puts into the world—whether positive or negative—will return threefold. Thus, Wiccans are encouraged to act with mindfulness and integrity, knowing that their choices ripple out into the universe.

For those new to Wicca, the first steps on this path may feel both exhilarating and daunting. The world of spells, rituals, and sacred symbols is rich with tradition and meaning, yet Wicca remains a deeply personal journey, one where each individual must find their own connection to the divine. There are no authoritative texts or singular paths; instead, there are countless books, teachers, and communities, each offering their own interpretations and insights.

Some may begin their practice alone, in quiet reflection beneath the open sky or with a simple altar in their home. Others may find their way through a coven, a community of like-minded individuals who gather to share knowledge, perform rituals, and support one another on their spiritual journeys. Both paths are valid, for Wicca honors the uniqueness of each individual's experience and encourages exploration and growth.

As practitioners deepen their connection to Wicca, they often find that it becomes more than a religion; it becomes a way of life. The cycles of the moon, the change of the seasons, and the beauty of the natural world become sacred touchstones, reminders of the divine presence in all things. Wicca teaches that the earth is alive and that we are a part of this living tapestry, not separate from it. This understanding fosters a profound sense of responsibility—to live lightly upon the earth, to respect its creatures, and to honor its rhythms.

In many ways, Wicca is a call to return to an ancient wisdom, to reclaim a way of being that modern society has forgotten. It is a call to slow down, to listen to the whispers of the wind and the songs of the birds, to feel the earth beneath one's feet and to recognize the sacred in all things. For those who hear this call, the Wiccan path offers not only a spiritual practice but a way to live in harmony with the world.

The relevance of Wicca in the modern world lies in its simplicity and its profound respect for life. It is a reminder that spirituality need not be complex or grandiose; it can be found in the quiet moments, in the natural world, and in the connections we share with one another. Wicca teaches that each person has the power to shape their own path, to seek the divine in their own way, and to live with kindness and respect for all beings.

In a world that often feels fragmented and disconnected, the Wiccan path offers a vision of wholeness, of interconnectedness, and of deep, abiding respect for the earth. It is a path that honors diversity, embraces individuality, and celebrates the beauty of the natural world. For those who choose to walk this path, Wicca is more than a religion—it is a way of being, a sacred journey through the ever-turning cycles of life.

Chapter 2
Ancient Traditions

The roots of Wicca stretch deep into the rich soil of ancient practices and beliefs, reaching back through millennia to touch the rituals and myths of early human civilization. Wicca is often considered a modern religion, but to understand it fully, one must explore the echoes of pre-Christian, pagan traditions that have shaped its essence. This journey backward reveals a web of beliefs that, despite being scattered across different lands and peoples, all share a profound reverence for nature, a sacred respect for the cycles of life and death, and an intricate tapestry of myth and magic. The Wiccan path, as it exists today, is woven from these ancient threads, bringing forth a legacy that has traveled through time, evolving yet staying true to its primal spirit.

Across the ancient world, in societies as far-reaching as the Egyptians, Greeks, Celts, and Norse, there existed practices and beliefs that centered around natural forces, divine archetypes, and cosmic cycles. The land itself was seen as imbued with spiritual significance, each mountain, river, and grove holding a life force, a spirit that demanded respect and could offer blessings. Sacred groves were not merely clusters of trees; they were places where one could feel the breath of the gods, hear their whispers, and seek their guidance. Temples, when built, were dedicated to gods and goddesses who represented the elements, the seasons, the harvest, the storms, and the mysteries of life and death.

The Wiccan tradition draws inspiration from these rich histories, and though it cannot claim direct lineage from them, it is a conscious reconstruction, an intentional revival of what these traditions valued and celebrated. The Celtic people, who inhabited large parts of Europe and Britain, are especially significant in the tapestry of Wicca's heritage. Their reverence for the earth, belief in the otherworldly realms, and elaborate rituals mark a tradition that mirrored many of Wicca's core values. For the Celts, nature was not merely scenery but a living, breathing force, imbued with spirits that needed to be honored and placated. Rituals often took place in sacred groves, where the boundaries between the human and spirit worlds were thin, and communication with the unseen could occur.

The Druids, the priestly class among the Celts, are often remembered as wise, mystical figures, guardians of ancient knowledge, and keepers of sacred rites. They did not write down their teachings, preferring oral transmission, a practice that shrouded their wisdom in secrecy but also protected it from outside interference. They were healers, diviners, and counselors, deeply connected to the cycles of the moon and sun, guiding their people with the knowledge of herbs, the stars, and the language of the elements. In many ways, the spirit of the Druidic practices lives on in modern Wicca, particularly in its reverence for nature, its emphasis on oral traditions, and its respect for ritual as a way of connecting with the divine.

In ancient Greece, too, one finds threads that align with Wiccan beliefs. The Greeks held a complex pantheon of deities, each embodying specific aspects of life and nature. The Greek mystery religions, such as the Eleusinian Mysteries, centered around death, rebirth, and initiation, themes that resonate within Wicca's understanding of the cycles of life. These mysteries offered a path to divine knowledge and transformation through symbolic rituals, designed not just to inform but to evoke profound inner experiences. They emphasized the descent into darkness followed by renewal, a journey mirrored in Wiccan celebrations of the Wheel of the Year, where each season marks a phase in the cycle of life, death, and rebirth.

Similarly, the Norse traditions bring forth another layer of depth to the Wiccan practice. The Norse cosmology, with its nine realms interconnected by the World Tree, Yggdrasil, presents a worldview where all things are bound by a cosmic order, where humans, gods, and nature are interwoven. Norse mythology is filled with powerful symbols and archetypes—the wise god Odin, who sacrifices himself to gain knowledge of the runes; the goddess Freyja, associated with love, magic, and death; and the cycle of Ragnarok, a tale of destruction followed by renewal. This reverence for cycles, and the belief that life is a web of interconnected energies, reflects a perspective that resonates strongly within Wicca, which also acknowledges the cycles of destruction and renewal as essential to the universe's balance.

While the roots of Wicca reach back to these ancient traditions, the Wiccan movement as we recognize it today began to take shape in the mid-20th century, through the work of figures like Gerald Gardner, an Englishman who is often considered the father of modern Wicca. Gardner, an anthropologist and folklorist, became fascinated by the remnants of British folk magic, and after World War II, he began to openly practice and promote a form of witchcraft he called "Wicca." Gardner claimed that Wicca was an ancient religion, secretly preserved through generations of covens that had managed to survive despite centuries of persecution. Whether or not this claim holds historical truth, Gardner's influence was profound, and his writings laid the foundation for Wicca as a cohesive, organized tradition.

Gardner's Wicca was deeply influenced by ceremonial magic, folk traditions, and the writings of early 20th-century occultists, such as Aleister Crowley and Margaret Murray. Murray, a British anthropologist, wrote about the concept of a "witch-cult" in Europe, positing that the people accused of witchcraft during the Inquisition were actually practitioners of an ancient fertility religion. Although Murray's theories have largely been discredited by modern scholars, her work captured the imagination of Gardner and others who sought to reconnect with what they saw as Europe's lost pagan heritage. Wicca, in many ways, became a synthesis of these historical influences, tempered by Gardner's own innovations and interpretations.

Following Gardner, other influential figures contributed to the growth and evolution of Wicca. Doreen Valiente, often called the "Mother of Modern Witchcraft," was one of Gardner's early followers and a talented poet. She helped refine Gardner's rituals, imbuing them with a more poetic and spiritual tone, and her contributions became central to the Wiccan liturgy. Together, Gardner and Valiente crafted rituals, spells, and invocations that would become the backbone of the Wiccan tradition, preserving the spirit of ancient paganism while adapting it to a modern world.

As Wicca spread beyond Britain and into the United States and other parts of the world, it began to diversify, developing different traditions and schools of thought. Alexandrian Wicca, founded by Alex Sanders, was an offshoot that placed a stronger emphasis on ceremonial magic and structure. Meanwhile, other branches, like Dianic Wicca, emerged, celebrating the divine feminine and emphasizing the worship of the Goddess alone. Eclectic Wicca, a more flexible and individualistic approach, allowed practitioners to draw from multiple sources, creating personalized practices that honored the unique spiritual path of each individual.

This diversity within Wicca reflects the pluralism of its ancient sources, where different cultures, deities, and rituals coexisted and sometimes intermingled. In Wicca, there is a respect for individuality and a recognition that each person's path may be different. For some, Wicca may involve devotion to specific deities from the Celtic or Norse pantheons; for others, it may be a more generalized practice centered on the Goddess and the God, or the elemental forces. This flexibility is one of Wicca's strengths, allowing it to remain a vibrant, adaptable spiritual path that can meet the needs of modern seekers.

The journey of Wicca from ancient traditions to a modern religion is not one of strict lineage or uninterrupted transmission. Rather, it is a revival, a reimagining of old wisdom for a new age. In a way, Wicca honors not only the ancient gods and spirits but also the resilience of the human spirit to seek meaning, to reforge connections with the past, and to create new expressions of the sacred. It is a reminder that spirituality is not stagnant but constantly evolving, just as the earth itself is in a state of perpetual change.

Today, Wicca continues to grow and evolve, drawing new generations of practitioners who feel the call of the earth, who seek a spirituality that is grounded in nature and respects the ancient wisdom of the past. While modern Wicca may differ from the practices of the Celts, Greeks, or Norse, it carries forward their reverence for the cycles of life, the power of ritual, and the belief in the interconnectedness of all things. Wicca is, in essence, a bridge between the ancient and the modern, a way for those in the present to connect with the primal energies of the earth and to honor the mysteries of existence.

In a world that often seems to have lost touch with its spiritual roots, Wicca offers a return to simplicity, a call to remember the old ways, and to celebrate life in all its forms. It is a reminder that the sacred is not found only in the heavens but also in the earth beneath our feet, the wind in the trees, and the light of the moon. The Wiccan path, informed by ancient traditions, invites each practitioner to walk this path with respect, humility, and a deep sense of wonder. As each Wiccan looks to the past, they also shape the future, carrying forward a legacy that honors both the ancient and the eternal.

Chapter 3
Divine Polarity

In the heart of Wiccan belief lies a profound reverence for balance—a cosmic dance between complementary forces, where light and dark, masculine and feminine, birth and death, merge into a harmonious whole. This duality is not simply a dichotomy but a reflection of the divine essence itself, which manifests as two interconnected aspects: the Goddess and the God. In Wicca, this concept of divine polarity—the sacred union of masculine and feminine energies—provides the foundation for understanding the nature of existence, the rhythms of nature, and the mysteries of the self.

The Goddess and the God are not merely figures in a pantheon; they are embodiments of life's dual forces, each holding equal importance and strength. This sacred pair represents an intricate web of balance, embodying the natural cycles and energies that animate the world. While the Goddess encompasses the mysteries of birth, creation, and nurturing, the God embodies strength, protection, and transformation. Their partnership is not hierarchical but deeply interwoven, reflecting an equality and interdependence that transcends any singular identity. Together, they are the primal powers from which all life flows, the original duality that shapes the cosmos.

To grasp the depth of divine polarity in Wiccan thought, one must look first to the Goddess, often seen as the primary deity, especially within feminist branches of Wicca where her worship is central. She is the Great Mother, the source of life, and the spirit of nature itself. As Maiden, Mother, and Crone, she holds the cycle of life within her, symbolizing youth, maturity, and wisdom. Her energy is felt in the blooming of flowers, the nurturing rain, and the wisdom of the old growth forests. The moon is her symbol, marking her phases and lighting her path as she moves through each aspect of herself. She is the queen of both life and death, guiding souls in birth and holding them in death, a reminder that creation and destruction are eternally bound.

The God, equally integral to Wiccan worship, represents the spark of life and the force of the sun. As the Lord of the Animals, he is both hunter and protector, embodying the untamed vitality of nature. He is often depicted with antlers or horns, symbols of his wild, primal nature and his deep connection to the animal kingdom. His power is transformative, linked to the energy of fire and the cycles of change. Just as the Goddess is associated with the moon, the God finds his resonance with the sun, which grows and wanes in strength throughout the year. His life unfolds in seasonal rhythms, born anew at the winter solstice, growing in strength through spring, and reaching his peak at the summer solstice, only to gradually return to the shadow until his rebirth. This eternal cycle of death and rebirth mirrors the changing seasons, the planting and harvest cycles, and the ebb and flow of life.

In Wiccan rituals, this union of the Goddess and the God is celebrated as the Great Rite, a sacred act symbolizing the unity of masculine and feminine energies. The Great Rite is more than a ritual act; it is a symbolic expression of the fundamental unity of opposites, an acknowledgment of the essential connection between all forms of life. In its symbolic form, the Great Rite is often performed by placing a ritual blade, representing the God, into a chalice, representing the Goddess. This act represents creation and the flow of life that arises from the balance of these forces. In doing so, Wiccans honor the divine polarity as a source of generative power, a spiritual and mystical bond that sustains the universe.

This concept of divine polarity reaches far beyond the mere roles of male and female. It is not a simplistic division but an understanding that all beings contain within them both masculine and feminine energies. In Wiccan thought, everyone has access to these qualities and can draw upon them in their spiritual practices. The Goddess and the God do not impose rigid definitions but encourage an exploration of these energies as they exist within each person. Masculine energy can be nurturing, just as feminine energy can be fierce and protective. These energies ebb and flow, shifting in response to the rhythms of nature and the inner life of each practitioner.

The relationship between the Goddess and the God also mirrors the ancient concept of duality found in many spiritual traditions. Like the Taoist yin and yang, these energies are complementary rather than opposing. Just as darkness gives way to light and winter to spring, the Goddess and the God coexist in a perpetual, balanced cycle. This interplay is a reminder that all things are connected and that life itself is born from the harmonious dance of opposites. For Wiccans, this understanding brings a profound sense of peace and purpose, for within the cycles of nature and the union of the divine lies the secret to harmony, both within oneself and with the universe.

In Wiccan seasonal observances, the relationship between the Goddess and the God is celebrated through the Wheel of the Year. The Wheel marks the turning points of nature, each festival embodying a stage in their mythic journey. The Sabbats, or seasonal celebrations, tell the story of their love, separation, death, and reunion—a timeless tale that reflects the changing energies of the earth. At Samhain, the God descends into the underworld, leaving the earth in the embrace of darkness. The Goddess, as the Crone, mourns his passing, holding the wisdom of the cycle and awaiting his rebirth. At Yule, the winter solstice, the God is reborn, bringing light and hope to the world once more. This cyclical story continues, with each Sabbat celebrating a phase in their journey together, a journey that mirrors the path of nature itself.

Through these seasonal rites, Wiccans experience the divine polarity not as a distant myth but as a living, dynamic force that flows through the world and within themselves. In the warmth of Beltane, where the God reaches his fullness and joins with the Goddess, practitioners celebrate fertility, creativity, and the joy of life. This celebration is a reminder of the sacred union, a time to honor the strength and beauty of both energies coming together in celebration of life's abundance. By partaking in these rituals, Wiccans not only pay homage to the Goddess and the God but also affirm their own place within the natural order, recognizing themselves as both products and participants of this divine cycle.

This duality offers a profound template for understanding the nature of spiritual growth. The Goddess teaches lessons of intuition, patience, and reflection, urging Wiccans to look within, to listen to the quiet voice of the heart, and to trust in the wisdom of the soul. Her cycles of waxing and waning, embodied by the moon, encourage practitioners to recognize their own internal rhythms, to embrace both light and shadow within themselves. The God, with his dynamic energy, inspires courage, transformation, and a willingness to engage with life's challenges. He represents the outward journey, the call to explore, to create, and to seek purpose in the world.

The dynamic between these two deities also invites Wiccans to cultivate balance within their lives, to integrate both reflection and action, intuition and intellect, softness and strength. In times of inner conflict or difficulty, Wiccans may call upon the Goddess for guidance, seeking comfort in her nurturing presence, or they may turn to the God for strength, drawing upon his energy to face their challenges with courage. This flexibility, this ability to turn to different aspects of the divine as needed, reflects the Wiccan belief that both energies are equally available and essential for a balanced, meaningful life.

The idea of divine polarity also shapes Wiccan relationships with others. Just as the Goddess and the God embody unity and mutual respect, Wiccans strive to cultivate relationships that reflect these values. Whether in friendships, romantic partnerships, or coven relationships, the ideal is one of balance, respect, and harmony. Just as no one force dominates in the natural world, no single individual should seek to control or overshadow others. Instead, Wiccan relationships are seen as partnerships, each person contributing their unique energy, wisdom, and gifts to a greater whole.

For many, the Goddess and the God are more than archetypes or symbolic figures; they are felt as real, personal presences. Through ritual, meditation, and personal practice, practitioners often establish a deep and intimate connection with these deities, experiencing their love, guidance, and protection in tangible ways. The Goddess and the God are seen as benevolent forces, always present and ready to support their followers in times of need. This connection provides comfort and reassurance, a reminder that the divine is always near, offering strength, wisdom, and love.

To honor the Goddess and the God is to honor the divine within oneself and within all of life. Wicca teaches that each person is a reflection of these sacred energies, that the Goddess and the God dwell within, guiding and inspiring from the heart of each individual. Through their worship, Wiccans seek not only to connect with these divine forces but to cultivate their own potential, to bring forth their own inner goddess or god, and to live in harmony with the world around them. In this way, divine polarity is not a distant concept but a living, breathing reality—a reminder that each soul carries within it the seeds of creation, and that each person is a unique, sacred expression of the universe.

Chapter 4
The Threefold Law

Within Wicca, the principle of the Threefold Law serves as a moral compass, guiding practitioners toward ethical choices and a mindful way of life. This foundational concept, often encapsulated in the phrase "what you send out returns to you threefold," embodies the Wiccan understanding of karma, justice, and personal responsibility. Unlike conventional views of morality, which are often based on commandments or external rules, the Threefold Law invites Wiccans to consider the energetic consequences of their actions on a profound level. It suggests that every thought, word, and deed carries a ripple of energy into the world, energy that eventually finds its way back to the source—magnified.

The Threefold Law operates on the principle that the universe functions as an interconnected web, where every action influences the whole. When a Wiccan sends out positive energy—whether through kindness, healing, or selfless action—that energy circulates and eventually returns with greater force. Similarly, negative energy, such as harm, deception, or ill will, creates an echo that also comes back to the individual, often amplified by threefold. This principle is not merely punitive but educational, emphasizing growth and the understanding that our choices, like seeds planted in fertile soil, grow into powerful effects that shape our lives and the world around us.

The origin of the Threefold Law within Wicca can be traced back to early teachings, notably in the works of Gerald Gardner, who is credited with formalizing many Wiccan beliefs.

Gardner emphasized the importance of ethical conduct in magical practices, aware that those who engage with subtle forces should approach them with respect and caution. Doreen Valiente, another significant figure in Wiccan history, expanded upon this, framing the Threefold Law as a moral guide within the broader context of Wicca's mystical and ritualistic framework. Valiente's poetic touch helped embed the Threefold Law in Wiccan liturgy, reminding practitioners to "do what ye will, an it harm none," thereby reinforcing the importance of ethical restraint.

This law functions as a spiritual mirror, reflecting back to practitioners their own intentions and actions. Wiccans learn that they are responsible not only for what they do but also for the thoughts and emotions they harbor. Emotions such as anger, envy, and resentment are understood to carry negative vibrations, which, when released, contribute to a cycle of harm that inevitably returns to the individual. Conversely, acts of compassion, forgiveness, and gratitude generate positive energy that benefits the practitioner and others. The Threefold Law encourages Wiccans to cultivate an inner awareness of these energies, promoting self-mastery and a mindful approach to the forces they work with.

In practice, the Threefold Law influences every aspect of Wiccan life, from spellwork and ritual to daily interactions and personal choices. When a Wiccan casts a spell, they do so with the awareness that their intentions must align with the principle of "harm none." This means that spells intended to manipulate, coerce, or harm others are generally avoided. Instead, Wiccans focus on spells for healing, protection, abundance, and personal growth, seeking to generate positive effects that will return in kind. This approach underscores the ethical responsibility inherent in Wiccan magic, which views power not as a tool for personal gain but as a means to bring balance, healing, and harmony to oneself and the wider world.

One might wonder why the Threefold Law amplifies the return of energy three times. This concept reflects the Wiccan belief in the universe's inherent balance, where actions are magnified to encourage self-awareness and growth. The return in threefold is thought to represent the effect on three levels: physical, emotional, and spiritual. Each action ripples through these dimensions, affecting the body, heart, and soul, reminding practitioners that their choices shape not only their outward reality but also their inner state and spiritual evolution. The Threefold Law is thus both a teacher and a guide, urging Wiccans to strive for harmony in their thoughts and deeds.

The Threefold Law is closely connected to the concept of karma found in Eastern philosophies, though there are notable differences. In traditional karma, actions generate effects that may span across multiple lifetimes, reflecting a cosmic justice that unfolds over time. The Threefold Law, by contrast, focuses more immediately on the present life, acting as a swift reminder of the impact of one's choices. The Law is not punitive or judgmental but instructive, encouraging personal growth and integrity. It empowers practitioners to become conscious co-creators of their reality, aware that every decision, no matter how small, has a meaningful effect.

While some view the Threefold Law as an absolute, others interpret it as a guiding principle rather than a literal rule. In this interpretation, the Law serves as a reminder to act with integrity and mindfulness, understanding that the universe responds in kind. These practitioners see the Threefold Law as a metaphor for the ways in which actions create an "echo effect," where positive or negative intentions shape the energy that surrounds them. The interpretation of the Law may vary across Wiccan traditions, yet its central message remains clear: to live with awareness, responsibility, and respect for the interconnectedness of all life.

For many Wiccans, the Threefold Law is a source of comfort, providing a sense of order and justice in a world that often seems chaotic. It reassures them that kindness and love will ultimately be rewarded, and that malice and selfishness will find their own repercussions. This belief allows Wiccans to release resentment and cultivate patience, knowing that the universe holds its own wisdom and will bring balance in time. The

Threefold Law invites practitioners to let go of the need for revenge or retribution, trusting that justice will manifest naturally without the need for interference.

In coven settings, the Threefold Law is often discussed and explored as part of ethical training. New initiates are encouraged to consider their actions carefully, understanding the consequences of magical work and the power of intention. Coven leaders may share stories of the Threefold Law in action, recounting personal experiences or folklore to illustrate its effects. These teachings are designed to instill a sense of responsibility, helping practitioners see the importance of aligning their actions with Wicca's core values. Through such guidance, Wiccans learn that their spiritual journey is not isolated but part of a larger, interconnected web.

The Threefold Law's influence reaches beyond Wiccan practices to shape a practitioner's broader worldview. Wiccans often extend the Law's principles to their interactions with others, fostering compassion and empathy. Many Wiccans are deeply committed to environmental stewardship, recognizing that actions taken against the earth will ultimately impact humanity. The Law thus fosters a sense of kinship with all life, encouraging respect for the earth's creatures, the natural environment, and future generations. For Wiccans, to harm the earth is to harm oneself, for all life is connected in an unbreakable circle.

In difficult times, Wiccans may turn to the Threefold Law as a reminder of resilience and patience. When faced with hardships, they reflect on their actions, seeking understanding and taking responsibility where necessary. In doing so, they open themselves to growth and transformation, seeing challenges as opportunities to realign with their highest selves. The Law encourages them to trust in the universe's wisdom, knowing that every experience holds a lesson and every action sows a seed. This perspective cultivates a sense of peace, acceptance, and empowerment, allowing practitioners to navigate life's complexities with grace.

Though it may seem simple, the Threefold Law offers profound insights into the nature of power, responsibility, and interconnectedness. It calls upon Wiccans to live consciously, recognizing that their choices ripple through the web of life, affecting not only themselves but all beings. The Law reminds practitioners that they are both creators and stewards, weaving their energy into the fabric of existence. This realization brings a deep sense of purpose, an understanding that one's life and actions are sacred expressions of the divine.

In this way, the Threefold Law transcends mere ethics; it becomes a spiritual practice, a daily reminder to live with intention, gratitude, and respect. It invites Wiccans to reflect upon their inner landscape, to cultivate positivity and integrity, and to walk their path with open hearts and wise minds. The Threefold Law is not a restrictive rule but a liberating force, guiding practitioners toward a life of harmony, balance, and connection with all that is.

For those who walk the Wiccan path, the Threefold Law stands as a beacon of hope and guidance, a promise that every act of love, kindness, and healing will return, magnified. It is a call to mindfulness, to live with integrity, and to honor the sacred web of life that binds us all. Through the Threefold Law, Wiccans come to understand that their lives are part of a greater whole, that they are creators of their destiny, and that, in the end, love and light will always find their way back.

Chapter 5
The Wheel of Life

In the Wiccan worldview, life unfolds in an eternal cycle, a continuous flow of birth, death, and rebirth that weaves through every aspect of existence. This cycle, often called the "Wheel of Life," is not merely an abstract concept but a lived reality, reflected in the natural world, the changing seasons, and the journey of the human soul. It is the wheel that turns, never stopping, each rotation carrying profound lessons and mysteries that Wiccans embrace as fundamental to their spiritual path. To walk the Wiccan path is to live in harmony with this wheel, to honor its phases, and to recognize one's place within the ever-turning dance of life.

The Wheel of Life is symbolized in Wiccan practice by the Wheel of the Year, a cycle of eight seasonal Sabbats, or festivals, that mark the changing energies of nature throughout the year. These Sabbats reflect the life of the land, the waxing and waning of the sun, and the interplay between light and darkness. Each festival has its own significance, yet all are interconnected, revealing the rhythmic pulse of life itself. Together, these eight Sabbats create a sacred calendar, guiding Wiccans to honor both the external seasons and the internal transformations they bring. The Wheel of Life is, in essence, a journey of spiritual growth, mirroring the cycles of nature and the profound truths found within them.

At the heart of the Wheel of Life is the understanding that existence is cyclic rather than linear. In Wicca, there is no finite end to life; rather, life flows from one stage to the next, constantly renewing and transforming. This concept of cyclic existence is mirrored in the agricultural cycles that have sustained humanity for millennia. Just as seeds are sown in spring, grow and bloom in summer, yield their harvest in autumn, and return to the earth in winter, so too does the spirit journey through phases of growth, fruition, release, and renewal. Each phase is essential, each a lesson in its own right, reminding Wiccans that death is not an ending but a transformation, a gateway to rebirth.

The Sabbats of the Wheel of the Year each represent stages within the cycle of life, and by observing them, Wiccans connect with the ebb and flow of nature's energies. The journey begins at Samhain, the Wiccan New Year, a time of introspection and honoring the dead. As the final harvest festival, Samhain is a point of transition, where the veil between the living and the dead is thin, allowing for communion with ancestors and spirits. It is a time of release, a moment to reflect on what must be let go, and to honor the cycles of death and renewal. Through the darkness of Samhain, Wiccans are reminded of the importance of honoring the past and preparing for the inward journey of winter.

With the arrival of Yule, the winter solstice, the Wheel turns to a moment of rebirth. The longest night gives way to the return of the sun, as the God is symbolically reborn, bringing light and hope to the world once more. Yule is a celebration of new beginnings, a promise that even in the heart of winter, life continues. In the quiet stillness of this season, Wiccans are encouraged to nurture their own inner light, to kindle the fires of hope and inspiration that will sustain them through the cold months. This rebirth of the sun mirrors the rebirth of the spirit, a reminder that every ending holds within it the seeds of new life.

As the Wheel turns to Imbolc, winter begins to soften, and the first signs of spring appear. Imbolc, dedicated to the goddess Brigid, is a festival of purification and preparation, a time to clear away the remnants of the old and make space for the new. Wiccans celebrate this period of renewal by lighting candles, a symbol of the growing light, and by dedicating themselves to goals and intentions for the coming year. Imbolc teaches the importance of preparation and faith, reminding practitioners that growth begins in unseen places, like seeds lying dormant beneath the snow, waiting to emerge.

The arrival of Ostara, the spring equinox, marks a time of balance, when day and night are equal. Ostara is a festival of fertility and awakening, a celebration of life returning to the land. As flowers bloom and animals emerge from hibernation, Wiccans honor the renewal of life, planting seeds both literally and metaphorically. Ostara encourages practitioners to embrace growth, to set intentions, and to nurture new beginnings. This is a time of hope and expansion, a reminder that life is in constant motion and that each soul, like the earth itself, is capable of endless rebirth.

Beltane, celebrated on the first of May, is a festival of passion, fertility, and creativity. It is a celebration of the union between the Goddess and the God, representing the fertility of the earth and the vibrancy of life. At Beltane, the fires are lit, dances are performed, and the joy of existence is embraced. This festival is a time of love, not only romantic love but also love for the self, for life, and for the world. Beltane reminds Wiccans to honor their desires, to celebrate their creativity, and to let passion guide them on their path.

The summer solstice, or Litha, marks the height of the sun's power. This is a celebration of abundance, vitality, and strength. The sun stands at its peak, casting light upon the world, symbolizing clarity and fulfillment. Litha is a time to honor the achievements and blessings that have come to fruition. Wiccans celebrate by gathering herbs, working with the energies of prosperity, and giving thanks for the abundance in their lives. As the longest day of the year, Litha also reminds Wiccans that life is cyclical and that even the sun's strength will eventually wane, leading back to the inward journey of autumn.

As the Wheel turns toward Lammas, or Lughnasadh, in early August, the first harvest begins. This is a time to give thanks for the fruits of the earth, to honor the labor and growth that have brought sustenance. Lammas teaches the value of gratitude and the importance of recognizing the cycles of effort and reward. Wiccans may bake bread, offer grain to the land, and celebrate the bounty that sustains them. Lammas also reminds practitioners to look within, to take stock of their accomplishments, and to prepare for the eventual release that autumn will bring.

The autumn equinox, or Mabon, marks a point of balance and reflection. As day and night stand equal once more, Wiccans celebrate the second harvest, gathering the last fruits of the season and giving thanks for the abundance of the year. Mabon is a time to pause, to reflect on the journey, and to prepare for the descent into winter. It is a moment of gratitude and balance, a reminder to find harmony within and to acknowledge both the light and the shadow. Mabon invites Wiccans to embrace the gifts of introspection, to recognize the lessons of the past, and to prepare for the quiet reflection of the coming months.

Through the Wheel of Life, Wiccans experience the flow of time as a cycle rather than a line, a continuous journey where each ending is also a beginning. This perspective shapes not only the way Wiccans perceive the natural world but also how they approach their own lives. Birth, death, and rebirth are not separate stages but interconnected experiences, each leading into the other, creating a seamless web of existence. For Wiccans, the soul's journey does not end with death; rather, it transforms, returning to the earth or moving into new realms, eventually to be reborn in another form or life.

This understanding of life as cyclical brings comfort and a sense of continuity. It encourages Wiccans to embrace change, to accept the inevitability of loss, and to trust in the process of renewal. The Wheel of Life teaches that grief and joy, light and dark, are all part of a larger balance, each essential to the whole. In moments of sorrow, Wiccans are reminded that winter will give way to spring, that death leads to rebirth, and that the spirit, like the earth itself, is forever renewed.

This awareness extends into Wiccan rituals, where the themes of birth, death, and rebirth are frequently honored. In initiations, Wiccans symbolically die to their old selves and are reborn into a new understanding. In rites of passage, such as handfastings, births, and memorials, Wiccans recognize and celebrate the turning points of life, each a step along the sacred path. By ritualizing these moments, Wiccans honor the journey and mark their place within the eternal cycle, creating a sense of purpose and belonging.

The Wheel of Life also influences Wiccans' approach to personal growth. Just as nature goes through phases of growth, decay, and renewal, so too does the human spirit. Wiccans understand that each phase of life brings unique lessons and challenges, that every winter has its wisdom, every spring its possibilities. This cyclical view fosters patience and acceptance, encouraging Wiccans to embrace their own evolution, to let go when necessary, and to welcome new beginnings with an open heart.

In a world that often rushes toward progress and fears endings, the Wiccan concept of the Wheel of Life offers a refreshing perspective. It teaches that endings are not failures but transitions, that life itself is a series of cycles that must be honored and embraced. For Wiccans, this understanding is a source of strength, a reminder that they are part of something vast and timeless. It is an invitation to dance with the rhythms of existence, to trust in the wisdom of the earth, and to walk the path with courage and grace, knowing that the wheel will always turn, bringing new life, new lessons, and new blessings.

Chapter 6
The Five Elements

In Wicca, the natural world is understood as a symphony of energies, each contributing its unique qualities to the harmonious whole. Central to this worldview are the Five Elements: Earth, Air, Fire, Water, and Spirit. These elements are not merely physical substances; they are forces, metaphors, and sacred presences that shape reality on both tangible and mystical levels. Each element embodies a set of qualities and powers, and together, they form the foundation of Wiccan practice, representing the interconnected web of existence.

For Wiccans, the elements serve as guides and companions, forces with which they can work to create change, find balance, and deepen their spiritual connection. In rituals and meditations, the elements are invoked to bring their energies into sacred space, allowing practitioners to attune themselves to the rhythms of the natural world. Each element carries its own wisdom, its own way of teaching, and its own way of healing. To understand these elements is to understand the essence of life itself and to recognize one's own nature within the greater universe.

Earth is the element of stability, groundedness, and material reality. It is associated with the North, and its presence is found in the soil, mountains, trees, and all things that embody the physical form. Earth is the foundation, the mother that nurtures and sustains all life. In Wicca, Earth is revered as the source of fertility and growth, the embodiment of abundance and resilience. When invoking Earth, Wiccans connect with the qualities of patience, endurance, and strength, drawing upon the solidity and reliability of the ground beneath their feet. Earth teaches the wisdom of slow, steady growth and the power of roots that run deep, unseen yet vital.

Practitioners work with the energy of Earth to ground themselves, to find balance in times of chaos, and to cultivate stability in their lives. Earth's influence is sought when Wiccans need to feel secure or when they wish to manifest physical or financial resources. In spellwork, stones, soil, and plants are often used as symbols of Earth's energy, each carrying the grounding vibration of this element. Earth teaches that all things grow in their own time and that true strength is found in resilience and patience. In Wiccan rituals, the energy of Earth is often represented by salt or stones, tangible reminders of the enduring power of the natural world.

Air is the element of intellect, communication, and inspiration. It is associated with the East, the direction of the rising sun and new beginnings. Air is the breath of life, the invisible force that animates all creatures and carries thoughts and ideas. In Wicca, Air represents the mind, the power of imagination, and the ability to bring ideas into form. It is the force of change and movement, encouraging clarity and insight. When Wiccans invoke Air, they connect with the qualities of openness, curiosity, and mental clarity, seeking inspiration and vision.

Air is the element of freedom, a force that lifts and expands. Its energy is light and quick, reminding practitioners of the importance of flexibility and the need to let go of limitations. Feathers, incense, and the movement of smoke are often used to represent Air's energy, each symbolizing the element's intangible nature. In spellwork, Air's qualities are called upon to enhance communication, to stimulate mental clarity, and to open channels of creativity. Air teaches that knowledge is ever-expanding and that wisdom flows like a breeze, unbound and ever-moving. In ritual, Air is often represented by incense or feathers, evoking its invisible presence and its power to transform.

Fire is the element of passion, transformation, and willpower. Associated with the South, Fire is the spark of life, the energy of creation and destruction. Fire burns away the old, clearing space for the new, and it fuels the drive to create and to strive. In Wicca, Fire represents courage, energy, and the pursuit of one's purpose. Its nature is both dangerous and essential, a force that can warm, inspire, or consume. Wiccans call upon Fire to ignite their intentions, to strengthen their will, and to awaken their inner power.

Fire's energy is intense, immediate, and ever-changing, embodying both inspiration and action. It is represented in rituals by candles, flames, or symbols of the sun, each a reminder of Fire's presence in all acts of creation. Fire's power is sought when practitioners need courage, motivation, or a sense of purpose. In spellwork, Fire's energy can break through obstacles, release pent-up emotions, and fuel transformation. Fire teaches that life is in constant motion and that true change often requires burning away the old. In Wiccan rites, Fire is frequently invoked with candles or fires, symbols of the warmth, light, and dynamic energy it brings.

Water is the element of emotion, intuition, and healing. Aligned with the West, the direction of sunset and the mysteries of the unknown, Water embodies fluidity, adaptability, and the flow of emotions. In Wicca, Water is revered as a source of cleansing and renewal, representing the subconscious mind and the depth of feelings. It is the element that encourages empathy, connection, and emotional growth. When invoking Water, Wiccans open themselves to the realm of dreams, intuition, and emotional healing, allowing the gentle flow of this element to cleanse and refresh their spirits.

Water's energy is soft yet powerful, capable of shaping rocks and carving landscapes. Its presence is represented by seashells, bowls of water, or chalices in ritual, each symbolizing the depths of emotion and the mystery of life's currents. In spellwork, Water is called upon to heal, to soothe, and to connect. Its qualities foster emotional resilience, helping Wiccans navigate their inner landscapes with grace and insight. Water teaches the importance of embracing change, of moving with life's tides rather than resisting them. In Wiccan practice, Water is often evoked with chalices, cauldrons, or shells, symbols of the element's nurturing and transformative power.

Spirit, or **Aether**, is the fifth element, the binding force that connects and unites all things. Spirit transcends direction, existing beyond the physical realm as the essence that infuses all creation. In Wicca, Spirit represents the divine, the infinite, the source of all life. It is the spark of consciousness, the presence of the divine within each soul, and the thread that binds all elements into one cohesive whole. Spirit is the bridge between the material and the mystical, a reminder of the sacred unity of all things.

Spirit is invoked in rituals as the core essence, the sacred center that aligns practitioners with the universe. It is the source of wisdom, inner truth, and enlightenment, a force that goes beyond words or symbols. In spellwork, Spirit is the energy that gives life to all intentions, empowering practitioners to align their will with the divine. Spirit teaches that all things are interconnected, that each being is both unique and part of the greater whole. Represented in Wiccan practice by a simple white candle or by the act of centering and grounding, Spirit embodies the ultimate truth: that everything is sacred, and that all life flows from the same source.

Together, these elements form a balanced, harmonious system, each one contributing its unique qualities to the whole. In Wiccan practice, this balance is essential, as it reflects the interconnectedness of all life. Earth grounds and stabilizes; Air inspires and uplifts; Fire transforms and empowers; Water soothes and heals; Spirit binds and unites. In rituals, Wiccans often create a sacred circle, calling upon each element to bring its qualities into the space. This circle becomes a microcosm of the universe, a reflection of the sacred balance that exists within and around all beings.

The elements are not static forces but dynamic energies that interact with one another, creating harmony through their differences. Earth may seem opposed to Air, just as Fire contrasts with Water, yet each element finds balance within the whole. For Wiccans, this understanding is more than symbolic; it is a spiritual truth that reveals the importance of balance and harmony. Just as nature thrives when elements work together, so too does the human spirit flourish when all aspects of the self are honored and integrated.

Working with the elements is a deeply personal and transformative practice in Wicca. By connecting with each element, practitioners gain insights into their own nature and learn to cultivate the qualities they need for personal growth. Earth teaches grounding and resilience; Air opens the mind to new perspectives; Fire fuels ambition and courage; Water nurtures compassion and intuition; Spirit unites all aspects into a harmonious whole. Through meditation, ritual, and spellwork, Wiccans build relationships with these elements, learning from their wisdom and embracing their power.

In Wiccan rituals, the elements are often represented on the altar, each with a corresponding tool or symbol. Pentacles, often made of stone or wood, represent Earth; wands represent Air; candles or athames (ritual knives) represent Fire; and chalices or cauldrons represent Water. These tools serve as conduits for the elements, helping practitioners channel and focus their energies. By working with these tools, Wiccans align themselves with the elemental forces, creating a sacred space that honors the balance of nature.

The elements also play a role in healing and personal transformation. Earth's grounding energy can be called upon for stability during difficult times, while Air's clarity helps with decision-making and mental focus. Fire can be used to release old habits or patterns, burning away what no longer serves. Water's gentle flow aids emotional healing, washing away pain and opening the heart. Spirit, the essence that unites all, is the energy of wholeness, reminding practitioners that healing is a return to the sacred self.

In the end, the Five Elements are more than symbols; they are living, breathing forces that speak to the soul. For Wiccans, they are teachers, allies, and reflections of the divine presence in all things. By honoring the elements, practitioners honor life itself, recognizing that each part of creation is sacred and that the journey of the spirit is one of balance, harmony, and connection with the universe. Through this connection, Wiccans find their place within the greater web of life, walking their path with gratitude and respect for the elements that shape their world.

Chapter 7
Elemental Kingdom

Beyond the physical and symbolic representations of Earth, Air, Fire, and Water lies a mystical realm known to Wiccans as the Elemental Kingdom. This enchanted domain is populated by ethereal beings who personify the elements and exist in a dimension slightly removed from our own. These entities, known as elementals, embody the very essence of their respective elements. Earth has its gnomes, Air its sylphs, Fire its salamanders, and Water its undines. Spirit, too, is said to have its beings—elusive and formless, representing the unity of all life. Each of these beings is not merely a symbol but an active force, an expression of the ancient intelligence that flows through the natural world.

To Wiccans, elementals are more than mystical creatures; they are guardians of the elemental energies and custodians of nature's harmony. Working with these beings allows practitioners to form a closer bond with the forces that shape reality, deepening their understanding of the world and enhancing their magical practices. However, approaching the elementals is not a simple endeavor. It requires respect, humility, and an understanding that these beings, though often helpful, operate on their own terms and follow the laws of nature, which are beyond human control.

Each elemental being carries unique attributes, personalities, and energies. They are attracted to environments that reflect their elemental essence, and it is said that they respond to those who approach with genuine reverence and intent. Working with the elementals is a way to honor the spirit of nature itself, a practice that teaches Wiccans to listen to the wisdom of the earth, sky, flame, and water, and to understand their role in the natural order.

The **gnomes**, the elemental beings of Earth, are often imagined as wise, sturdy creatures who dwell in forests, caves, and mountains. These beings are closely connected to the land, guarding the hidden treasures and deep roots of the earth. Gnomes are known for their loyalty, patience, and strength, qualities that reflect the grounded energy of Earth itself. In Wiccan lore, gnomes are considered guardians of stability and material abundance. They are believed to have ancient wisdom, understanding the secrets of stones, crystals, and metals. Those who wish to work with gnomes often seek grounding, stability, or protection. Offerings of natural items such as stones, crystals, or dried herbs may be left in gardens or at the base of trees to honor the gnomes and invite their energy.

Working with gnomes requires a respectful approach, as they are known to value sincerity and effort. They are most responsive to those who respect the land, care for plants, and seek to preserve the earth's natural beauty. When invited into magical work, gnomes lend a solidifying presence, helping to anchor spells for abundance, growth, and protection. Yet, they are also cautious, wary of those who take from the earth without giving back. To honor the gnomes is to honor the earth, to tread lightly, and to understand that true wealth comes from respecting and caring for the land.

The **sylphs** are the elementals of Air, beings of light and ethereal beauty who reside in the winds and clouds, dancing on breezes and drifting through the open skies. Sylphs are associated with intellect, inspiration, and freedom, reflecting the swift, flowing energy of Air. In Wiccan traditions, sylphs are considered guardians of knowledge and communicators of higher wisdom. They are drawn to those with an open mind and a sense of curiosity, favoring those who seek to understand life's mysteries and explore the unseen realms. Sylphs are thought to inspire creativity, bring clarity to the mind, and carry messages from the spirit world.

When working with sylphs, Wiccans often turn to meditation, breathwork, or time spent outdoors, particularly on windy days. Sylphs respond to the sound of music, the rustling of leaves, and the whisper of words carried on the air. They can be called upon to bring insight, stimulate mental agility, or to enhance divination practices. Represented by feathers, bells, or incense, sylphs offer a sense of liberation, helping practitioners release mental clutter and open themselves to new ideas. Yet, they are as elusive as a breeze, impossible to control, teaching that true wisdom cannot be held but must be experienced.

The **salamanders**, the fiery elementals, embody the wild, transformative power of Fire. These beings are fierce, dynamic, and filled with energy, residing in flames, lava, and the intense heat of the sun. Salamanders are associated with passion, courage, and creativity. They are the spark that ignites change, the force that pushes boundaries, and the energy that fuels ambition. Wiccans call upon salamanders when they need to awaken inner strength, find motivation, or initiate transformation. Working with salamanders is not for the faint-hearted, as they embody the intense and often unpredictable nature of Fire.

In Wiccan practice, salamanders are represented by candles, fires, or symbols of the sun. They are honored in rituals that involve purification, courage, or the release of limiting beliefs. Salamanders respond to those who have a clear purpose and a courageous heart, but they also demand respect, for Fire can be both a creator and a destroyer. In working with salamanders, Wiccans learn to channel their own passions constructively, to ignite their inner fire without being consumed by it. Salamanders remind practitioners that transformation requires both courage and control, a willingness to let go of the old to make way for the new.

The **undines** are the elementals of Water, fluid and mysterious beings who dwell in rivers, lakes, oceans, and even the rain. Undines are associated with emotion, intuition, and healing, reflecting Water's ability to cleanse and soothe. In Wiccan belief, undines are deeply sensitive and compassionate, often drawn to those who seek healing or emotional release. They are considered guardians of the heart, helping practitioners explore their inner worlds and connect with their deepest feelings. Those who wish to work with undines often seek to enhance their intuition, deepen their empathy, or heal emotional wounds.

Undines are honored with offerings of flowers, shells, or water left near natural bodies of water. In ritual, undines are called upon to cleanse, to heal, and to bring insight into one's emotions. They are thought to bring dreams, visions, and an awareness of the subconscious. Working with undines requires an openness to vulnerability, a willingness to flow with life's changes. Undines teach that emotions, like water, must move and shift, that stillness brings stagnation, and that healing comes from embracing one's own depths. They offer comfort in times of sorrow, teaching that all emotions are valid and that true strength comes from accepting oneself fully.

Finally, the formless entities of **Spirit** represent the element of unity, the binding force that connects all things. Spirit elementals are elusive, often described as beings of pure light or energy, embodying the mystery and transcendence of the divine. Unlike the other elementals, Spirit beings do not reside in any particular location but exist everywhere, in all things, at all times. They are seen as guides to higher consciousness, helpers in spiritual growth, and teachers of the interconnectedness of life. In Wicca, Spirit is the fifth element, present in every ritual and every moment of reflection, reminding practitioners of their connection to all existence.

Working with Spirit beings requires a deep level of awareness and openness. These entities are less accessible than the elementals of Earth, Air, Fire, or Water, appearing only when the practitioner is ready to transcend ordinary understanding. Spirit beings do not respond to offerings or symbols; instead, they are honored through meditation, spiritual practice, and acts of kindness. They are called upon to bring insight, to help one find purpose, or to guide one's spiritual journey. Spirit beings teach that we are all part of a vast, infinite whole, that separation is an illusion, and that true wisdom lies in understanding our unity with all life.

For Wiccans, working with the elementals is a practice of respect, connection, and learning. These beings are not to be commanded or used but approached as allies, honored for their wisdom and power. Each elemental brings its own lessons, its own way of guiding practitioners back to their truest selves. Gnomes teach resilience and patience, sylphs inspire mental clarity and freedom, salamanders ignite transformation and courage, undines foster healing and intuition, and Spirit beings connect all aspects into a unified whole.

The Elemental Kingdom serves as a bridge between the physical and spiritual worlds, reminding Wiccans of the unseen forces that shape existence. By building relationships with these beings, Wiccans learn to listen to the whispers of nature, to see the magic in the ordinary, and to understand that every part of life is sacred. These beings invite practitioners into a world of wonder and mystery, teaching that all life is interconnected and that every creature, every rock, every tree is imbued with spirit.

In honoring the elementals, Wiccans also honor the cycles of nature, recognizing that each season, each element, and each being has a role to play in the greater harmony of life. Through rituals, offerings, and acts of reverence, Wiccans cultivate a sense of kinship with the natural world, learning to walk lightly, to give as they receive, and to live in balance. The elementals are both teachers and companions, reflections of the divine that help practitioners remember their own place within the sacred web of existence. For those on the Wiccan path, the Elemental Kingdom is a source of inspiration, a reminder of the magic that lies within and around us, waiting to be honored, understood, and celebrated.

Chapter 8
Vital Energy

In the stillness of an ancient forest, in the rush of waves on a forgotten shore, or in the quiet rhythm of a heart beating, there pulses an invisible force known to Wiccans as vital energy. This life force, also called "universal energy" or "chi" in other traditions, is the very essence of life, the invisible current that flows through all things, connecting every creature, tree, river, and stone. It is the pulse of existence, the hidden thread that binds the universe together. In Wicca, vital energy is understood as both the breath of the earth and the soul of the self, a sacred energy that practitioners can sense, harness, and channel to bring harmony, healing, and transformation.

This concept of vital energy is not unique to Wicca; it appears in many spiritual traditions across the world. Known as "prana" in Hinduism, "mana" in Polynesian cultures, and "ki" in Japanese philosophy, vital energy is the foundation of life itself. However, in Wicca, this energy is approached through a deeply personal, nature-centered perspective. Wiccans understand that vital energy is not only present in people but also in plants, animals, bodies of water, and even the stones of the earth. Everything in existence, from the smallest pebble to the vast sky, contains a spark of this life force, each contributing to the great web of interconnected energies.

Learning to perceive and work with vital energy is a foundational skill for Wiccans, one that forms the basis of their spiritual and magical practices. To sense this energy is to awaken to the mysteries of life, to feel the flow of the universe, and to recognize one's place within it. This awareness is not gained through intellect alone; it is a felt experience, cultivated through quiet observation, meditation, and mindful engagement with the world. In time, a practitioner learns to move with this energy, to respect its rhythms, and to align their own actions with its natural flow.

In Wiccan practice, vital energy is often visualized as a glowing, pulsating light or a gentle warmth that moves within and around the body. This energy can be felt in many ways: as a tingle along the skin, a warmth in the hands, or a subtle pressure in the air. When performing rituals or spells, Wiccans draw upon this energy, gathering it within themselves and channeling it toward their intentions. By learning to sense and direct vital energy, practitioners can focus their will, amplify their intentions, and connect more deeply with the natural world.

One of the primary methods of connecting with vital energy is through grounding, a practice that allows Wiccans to attune themselves to the earth's energy. Grounding is a process of releasing excess or stagnant energy into the earth, drawing in fresh, stable energy in return. To ground oneself is to feel rooted, centered, and aligned with the earth's own pulse. Wiccans often imagine roots extending from their body deep into the earth, anchoring them and allowing energy to flow freely. This practice fosters a deep sense of calm and stability, creating a foundation from which one can access and work with vital energy effectively.

Once grounded, a Wiccan can begin to work with energy through visualization, breathwork, and focused intention. Visualization is a powerful tool in Wiccan practice, allowing practitioners to shape and guide energy through the mind's eye. For example, when preparing for a spell, a Wiccan might visualize energy gathering within their body as a warm, golden light. With each breath, this light grows brighter, filling them with a sense of strength and purpose. When the time is right, they release this energy, directing it toward their goal with clarity and focus. This act of visualization is not merely symbolic; it is a way of engaging with the flow of energy, transforming thought into action, intention into reality.

Breathwork, too, is a key technique for sensing and directing vital energy. The breath is intimately connected to life force, a rhythm that mirrors the cycle of giving and receiving, of drawing in and letting go. In Wiccan practices, controlled breathing can be used to enhance one's sensitivity to energy, to calm the mind, or to gather strength before a ritual. By breathing deeply and mindfully, a practitioner can tune into their own energy field, sensing any areas of tension or imbalance. As they exhale, they may imagine releasing any stagnant or negative energy, allowing their breath to carry it away. Inhaling, they draw in fresh, revitalizing energy from the air, filling their body with a renewed sense of life and clarity.

Vital energy is also cultivated through regular interaction with nature. The natural world is filled with sources of this life force, and by spending time in wild places, Wiccans can recharge their own energy fields. Walking barefoot on the earth, touching trees, feeling the warmth of the sun, and listening to the sounds of the forest are all ways of absorbing the earth's energy, a practice that strengthens the bond between the practitioner and the living world. Nature itself becomes a teacher, showing the rhythms and cycles of energy in the growth of plants, the flow of rivers, and the patterns of weather.

In Wicca, the act of drawing down energy from the sun and the moon is a way to harness specific types of vital energy. Solar energy is associated with vitality, strength, and clarity, while lunar energy is linked to intuition, dreams, and emotional balance. During rituals, Wiccans may align their energy with the sun's rays, drawing in warmth and motivation for dynamic spells and intentions. On nights of the full moon, they may stand under its light, opening themselves to the moon's subtle, mystical influence, enhancing their intuitive faculties and their connection to the unseen.

Understanding vital energy also means recognizing the ways in which this energy can become blocked or depleted.

Negative emotions, stress, and unhealthy environments can disrupt the flow of life force, leading to physical, mental, and spiritual fatigue. Wiccans believe that when energy becomes stagnant, it can manifest as tension, anxiety, or even illness. Therefore, maintaining a healthy flow of energy is essential for both spiritual growth and personal well-being. Practices like smudging, crystal work, and regular meditation help cleanse and rejuvenate the energy body, releasing negativity and restoring balance.

Smudging, the act of burning sacred herbs like sage or lavender, is a common practice for clearing stagnant or negative energy. The smoke is believed to carry purifying properties, lifting away harmful energies and bringing a sense of renewal. Wiccans may use smudging to cleanse their aura, their home, or their ritual space, ensuring that the energy is fresh and conducive to spiritual work. In doing so, they create an environment that supports a healthy flow of life force, one that nurtures both body and spirit.

Crystal work is another method by which Wiccans interact with vital energy. Crystals are seen as repositories of earth energy, each carrying a unique vibration that can influence the energy field. For example, clear quartz is known for its amplifying properties, enhancing the flow of energy, while amethyst promotes calm and spiritual awareness. By placing these stones on the body or within a sacred space, Wiccans can tune into their energy, using the crystal's resonance to balance and align their own. Crystals serve as conduits, helping practitioners connect with the deeper layers of earth energy and bringing harmony to their energy fields.

Wiccans understand that vital energy is not only an external force but also an internal one. They are conscious of their own energy field, or "aura," which radiates from the body and interacts with the world around it. The aura is seen as an extension of the self, reflecting thoughts, emotions, and physical well-being. When a Wiccan feels fatigued or out of balance, they may examine their aura, sensing any disruptions in the flow of energy. Through meditation, visualization, and healing techniques, they work to cleanse and strengthen their aura, ensuring that their life force remains vibrant and resilient.

One of the most transformative ways of engaging with vital energy is through healing work. In Wiccan healing practices, practitioners may lay hands upon themselves or others, directing energy to where it is most needed. This practice, sometimes known as "energy healing," involves channeling life force into areas of imbalance, bringing relief and restoration. By aligning with the universal energy flow, Wiccans seek to awaken the body's own healing capacities, helping the spirit to realign with its natural state of wellness. Healing work reminds practitioners that life force is not only a mystical concept but a tangible, nurturing presence that can be drawn upon for strength and comfort.

Ultimately, working with vital energy is a path to self-awareness, a journey into the unseen realms of the self and the universe. By cultivating sensitivity to this energy, Wiccans deepen their connection to the mysteries of life, seeing the world as a living, breathing whole. They recognize that every creature, every tree, every drop of rain carries a spark of the divine and that this spark flows through them as well. In Wiccan belief, the more one honors and works with vital energy, the more attuned one becomes to the sacred in all things, experiencing life not as a series of separate events but as a seamless tapestry of interwoven forces.

The practice of working with vital energy transforms the ordinary into the extraordinary, revealing the magic that resides in every breath, every heartbeat, and every sunset. It teaches practitioners that they are not separate from nature but an expression of it, that their very existence is a testament to the boundless creativity of life. Through this understanding, Wiccans walk their path with gratitude, knowing that they are a part of a vast, living universe, one that flows with life force, beauty, and endless possibility. Vital energy, in all its mystery and power, is both the source and the destination, the sacred pulse of existence that guides and sustains the Wiccan soul.

Chapter 9
Sacred Space

In Wicca, the act of creating sacred space is a practice of profound significance. To consecrate a space is to transform it into a place where the veil between the worlds thins, where the mundane meets the divine, and where energies align to support ritual, meditation, and personal growth. Sacred space is not bound by any particular location; it can be created indoors, outdoors, within a small corner of a room, or upon the vast earth beneath the sky. Wherever it may be, a sacred space becomes a sanctuary, a place of power, calm, and intention. It is here that Wiccans step into a world beyond the ordinary, entering a realm that is attuned to the energies of nature, spirit, and self.

The preparation of sacred space is an invitation to mindfulness, a ritual in itself. Each step in the process—from choosing the location to purifying the area and casting a circle—holds meaning and purpose. By creating sacred space, practitioners set aside a moment and a place for spiritual connection, committing themselves fully to the experience. This act of dedication shifts the practitioner's consciousness, opening them to the deeper currents of energy and guiding them to the threshold of the sacred.

The first step in creating sacred space is selecting an appropriate location. This choice is deeply personal and often guided by intuition. For many Wiccans, the ideal location is somewhere in nature: a secluded grove, a quiet meadow, or a peaceful beach where the natural energies are strong and undisturbed. In nature, sacred space is enhanced by the presence of elemental forces, the earth beneath, the sky above, and the life that flourishes in between. Yet sacred space can be created anywhere, even in the quietest corner of a bedroom, as long as it is chosen with intention. What matters is the reverence brought to the space, the recognition that it is being set apart from ordinary life for a time.

Once the location is chosen, the next step is **cleansing**. Cleansing is the act of purifying the space, removing any stagnant or disruptive energies so that the area is receptive to sacred work. This process can be done with simple tools such as salt, herbs, incense, or even a bowl of water. Sage, rosemary, or lavender are commonly used herbs in Wiccan practice, burned as incense to cleanse the air. As the smoke drifts through the space, it is imagined as carrying away any negative or chaotic energies, clearing the space and creating a neutral, harmonious environment. If the practice is done indoors, opening windows can further assist this process, allowing fresh air to carry away old energies.

Salt is also a powerful tool for cleansing and is sometimes sprinkled in a circle around the space or placed at each of the four directions. Salt is known for its grounding properties, symbolizing the element of Earth and offering a sense of stability and protection. In Wiccan tradition, it is often mixed with water to create holy water, which is then sprinkled around the space or used to wash surfaces, infusing them with purity and intention. Water, too, carries purifying energy, especially when gathered from a natural source like a river, spring, or ocean. For those who wish to connect more deeply with the Water element, a bowl of blessed water may be placed within the sacred space, offering a sense of flow and emotional clarity.

With the space physically and energetically cleansed, the next step is to **call upon the four directions**—North, East, South, and West—and the elements associated with them: Earth, Air, Fire, and Water. This invocation creates a balanced, harmonious environment where all forces are represented, supporting the ritual work that follows. Beginning in the East, which represents

Air and new beginnings, Wiccans honor each direction in turn, moving clockwise around the circle. Each direction is often invoked with a simple phrase or invocation, acknowledging the element and inviting its energy into the space. This process is not only a call for protection and support but also an act of respect for the natural forces that surround and sustain all life.

The **casting of the circle** is one of the most important steps in creating sacred space. To cast a circle is to establish a boundary between the sacred and the mundane, a space where time feels suspended, and the mind shifts into a deeper state of awareness. The circle is more than just a boundary; it is a microcosm of the universe, a place where the energies of the earth and sky, the elements and spirit, converge in harmony. Wiccans often visualize the circle as a sphere of light extending above and below them, encompassing the entire space and creating a safe, protected environment.

Casting a circle can be done with a ritual tool, such as an athame (a ceremonial blade), a wand, or even a simple hand gesture. The practitioner walks clockwise around the space, envisioning energy flowing from the tool or their hand, forming an unbroken line of light. This light represents the barrier that keeps out unwanted influences and holds in the energy raised within the circle. Once the circle is cast, it is treated with reverence; nothing is taken in or out without careful intention, preserving the sanctity of the space.

Within this consecrated space, **an altar** may be arranged, serving as a focal point for the ritual. The altar holds tools, symbols, and offerings that support the practitioner's intention, each item placed thoughtfully and with purpose. Traditional items on a Wiccan altar often include representations of the elements, such as a pentacle for Earth, incense for Air, a candle for Fire, and a chalice of water. Each item acts as a bridge between the physical and spiritual realms, grounding the practitioner's intentions and inviting the presence of the elements. The altar itself becomes a sacred landscape, a place where the energy of the practitioner and the divine energies converge.

With the circle cast and the altar prepared, the practitioner may then **invoke the deities** or spiritual forces they wish to work with. This invocation is a heartfelt call, an invitation for divine guidance and presence within the space. Wiccans often honor both the Goddess and the God, seeing them as dual aspects of the divine, representing balance and unity. Invocations can be spoken, chanted, or simply felt in silence, depending on the practitioner's personal preference. This step personalizes the sacred space, aligning it with the practitioner's specific spiritual path and intentions.

In the silence of sacred space, a Wiccan practitioner experiences a shift in perception, an awareness of energies that go unnoticed in daily life. Time seems to slow, the air feels charged, and a sense of peace descends. Here, in this consecrated space, the practitioner feels connected to the earth, to the sky, and to the vast, unseen realms that lie beyond ordinary sight. Sacred space is a place of communion, a bridge between worlds where messages may be received, insights gained, and transformation initiated. Each sound, each movement, and each word within the circle is imbued with heightened meaning, amplifying the practitioner's intentions and aligning them with the greater forces of nature and spirit.

When the ritual is complete, **the circle must be closed with the same care with which it was cast**. Just as casting the circle is an act of opening a door to the sacred, closing it is a respectful farewell, a gratitude-filled return to the ordinary world. The practitioner walks counterclockwise, visualizing the energy of the circle dissolving and returning to the earth, thanking each direction and element in turn. This act of releasing the circle restores the space to its everyday state, yet it leaves a subtle residue of sacredness, a reminder that even the mundane holds echoes of the divine.

The act of creating sacred space is a deeply personal ritual, one that reflects the unique energies and intentions of each practitioner. It is a practice that can be simple or elaborate, yet its purpose remains the same: to create a sanctuary where the practitioner can engage with the mysteries of existence. In this space, Wiccans find a sense of belonging and a place where they can safely explore their spirituality. It is a space that speaks to the soul, offering a moment of pause, a place of reflection, and a connection to something greater than oneself.

Sacred space is both a container for energy and a vessel of intention. Each time it is created, it becomes a new experience, shaped by the unique qualities of the moment. In this way, Wiccans are reminded that the sacred is not a static concept but a living presence, one that changes, evolves, and grows with each practitioner's journey. The act of creating sacred space is a practice of devotion and presence, an invitation to step into the flow of life with reverence, gratitude, and awareness.

Through the practice of creating sacred space, Wiccans learn that every space has the potential to become sacred, that every action can be a ritual, and that every moment holds the possibility of communion with the divine. By consciously choosing to create and honor sacred space, Wiccans bring their spirituality into the present moment, weaving their intentions into the fabric of existence. This practice is both an art and a discipline, a reminder that the sacred is always within reach, waiting to be recognized and celebrated.

In sacred space, Wiccans find a home for their spirit, a place of peace and power, a sanctuary from which they can venture forth, renewed and inspired. Here, in this quiet, hallowed ground, they reconnect with the elements, the gods, and their own innermost selves. And as they step back into the world, they carry with them the memory of this sacred space, knowing that the divine is not confined to the ritual circle but flows through all of life, present in every breath, every leaf, every star, and every heart.

Chapter 10
Personal Altar

At the heart of Wiccan practice lies the altar—a sacred, personal space that serves as both a reflection of one's inner spirit and a gateway to the divine. The altar is not only a focal point for rituals and spells but also a sanctuary, a place where the spiritual and material worlds meet. A Wiccan altar, whether simple or elaborate, holds objects and symbols that resonate with the practitioner, embodying their intentions, honoring the deities they revere, and representing the elements that sustain life. Through the careful arrangement of each item, the altar becomes a mirror of the practitioner's soul, a personal and sacred expression of their path.

In Wicca, an altar is seen as a living entity, imbued with energy and purpose. It is where spells are cast, offerings are made, and meditations are deepened. The altar holds objects that are meaningful, symbols that speak to the spirit, and tools that assist in magical work. Some practitioners create altars that are dedicated to specific deities, while others build altars that change with the seasons or reflect particular aspects of their journey. The beauty of the Wiccan altar lies in its flexibility; it is a reflection of the practitioner's evolving connection with the divine, a space that can grow and change as they do.

The first step in creating a personal altar is to **choose its location**. While an altar can be set up anywhere—on a small table, a shelf, or even a windowsill—the chosen space should feel private and sacred to the practitioner. Many Wiccans select a quiet corner of their home, a place where they can focus without distraction. Others create outdoor altars, tucked beneath trees or beside running water, where they can commune with nature while honoring the elements. The location should feel comfortable, a place where the practitioner can sit or stand with ease, free to meditate or work without interruption.

Once the location is chosen, the altar is cleansed and consecrated, setting it apart from the ordinary world. Cleansing the space removes any residual energies, creating a fresh and neutral environment. This can be done with tools like sage, incense, or a simple sprinkle of salt and water. The act of cleansing transforms the area, signaling to the practitioner and the energies around them that this is a place for spiritual work. With each cleansing, the altar becomes increasingly attuned to the practitioner, holding their intentions and resonating with their energy.

The **selection of altar items** is a personal and intuitive process, guided by what the practitioner feels connected to. Some common items on a Wiccan altar include representations of the four elements, symbols of the Goddess and the God, candles, crystals, and ritual tools. Each item is chosen with care, reflecting the practitioner's intentions and the energies they wish to invite into their space. For example, a small bowl of earth or a stone might represent the grounding presence of Earth, while a feather symbolizes the lightness and clarity of Air. A candle might stand for Fire, while a shell or cup of water embodies the gentle flow of Water.

Symbols of the deities are also often placed on the altar, acknowledging the presence of the divine in the practitioner's life. These symbols can take many forms—a statue, a candle, a piece of artwork, or even a simple stone that has been dedicated to the Goddess or God. Each item is not just an object but a vessel of meaning, a reminder of the spiritual connection that guides the practitioner's path. For some, a single candle or flower might suffice, while others might include elaborate representations of both masculine and feminine energies, creating a balanced space that honors both.

Candles are central to most Wiccan altars, representing the element of Fire and serving as a source of light and focus. The flame of a candle symbolizes transformation, clarity, and spiritual awakening. Many practitioners light a candle at the beginning of each ritual or meditation, signifying the transition from the mundane to the sacred. Different colored candles can be chosen to reflect specific intentions or energies—green for healing, red for courage, blue for peace, or white for purity and protection. The candle flame itself becomes a point of meditation, a reminder of the inner fire that burns within each soul.

Crystals are another common addition to the Wiccan altar. Each crystal carries its own unique vibration and energy, enhancing the spiritual atmosphere of the altar. Clear quartz, for example, is known for its amplifying properties, making it a versatile tool in any ritual. Amethyst, with its soothing purple hue, encourages spiritual insight and emotional healing. Rose quartz fosters love and compassion, while citrine attracts abundance and creativity. By placing these stones on the altar, practitioners align their space with the energies that resonate with their intentions, creating a harmonious environment that supports their work.

Ritual tools such as the athame, chalice, wand, and pentacle are also commonly found on Wiccan altars. Each tool serves a distinct purpose in ritual and magical practice. The athame, a ceremonial blade, represents the element of Fire or, in some traditions, Air. It is used to direct energy, to cast circles, and to focus intention. The chalice, representing Water, is used for offerings and as a symbol of the Goddess. The wand, often associated with Air or Fire, is a tool for invoking spirits, directing energy, and communicating with the unseen. The pentacle, a disc marked with the five-pointed star, represents Earth and is a symbol of protection, grounding, and balance.

Arranging these items on the altar is an act of ritual in itself. Many Wiccans arrange the altar in a way that mirrors the four cardinal directions, placing symbols of Earth in the North, Air in the East, Fire in the South, and Water in the West. This arrangement reflects the balance and harmony of the elements, creating a miniature world within the altar space. However, each altar is unique, and practitioners are encouraged to follow their intuition, placing items where they feel they belong. The altar is a personal reflection, a space that aligns with the practitioner's inner vision and spiritual path.

In addition to these foundational items, many practitioners add personal touches that make the altar uniquely theirs. Some may place photos of loved ones, charms, feathers, flowers, or small trinkets that carry special meaning. Seasonal items are also common, allowing the altar to reflect the turning of the Wheel of the Year. For instance, in spring, fresh flowers or green leaves might adorn the altar, while autumn brings fallen leaves, acorns, and symbols of the harvest. This practice keeps the altar alive, changing with the seasons and resonating with the energy of the moment.

To activate the altar, practitioners often dedicate it with a prayer or blessing, stating their intentions and inviting divine guidance. This dedication is a way of imbuing the altar with purpose, marking it as a sacred space for spiritual growth, magical work, and communion with the divine. A simple invocation, such as "Blessed be this altar and all that I do here," can consecrate the space, setting it apart from the ordinary and aligning it with the energies of love, wisdom, and peace. With each ritual, the altar becomes more powerful, a vessel that holds and amplifies the practitioner's intentions.

The altar is not a static space but a living, evolving entity. It can be rearranged, refreshed, and revitalized as the practitioner's needs and intentions change. Over time, the altar becomes an extension of the practitioner's energy, a place that resonates with their spirit and holds their deepest aspirations. It is a space for reflection, for connection, and for transformation—a place to return to, time and again, to find clarity, comfort, and strength. The altar becomes a trusted companion on the spiritual path, a constant presence that grounds the practitioner and reminds them of their purpose.

In the quiet moments before the altar, practitioners may find themselves entering a meditative state, a deep stillness where thoughts fall away, and only presence remains. This is the heart of altar work—the communion with the divine that transcends words and symbols. As candles flicker and incense smoke curls through the air, the practitioner feels a sense of peace, of coming home to the sacred. In these moments, the altar is more than a collection of objects; it is a doorway to the infinite, a place where one's spirit touches the mysteries of existence.

For many Wiccans, the personal altar becomes a center of daily life, a place to greet the day, to give thanks, or to seek guidance in times of uncertainty. Through the act of visiting the altar regularly, practitioners establish a rhythm, a practice of devotion that strengthens their connection to the divine. The altar becomes a mirror of their journey, reflecting the changes, the growth, and the insights gained along the way. In this sacred space, practitioners honor the cycles of life, the power of intention, and the beauty of their own path.

The Wiccan altar is a reminder that the sacred is always close, that the divine can be honored in simple, personal ways. It is a place of wonder and wisdom, a sanctuary where one's spirit is free to explore, to dream, and to create. As practitioners build and tend to their altars, they cultivate a deeper understanding of themselves and their relationship with the world. The altar is a symbol of this journey, a place of unity and connection that serves as a bridge between the self and the infinite.

In the end, the personal altar is as unique as each practitioner. It is a space that evolves with the soul, a reflection of the love, reverence, and mystery that lie at the heart of Wicca. It is a place to honor the elements, to connect with the divine, and to find strength within oneself. For Wiccans, the altar is more than a ritual tool—it is a beloved space, a friend, and a guide on the path of wisdom, reminding them that the sacred is woven into every moment, every breath, and every heartbeat.

Chapter 11
Sacred Tools

In Wiccan practice, sacred tools hold a vital place, bridging the gap between the physical and spiritual worlds. Each tool is carefully selected, consecrated, and used with purpose, becoming an extension of the practitioner's will and intention. Unlike ordinary objects, these tools are imbued with symbolic power and represent the elements, divine energies, and archetypal forces. They assist in directing energy, focusing intent, and channeling the practitioner's inner power. Though each tool has its unique role and meaning, they all share a purpose—to aid the practitioner in their spiritual journey and to deepen their connection with the energies of the Wiccan path.

For Wiccans, working with sacred tools is not about the object itself but the intention and energy behind its use. These tools are treated with great respect, kept in a clean and honored space, and handled with reverence. They are not just instruments but spiritual companions, each one representing a unique aspect of the natural world and the divine. Some tools are traditional, while others are chosen according to personal preference or intuitive guidance, making each Wiccan's collection of tools uniquely theirs.

One of the most significant sacred tools is the **athame**. The athame is a ritual knife, typically with a double-edged blade and a black handle, used primarily for directing energy rather than cutting physical objects. Associated with the element of Fire (or Air in some traditions), the athame is a symbol of willpower, strength, and transformation. It is used to cast circles, to invoke the elements, and to focus energy during ritual work. The athame's sharp blade symbolizes clarity, decisiveness, and the power to shape reality according to one's intent. Its purpose is to channel the practitioner's will, guiding energy with precision and strength.

The athame is often personalized, with some Wiccans choosing to engrave symbols, runes, or sigils on the handle or blade. These markings reflect the practitioner's unique spiritual identity, embedding the athame with personal energy and purpose. While the athame may be central to formal rituals, it is also deeply personal, a reflection of the practitioner's inner power. It is typically consecrated before use, a process that aligns it with the energies of the practitioner and the divine, transforming it from a simple object into a sacred tool.

The **wand** is another significant tool in Wiccan practice, embodying a gentler form of energy direction. Traditionally associated with the element of Air (or Fire, depending on the tradition), the wand is used to invoke deities, spirits, or elemental energies, guiding the flow of energy in rituals and spells. Wands are often crafted from wood, with each type of wood carrying its own symbolic properties. Oak represents strength and wisdom, willow embodies intuition and flexibility, and hazel is known for its connection to divination. Some wands are decorated with crystals, feathers, or carvings, adding layers of symbolism and personal meaning.

Wands are commonly used in rituals that require invocation, communication, or blessing. They can also be used to draw symbols in the air, to mark sacred boundaries, or to direct energy within a circle. The wand is a versatile tool, adaptable to various forms of magical work, and serves as an extension of the practitioner's intent. Like the athame, the wand is consecrated, aligning it with the energies it will channel, making it a trusted companion in ritual.

The **chalice** is a sacred vessel representing the element of Water and symbolizing the Goddess, receptivity, and the womb of creation. Often made of silver, ceramic, or glass, the chalice holds liquids during ritual, most commonly water, wine, or herbal infusions. In some rituals, the chalice is used to represent the feminine principle, especially in ceremonies involving the Great Rite, which symbolizes the union of the masculine and feminine energies. The chalice may be filled with water during rituals as an offering to the elements or the deities, embodying the qualities of intuition, emotional depth, and healing.

The chalice is often placed on the altar during ceremonies, serving as a focal point for connection with the Goddess and the element of Water. It reminds practitioners of the importance of receptivity, nurturing, and inner reflection. The chalice is also used in ritual blessings, where practitioners may drink from it or use its contents to anoint themselves or others, infusing them with the qualities associated with the Goddess and Water. The act of drinking from the chalice is seen as a form of communion, a moment of unity with the divine and the energies of life.

The **pentacle** is a five-pointed star within a circle, representing Earth and symbolizing protection, balance, and the unity of the elements. In Wiccan tradition, each point of the pentacle corresponds to one of the five elements: Earth, Air, Fire, Water, and Spirit. Placed on the altar, the pentacle serves as a grounding tool, a reminder of the interconnectedness of all life. Traditionally made from wood, metal, or clay, the pentacle is often inscribed with symbols or sigils that align with the practitioner's intentions.

During rituals, the pentacle is used to consecrate other tools, hold offerings, or ground energy. It acts as a stabilizing force, anchoring the energy of the circle and providing a focal point for manifestation work. By placing items on the pentacle, Wiccans bless and infuse them with the qualities of Earth, ensuring that they are energetically balanced and protected. The pentacle embodies the Wiccan philosophy of unity and serves as a powerful emblem of connection with the earth.

The **cauldron**, a symbol of transformation and rebirth, holds a special place in Wiccan practice. Associated with the Goddess, the cauldron represents the womb, the cycle of life, and the mysteries of death and rebirth. Traditionally made of cast iron, the cauldron can hold water, herbs, or fire, and is used in various rituals and spells. It is a tool for brewing potions, burning offerings, or scrying (gazing into water or fire to gain insight). The cauldron serves as a miniature vessel of creation, a reminder of the eternal cycles that govern life and death.

In rituals, the cauldron is used to burn paper or herbs as an act of release or transformation, symbolizing the practitioner's willingness to let go of what no longer serves them. Water placed within the cauldron may be used for scrying, allowing the practitioner to access insights from the subconscious mind. The cauldron is a versatile tool, embodying the transformative power of the Goddess and reminding practitioners of the cyclical nature of existence.

The **incense burner** is another key item on the Wiccan altar, representing the element of Air and serving as a tool for purification and focus. Incense is burned to cleanse the space, to honor the spirits, or to mark the beginning of ritual. The smoke from incense is believed to carry prayers and intentions to the spirit realm, connecting the practitioner with higher energies. Different types of incense are used for specific purposes—sage for purification, frankincense for spiritual connection, sandalwood for grounding, and lavender for peace.

The act of lighting incense becomes a ritual in itself, a way of preparing the mind and body for the spiritual work ahead. The rising smoke symbolizes the lifting of thoughts and intentions, helping practitioners attune to the subtle energies of the sacred space. Incense is also used to cleanse other tools, wafting the smoke around them to clear away any residual energies. In this way, the incense burner acts as both a tool of transition and a bridge between worlds.

Each tool on the altar is **consecrated** before use, a process that aligns it with the energies of the practitioner and the divine. Consecration involves a ritual of blessing, where the tool is purified and dedicated to its intended purpose. This act of consecration is often done with the four elements—sprinkling the tool with salt (Earth), passing it through incense smoke (Air), holding it near a candle flame (Fire), and sprinkling it with water (Water). Through this ritual, the tool is transformed, becoming a sacred object that holds the practitioner's energy and intentions.

Consecrated tools are handled with care, cleaned regularly, and stored in a respectful manner. They may be wrapped in cloth, placed in a special box, or kept in a designated space on the altar. This care reflects the practitioner's respect for the energies each tool holds and their dedication to the path. The tools are not treated as possessions but as allies, each contributing to the balance and effectiveness of the practitioner's spiritual work.

Over time, sacred tools become deeply attuned to the practitioner's energy, creating a bond that enhances their effectiveness in ritual. Just as a musician forms a connection with their instrument, a Wiccan forms a connection with their tools, understanding their unique energy and qualities. This bond brings a sense of familiarity and trust, allowing the practitioner to work more intuitively and confidently in ritual. Each tool becomes an extension of the self, reflecting the practitioner's intentions, beliefs, and journey on the Wiccan path.

In the end, sacred tools serve as a bridge between the seen and unseen worlds, helping practitioners connect with the divine, the elements, and their own inner wisdom. They are more than objects; they are symbols of the practitioner's commitment to growth, transformation, and spiritual exploration. Through the mindful use of these tools, Wiccans honor the sacred, deepen their practice, and walk their path with reverence, purpose, and joy.

Chapter 12
Ritual Garments

In the Wiccan tradition, ritual garments serve as a physical and symbolic way to step into the sacred. These garments are not merely items of clothing but are treated as expressions of the practitioner's spiritual state, purpose, and connection to the divine. Wearing ritual attire is a way to leave behind the everyday and enter a space of reverence and intention. Each fabric, color, and design holds meaning, helping the practitioner align with the energies they wish to invoke. To don ritual garments is to signal the mind and body that the time has come for transformation, that one is stepping into the realm of the sacred.

Ritual garments vary greatly among Wiccans, as personal preference, tradition, and intention play significant roles in their selection. For some, simple robes or tunics serve as the primary attire, while others may incorporate jewelry, sashes, or cloaks adorned with symbols of personal meaning. The garments chosen are not simply for aesthetic appeal; they are aligned with the practitioner's energy and intentions, helping to create a connection between the individual and the forces they call upon. In many ways, these garments become as much a part of the ritual as the altar, the tools, and the invocations, enhancing the energy and focus of the practitioner.

For many practitioners, the choice to wear ritual attire is a deeply personal one. Some may wear garments only for formal ceremonies or group rituals, while others incorporate them into their solitary practice as a means of deepening their connection to the divine. Regardless of when or where they are worn, ritual garments serve to bridge the gap between the ordinary and the extraordinary, allowing the practitioner to step out of the everyday world and into a state of sacred awareness. Each time they are donned, the garments become a reminder of the path, a symbol of devotion, and a means of aligning with the energies of nature and spirit.

The Ritual Robe is perhaps the most commonly used garment in Wiccan practice. It is often simple in design, with a flowing shape that allows for comfort and freedom of movement. Traditionally, robes are made from natural fabrics like cotton, linen, or silk, materials that are believed to carry the earth's energy and support the practitioner's connection to nature. A robe can be plain or adorned with symbols, embroidery, or colors that hold specific meanings. Some practitioners prefer a robe that is reserved solely for ritual use, treating it as sacred attire that is never worn outside of ceremonial work.

Each color of robe carries its own energy and symbolism, allowing practitioners to align their attire with the intention of the ritual. A black robe is commonly worn for protection and grounding, as black is known for its ability to absorb and neutralize negative energy. White robes are associated with purity, clarity, and connection to Spirit, making them suitable for rituals involving healing, divination, or communion with higher energies. Green robes may be worn for nature-focused rites, fertility spells, or work with Earth energy, while red robes represent passion, courage, and the fiery energy of transformation. The choice of color is a way to tune oneself to the specific vibration needed for each ritual, allowing the robe to become a conduit for the desired energy.

The Cloak is another garment frequently used in Wicca, providing a sense of protection and mystery. Many Wiccans wear cloaks with hoods, which can be drawn over the head to create a sense of enclosure and focus. The cloak is often seen as a shield, a garment that encircles the wearer and allows them to carry their sacred space with them, especially in outdoor settings. When wrapped in a cloak, the practitioner is reminded of their connection to the elements, to the night sky, and to the mysteries they seek to honor. Cloaks, like robes, are often made from natural fibers and may be black, dark blue, or green to blend with nature, providing a feeling of invisibility and closeness to the earth.

Some Wiccans incorporate **ritual sashes or belts** into their attire, adding layers of meaning to their garments. A sash can be worn around the waist or across the shoulder, representing dedication to a particular aspect of the craft or signifying an important milestone, such as initiation or advancement within a coven. Belts and sashes may be color-coded according to the elements, with green for Earth, yellow for Air, red for Fire, and blue for Water. These garments are often handmade, crafted with intention and care, and may include beads, charms, or knots that carry personal meaning or reflect the practitioner's goals. Each knot or bead can be imbued with energy during its creation, transforming the sash or belt into a talisman of protection, focus, or guidance.

Jewelry also holds a significant place in ritual attire, often serving as a form of magical tool or amulet. Many Wiccans wear rings, necklaces, bracelets, or earrings that carry symbols of their beliefs, such as pentacles, crescent moons, or crystals. These items are not simply adornments; they are powerful symbols that carry the wearer's energy and intentions. A pendant with a pentacle, for example, may be worn for protection, while a moonstone ring connects the wearer to lunar energy and enhances intuition. Jewelry is often consecrated before it is worn, transforming it into a piece of ritual equipment that resonates with the practitioner's personal energy.

The colors of ritual attire play an essential role in Wiccan practice, each color chosen for its vibrational qualities and associations. While black is known for its grounding and protective qualities, white is revered for its purity and spiritual connection. Red, as the color of blood and fire, symbolizes life force, courage, and transformation. Green represents growth, fertility, and harmony with nature, while blue evokes the qualities of peace, healing, and the ocean's depth. Purple is associated with spirituality, psychic awareness, and connection to the divine, making it an ideal choice for rituals of meditation or inner vision. The practitioner's choice of color is often guided by intuition and the specific energies they wish to invoke, allowing the garments to support their intentions on a subtle but powerful level.

For those who practice in groups, ritual attire often serves as a unifying element, creating a sense of cohesion and shared purpose. In some covens, members wear matching robes or cloaks, aligning them visually and energetically. This uniformity symbolizes unity and harmony, reinforcing the group's collective energy and purpose. While each practitioner brings their individuality to the circle, the shared attire serves as a reminder of the group's common goals and values, creating a collective sense of sacred space.

Preparation and consecration of ritual garments are important steps that align the attire with its intended purpose. Before wearing ritual garments, many Wiccans will cleanse them through smudging with sage or incense, sprinkling them with blessed water, or placing them under the light of the full moon. This cleansing removes any residual energies, creating a garment that is fresh and attuned to the practitioner's own energy. Some may also speak a blessing or intention over the garments, dedicating them to their spiritual path and infusing them with personal power.

Each time ritual garments are worn, they become more deeply attuned to the practitioner's energy, creating a bond that strengthens with use. Over time, these garments carry the memories of rituals past, the energy of prayers spoken, and the intentions set within the sacred space. They become imbued with the essence of the practitioner's journey, a tangible expression of their growth and dedication. Some Wiccans reserve their ritual garments solely for special ceremonies, while others wear them for solitary practices, creating a consistent routine that prepares the mind and body for spiritual work.

For those who prefer to practice without formal attire, **ritual nudity**, or "skyclad" practice, is also a respected tradition within Wicca. The term "skyclad" means practicing without clothing, a state that symbolizes openness, purity, and freedom from societal constraints. Many practitioners feel that practicing skyclad allows for a deeper connection to the elements and a heightened sense of self. It is a way of approaching the divine without barriers, honoring the body as a natural and sacred vessel. However, this practice is deeply personal, and each practitioner chooses whether to incorporate it based on their comfort, beliefs, and the setting of their practice.

In Wicca, ritual garments serve as a bridge between the inner and outer worlds, helping practitioners embody the qualities they seek and aligning them with the energies of their intentions. Whether through robes, cloaks, jewelry, or color, these garments create a sensory experience that enhances the ritual, grounding the practitioner and creating a sense of reverence. To put on ritual attire is to step into one's spiritual identity, to embrace the sacred within and around, and to honor the path one walks.

Each time they are donned, ritual garments transform the practitioner's space, marking it as a place of magic and mystery. Through these garments, Wiccans connect to the timeless rhythms of nature, the presence of the divine, and the power within themselves.

Chapter 13
Triple Goddess

In Wiccan spirituality, the divine feminine is often envisioned as the Triple Goddess, a symbol of the sacred feminine unfolding in three interconnected aspects: the Maiden, the Mother, and the Crone. This trinity captures the cycles of life, reflecting the natural progressions of birth, growth, death, and rebirth. The Triple Goddess is not only a representation of divine power; she is also a reflection of human experience and the rhythms of the earth. In her various forms, the Goddess offers guidance, protection, and wisdom, becoming a presence that Wiccans can relate to on deeply personal and universal levels.

The idea of the Triple Goddess finds its origins in ancient mythologies from around the world. Many early cultures recognized divine figures with multiple aspects, often aligned with the cycles of the moon, the changing seasons, or the stages of life. Over time, the concept evolved into the Triple Goddess known in Wicca, whose presence encompasses the beauty, creativity, and wisdom of the feminine principle. For Wiccans, connecting with the Triple Goddess is a way of understanding the phases of life, embracing change, and honoring the cycles of nature that are mirrored within each person.

The **Maiden** is the first aspect of the Triple Goddess, symbolizing youth, new beginnings, and untamed potential. She represents the energy of springtime, a season of renewal and growth when the earth awakens with life. The Maiden's spirit is vibrant, curious, and filled with the promise of new adventures. She embodies freedom, innocence, and discovery, inviting

Wiccans to approach life with openness and wonder. In the Maiden, Wiccans find a source of inspiration for new projects, personal growth, and the courage to explore unknown paths.

Aligned with the waxing moon, the Maiden's energy is building, dynamic, and forward-looking. She encourages practitioners to plant the seeds of intention, to nurture dreams, and to embrace the excitement of possibility. When Wiccans invoke the Maiden, they seek her guidance for beginnings—new relationships, creative endeavors, or personal transformations. The Maiden teaches that growth requires both patience and courage, that each new step on the journey is part of a greater unfolding. Her energy is playful and bold, reminding practitioners of the beauty of exploration and the power of trusting their own potential.

The Maiden is often symbolized by flowers, crescent moons, or bright colors that evoke the fresh energy of spring. In ritual, Wiccans may call upon the Maiden when they need motivation, clarity, or a sense of renewal. She is a reminder that each beginning carries within it the potential for growth, that the first step is sacred and that life itself is a journey of constant discovery. By embracing the Maiden's qualities, Wiccans reconnect with the youthful spirit within, the part of themselves that is always ready to explore, to learn, and to create.

The **Mother** is the second aspect of the Triple Goddess, representing fertility, nurturing, and abundance. She is aligned with the full moon, a time of fullness, fruition, and realization. In the Mother, Wiccans see the power of creation and the ability to bring dreams into reality. She is the goddess of summer, the earth in full bloom, the harvest that sustains life. The Mother embodies compassion, love, and protection, offering her strength to those who seek her guidance and care. Her energy is expansive and life-giving, a source of unconditional support and nurturing.

For Wiccans, the Mother represents the act of nurturing oneself, others, and the earth. She teaches that true power lies not in control but in the ability to care, to foster growth, and to offer love freely. In the Mother's presence, Wiccans are reminded of the importance of balance, the need to tend to their own needs while supporting the well-being of others. Her wisdom is that of experience, understanding that growth requires time, patience, and dedication. When Wiccans invoke the Mother, they seek her blessings for abundance, health, and harmony, drawing upon her strength to manifest their intentions.

The Mother is often represented by symbols of fertility, such as grains, fruits, or flowers in full bloom, as well as the full moon that shines with her presence. In rituals, Wiccans call upon the Mother for guidance in nurturing relationships, for support in times of difficulty, or for aid in manifesting goals. She is a powerful figure, embodying both strength and tenderness, reminding practitioners of the importance of giving and receiving in equal measure. By connecting with the Mother, Wiccans embrace the part of themselves that is capable of love, compassion, and the courage to bring forth life in all its forms.

The **Crone** is the third aspect of the Triple Goddess, symbolizing wisdom, transformation, and the mysteries of death and rebirth. She is aligned with the waning and dark moon, a time of introspection, release, and closure. The Crone's energy is that of autumn and winter, when the earth turns inward, preparing for renewal. She is the wise woman, the keeper of secrets, and the guide to the mysteries of the unseen. The Crone teaches Wiccans that death is not an end but a necessary part of life's cycle, a transformation that brings renewal and growth.

In the Crone, Wiccans find the strength to release what no longer serves them, to face fears, and to embrace the unknown. Her energy is quiet yet powerful, filled with insight and understanding. The Crone is a figure of resilience and wisdom, a reminder that life's trials and challenges bring knowledge that cannot be gained through ease alone. When Wiccans invoke the Crone, they seek her guidance for inner work, shadow work, and the process of letting go. She is the teacher of transformation, offering her wisdom to those who are ready to journey within and find strength in their own depths.

The Crone is often symbolized by the waning moon, bare trees, or objects that evoke the mystery of night and the power of endings. In ritual, Wiccans call upon the Crone for insight, for the courage to face transitions, or for assistance in healing wounds from the past. She teaches that true wisdom lies in accepting the cycles of life, that every ending is a doorway to new beginnings, and that the darkness holds its own form of light. By connecting with the Crone, Wiccans honor the part of themselves that holds knowledge, resilience, and the ability to embrace life's full spectrum.

Together, the Maiden, Mother, and Crone form a trinity that encompasses the entire spectrum of existence. In each phase of the Triple Goddess, Wiccans find guidance for their own journey, recognizing that life is an ever-turning wheel of change, growth, and transformation. Each aspect of the Goddess reflects the stages that every soul encounters, from the innocence and curiosity of youth to the nurturing and creativity of maturity, and finally to the wisdom and acceptance of life's twilight. Through the Triple Goddess, Wiccans learn to honor each phase of life, understanding that every stage holds its own unique beauty and purpose.

The cycles of the Triple Goddess are mirrored in the natural world, reflecting the waxing, full, and waning phases of the moon and the turning of the seasons. The moon, a powerful symbol of the Goddess, goes through her own transformations, shifting from Maiden to Mother to Crone each month. Wiccans draw inspiration from the moon's journey, seeing in her phases a reminder of the natural rhythms that govern all life. Just as the moon waxes and wanes, so too does human life, each phase a necessary step on the path to wholeness.

In rituals, Wiccans may choose to work with one aspect of the Triple Goddess depending on the intention and energy they wish to invoke. For new beginnings, inspiration, or courage, they might call upon the Maiden, asking for her guidance in taking the first steps. For support, nurturing, or manifesting goals, the Mother is invoked, her presence bringing strength and abundance.

For reflection, release, or seeking inner wisdom, the Crone is called upon, offering her insight and her acceptance of life's mysteries. The Triple Goddess is not distant; she is a living force that Wiccans can connect with, a source of support, comfort, and wisdom at every stage.

Through the Triple Goddess, Wiccans celebrate the beauty of the feminine spirit, seeing her as both a protector and a guide, a source of empowerment and transformation. The Triple Goddess is not limited to women alone; her qualities are universal, and her wisdom speaks to all who seek to understand themselves and their place within the cycles of life. She embodies the sacred within each soul, inviting all to embrace their journey with openness, love, and respect for the wisdom that comes from experience.

The Triple Goddess, in all her forms, teaches that life is sacred, that every phase has its own purpose, and that the path of growth is one of embracing both light and shadow. She is a reminder that within each person lies the Maiden's curiosity, the Mother's love, and the Crone's wisdom, all coexisting and guiding the journey toward self-realization and unity with the divine. In honoring the Triple Goddess, Wiccans honor the cycles of nature, the mysteries of existence, and the divine essence that flows through all life. Through her, they find strength, compassion, and the courage to embrace life in its fullness, trusting in the beauty of each phase of the journey.

Chapter 14
Horned God

In Wiccan belief, the Horned God stands as the counterpart to the Triple Goddess, embodying the sacred masculine energies of the natural world. He is both the wild, untamed spirit of the forest and the nurturing force that guides, protects, and sustains life. As Lord of Animals, Sun, and Guardian of the cycles of life and death, the Horned God represents the primal energies that shape existence, offering Wiccans a path to understand and connect with the rhythms of nature. His presence is both fierce and gentle, embodying strength, wisdom, and a deep reverence for life.

The Horned God appears in many forms across various cultures and mythologies, reflecting humanity's ancient connection to the land and the seasons. He is often envisioned with antlers or horns, symbols of his link to the animal kingdom, his wild spirit, and his role as protector. In ancient Celtic traditions, he was known as Cernunnos, the god of forests, fertility, and wealth, depicted with horns and surrounded by animals. In Greco-Roman myth, he appeared as Pan, the woodland god of music and nature. These archetypes, though varied, share the essence of the Horned God—a deity who embodies the untamed forces of nature and the cyclical nature of life.

In Wiccan practice, the Horned God is honored as a vital force that brings balance to the Goddess. Together, they represent the sacred duality of life: the union of masculine and feminine, light and dark, creation and destruction. Just as the Goddess is seen in her Triple form as Maiden, Mother, and Crone, the Horned God appears in different aspects, each one representing a phase of the cycle of life, death, and rebirth. He is seen as a teacher, a guide, and a protector, helping Wiccans find strength within themselves and harmony with the world around them.

The first aspect of the Horned God is **Lord of Animals**, a role that aligns him closely with the forces of Earth and the creatures that inhabit it. As the Lord of Animals, he is both hunter and protector, embodying the instincts, wisdom, and primal energy of the animal kingdom. In this form, the Horned God teaches Wiccans to respect the natural world, to honor the lives of all creatures, and to understand the balance between predator and prey. He is a reminder of the wild spirit within each person, the untamed energy that longs for freedom and connection with the earth.

In ritual, the Horned God as Lord of Animals may be invoked for strength, guidance, and the courage to embrace one's instincts. His energy is grounding, offering practitioners a way to connect with their own primal nature and the wisdom of their bodies. Wiccans honor him as the spirit of the forest, the force that keeps the cycles of nature in balance, and the guardian of life's mysteries. His symbols often include antlers, animal bones, and representations of wild creatures, each one a reminder of the sacredness of all life and the interconnectedness of all beings.

The Horned God's second aspect is **Lord of the Sun**, representing vitality, illumination, and the creative force of light. As the Sun God, he is aligned with the changing seasons, particularly the solstices, where his power rises to its zenith or descends into shadow. His presence is felt in the warmth of summer, in the brightness of day, and in the life-giving light that sustains the earth. The Horned God as Lord of the Sun embodies strength, resilience, and the ability to shine through even the darkest times, offering a path to growth, clarity, and purpose.

In Wiccan celebrations of the Wheel of the Year, the Sun God's journey is honored in seasonal festivals that reflect his cycle of birth, life, and eventual sacrifice. At Yule, the winter solstice, he is born anew, bringing hope and light to the world at its darkest hour. As he grows stronger through spring and summer, he reaches his peak at Litha, the summer solstice, radiating life-giving energy before slowly beginning his descent toward the shadow of winter. In this journey, Wiccans see the natural rhythms of life mirrored, a reminder that every peak is followed by a return to rest, and every end is a beginning.

To connect with the Sun aspect of the Horned God, Wiccans may incorporate solar symbols, such as gold candles, sunflowers, or bright crystals like citrine and amber. His energy is invoked for strength, confidence, and clarity, for projects that require vitality and perseverance, and for guidance during times of uncertainty. The Horned God as Lord of the Sun teaches that life itself is a cycle of illumination and shadow, encouraging practitioners to seek balance, to grow, and to understand the importance of each season in their own journey.

The third aspect of the Horned God is **Guardian of the Underworld**, the keeper of secrets, death, and transformation. In this form, he is the God of the shadow, guiding souls through the mysteries of death and offering rebirth in new forms. He embodies the wisdom of endings, the power of release, and the profound transformation that occurs when one accepts the inevitability of change. The Guardian of the Underworld is not a figure to be feared; rather, he is a guide who helps practitioners confront their own fears, embrace transformation, and find strength in the unknown.

As Guardian of the Underworld, the Horned God is associated with Samhain, the festival marking the end of the harvest and the thinning of the veil between worlds. During Samhain, Wiccans honor the spirits of their ancestors and seek guidance from those who have passed beyond the physical realm. The Horned God, in his underworld aspect, serves as a bridge between life and death, a reminder that every end holds within it the seeds of rebirth. His energy encourages Wiccans to face the mysteries of death with courage, knowing that the cycles of nature ensure renewal and that the spirit endures beyond physical form.

In ritual, the Horned God as Guardian of the Underworld may be invoked for guidance during difficult transitions, for support in shadow work, or for help in releasing what no longer serves. His symbols include skulls, bones, black candles, and representations of animals like the owl or wolf, each connected to the mysteries of transformation. By connecting with this aspect of the Horned God, Wiccans learn to trust in the process of change, to find wisdom in endings, and to recognize the power that lies in surrendering to life's natural flow.

The Horned God, through each of his aspects, teaches Wiccans to honor the cycles of life, to respect both strength and vulnerability, and to find harmony within themselves and with nature. He is both wild and wise, fierce and compassionate, embodying a balanced approach to life that respects both action and introspection. As the consort of the Goddess, he represents the dynamic, generative force that, together with the nurturing energies of the Goddess, sustains the natural world. His presence reminds practitioners that masculine energy is not about domination but about partnership, protection, and respect for all life.

In some Wiccan traditions, the Horned God is not a single deity but a collective archetype encompassing various gods associated with nature, fertility, and the wilderness. Each deity, whether it be Cernunnos, Pan, or Herne, reflects a different facet of the Horned God, bringing unique insights and qualities. This flexibility allows practitioners to connect with the aspect of the Horned God that resonates most deeply with them, forging a personal relationship with the divine masculine that reflects their own beliefs and experiences.

For many Wiccans, invoking the Horned God is an act of grounding and centering, a way of connecting with the primal energies that flow through all of existence. His presence brings a sense of stability and confidence, encouraging practitioners to stand firmly in their power, to trust in their instincts, and to respect the cycles of life and death. The Horned God teaches that true strength is found in harmony with nature, that wisdom lies in understanding one's own inner wilderness, and that growth often requires both light and shadow.

In honoring the Horned God, Wiccans embrace the duality of life, understanding that both creation and destruction are necessary for balance. He is a reminder that every journey is part of a larger cycle, that every death brings new life, and that the wildness within is a source of wisdom and connection. By working with the Horned God, Wiccans find strength in their own spirit, the courage to face their fears, and the grace to walk their path with respect for all life.

The Horned God stands as a guardian of the natural world, a symbol of masculine energy that is deeply intertwined with the earth, the sun, and the mysteries of transformation. His presence offers guidance, comfort, and strength, reminding Wiccans that they are part of a vast, interconnected web of life. Through him, practitioners find balance within themselves, learning to honor both their inner fire and their capacity for growth and change. In the Horned God, Wiccans see the beauty of life's cycles, a reminder of the power within and around them, always guiding them on their path toward unity with nature and the divine.

Chapter 15
Divine Pantheons

The Wiccan path, while rooted in its own spiritual practices, is enriched by a vast tapestry of deities from various cultures and historical periods. Known as divine pantheons, these collections of gods and goddesses represent different aspects of life, nature, and the universe, each bringing unique qualities, stories, and wisdom. For Wiccans, exploring and choosing deities from these pantheons is a personal and often transformative journey, one that allows them to connect with the divine in ways that feel meaningful and deeply resonant. By working with different gods and goddesses, practitioners find inspiration, guidance, and support, weaving diverse expressions of divinity into their spiritual practice.

Wiccans do not view pantheons as rigid or exclusive; rather, they see each deity as a unique representation of universal forces. Many practitioners take an eclectic approach, honoring deities from multiple cultures, finding that different gods and goddesses resonate with specific needs, life stages, or areas of spiritual work. This openness allows Wiccans to craft a deeply personal path, one that reflects both ancient wisdom and individual experience. The selection of deities is often guided by intuition, study, and personal connection, encouraging Wiccans to explore diverse traditions while honoring the essence of each god or goddess they invoke.

Among the many pantheons that Wiccans might draw upon, the **Celtic pantheon** holds a prominent place, deeply intertwined with nature, seasons, and the mysticism of the land.

Deities like Brigid, a goddess of fire, healing, and creativity, and Cernunnos, the horned god of the forest and animals, embody qualities that are central to Wiccan practice. The Celts saw their gods and goddesses as intimately connected to the elements and landscapes around them, and their myths are filled with reverence for the cycles of life, death, and rebirth. When a Wiccan invokes Brigid, for example, they may be seeking guidance in creative pursuits, healing, or self-empowerment, while calling upon Cernunnos may bring a deeper connection to the earth and its creatures.

Working with Celtic deities often involves a respect for nature and a focus on the inner qualities these gods and goddesses represent. For instance, the Morrigan, a complex goddess associated with battle, sovereignty, and transformation, is called upon by those seeking inner strength and the courage to face life's challenges. By honoring these deities, Wiccans are reminded of the natural world's power, the beauty of resilience, and the importance of embracing the mysteries within. The myths of the Celtic gods are woven with lessons in transformation, courage, and the wisdom that comes from respecting the cycles of nature.

The **Greek pantheon** also provides rich sources of inspiration for Wiccan practitioners. Figures like Demeter, goddess of the harvest, and Apollo, god of the sun, music, and healing, represent forces that resonate with Wiccan beliefs in the sacredness of nature and the cycles of life. Greek gods and goddesses are known for their complex personalities, embodying a wide range of human traits that make them relatable and approachable. Their myths offer powerful stories of love, sacrifice, wisdom, and transformation, each story carrying lessons that practitioners may draw upon in their own lives.

A Wiccan might invoke Demeter to bless the harvest season, to seek comfort in times of loss, or to honor the motherly qualities of nurture and protection. Aphrodite, the goddess of love and beauty, may be called upon in rituals involving self-love, attraction, and emotional healing. Each Greek deity brings specific energies, making them suitable for different forms of magical work and personal exploration. Through their stories, Wiccans find guidance in navigating the complexities of emotion, relationship, and self-discovery.

Another significant source of divine archetypes in Wicca is the **Norse pantheon**, known for its strong associations with fate, courage, and natural elements. Norse deities such as Odin, the wise and enigmatic god of wisdom and prophecy, and Freyja, goddess of love, war, and magic, are invoked by Wiccans seeking insight, courage, or deeper knowledge of themselves. Odin's journey of self-sacrifice on the World Tree Yggdrasil, where he hung for nine days to gain the wisdom of the runes, is a potent symbol of the search for inner truth and transformation. Freyja's connection to both love and battle reflects the balance of tenderness and strength that many practitioners seek to embody.

The Norse pantheon, with its focus on cycles of creation and destruction, resonates with the Wiccan view of life as a series of interconnected cycles. Each Norse deity offers lessons in resilience, honor, and personal power. Thor, the thunder god, is often invoked for protection, strength, and the courage to overcome obstacles. His presence reminds practitioners of the power that lies within and the importance of standing firm in one's beliefs. The myths of the Norse gods, filled with tales of bravery and fate, encourage Wiccans to embrace their own paths with a similar sense of purpose and dedication.

The **Egyptian pantheon** brings a sense of ancient mystery and wisdom, with deities like Isis, the mother goddess of magic and healing, and Anubis, the jackal-headed god of the afterlife. Egyptian gods are often associated with the cycles of life, death, and rebirth, as well as with the elements of nature. Isis, revered for her protective and nurturing qualities, is a powerful figure for Wiccans seeking healing, compassion, and insight into the mysteries of life. Her story of resurrection and transformation, as she restores her husband Osiris to life, speaks to the Wiccan belief in the cycles of renewal and the power of love.

Egyptian deities are also associated with specific magical practices. For instance, invoking Thoth, the god of wisdom and writing, can aid in divination, study, or communication, enhancing clarity and understanding. Sekhmet, the lioness goddess of war and healing, embodies the fierce yet compassionate aspects of transformation, and is often called upon in rituals for protection and personal empowerment. The Egyptian pantheon offers a wide range of energies that can guide practitioners through different aspects of their spiritual journey, reminding them of the sacred and eternal nature of existence.

In choosing which pantheon to work with, many Wiccans rely on a combination of **research and intuition**. Learning about a deity's origins, symbols, and myths helps practitioners understand the qualities and powers associated with each god or goddess. However, the decision is often guided by a feeling of resonance or connection—a sense that a particular deity is calling to them or reflects an aspect of themselves they wish to explore. Wiccans believe that the relationship between practitioner and deity is reciprocal, an exchange of energy that grows through respect, dedication, and open-hearted intention.

When honoring deities from various pantheons, Wiccans approach each god or goddess with reverence, aware of the cultural context in which these deities were originally worshiped. This respect is crucial, as each deity carries a unique history and cultural identity. Some practitioners prefer to work solely within a specific pantheon, finding that it deepens their connection to a particular culture's worldview. Others blend deities from different pantheons, creating a diverse spiritual practice that honors the unique energies each deity brings.

The practice of **building a personal pantheon** is an integral part of many Wiccan paths, allowing practitioners to create a spiritual network of divine figures that resonate with their own lives and intentions. These chosen deities become spiritual allies, companions, and mentors, each one offering specific guidance or support. Some practitioners build their pantheon over time, gradually adding gods and goddesses who speak to them, while others may work closely with a few deities throughout their lives. Each relationship is unique, evolving as the practitioner grows and as new insights and experiences shape their path.

The **invocation of deities** from these pantheons during ritual is a sacred act, a calling of the divine energies into the practitioner's space and heart. Invocations may be spoken, chanted, or visualized, each word or thought inviting the presence of the god or goddess into the ritual. When calling upon a deity, Wiccans often use symbols, offerings, or colors associated with that god or goddess, creating a space that is welcoming and aligned with their energy. The act of invocation is an invitation, a gesture of trust and openness, allowing the practitioner to receive the guidance, protection, or wisdom the deity offers.

In return, Wiccans **offer respect, gratitude, and devotion** to the deities they work with. This can take many forms, from simple offerings of food, herbs, or flowers to acts of service and dedication. Many Wiccans maintain an altar space for their chosen deities, placing statues, candles, or symbols that honor their presence. These acts of devotion are more than ritual gestures; they reflect the practitioner's ongoing relationship with the divine, a bond that strengthens through mutual respect and love.

The exploration of divine pantheons in Wicca is not just a study of mythology but a journey of personal and spiritual discovery. Through their relationships with deities, Wiccans gain insights into their own nature, learn to honor the cycles of life, and find the courage to face the unknown. Each god and goddess becomes a teacher, a mirror, and a guide, helping practitioners navigate their path with wisdom, strength, and compassion. This blending of pantheons creates a spiritual practice that is as diverse as it is unified, a reflection of the many ways that the divine manifests in the world and within each soul.

Ultimately, the divine pantheons are a reminder of the interconnectedness of all life, of the many expressions of the sacred that exist across cultures, times, and places. By working with these deities, Wiccans honor the richness of the world's spiritual heritage, celebrating the diversity and unity of the divine.

Through the gods and goddesses they invoke, Wiccans find connection, purpose, and a deeper understanding of themselves and the mysteries of existence. The pantheons serve as a bridge between the individual and the cosmos, inviting each practitioner to step into a sacred dance with the divine.

Chapter 16
Spirit Guardians

In Wiccan tradition, Spirit Guardians, often known as the Guardians of the Directions, serve as powerful protectors and guides in ritual practice. These beings are called upon to safeguard the sacred space, to bring balance, and to assist practitioners in connecting with the elemental forces that structure and sustain the natural world. Each Guardian is associated with a cardinal direction—North, East, South, and West—and embodies the energy of one of the four classical elements: Earth, Air, Fire, and Water. In some practices, a fifth Guardian, Spirit, is also invoked, representing unity and the divine presence that binds all things together.

The calling of Spirit Guardians is more than a ritual gesture; it is an invitation for these energies to support and empower the practitioner's work. When the Guardians are summoned, they bring a unique essence to the sacred space, enhancing the focus and purpose of the ritual. Each Guardian holds wisdom and strength, offering a pathway to connect with the elemental energies that shape the universe. By honoring the Guardians of the Directions, Wiccans acknowledge their place within the natural world and align themselves with the powerful forces that move through all of existence.

To begin working with Spirit Guardians, Wiccans prepare by **casting a circle** and establishing a sacred space. The circle acts as a boundary between the mundane world and the spiritual realm, creating a protective and focused environment for ritual work. Within this circle, the Guardians are called upon from their respective directions, each one bringing an energy that enhances and protects the space. The act of summoning the Guardians is performed with reverence, as these beings are seen not only as protectors but also as respected allies.

The **Guardian of the North** is the embodiment of Earth energy, representing stability, grounding, and the nurturing aspect of the natural world. North is often viewed as the direction of strength, patience, and endurance, and the Guardian of the North is associated with mountains, forests, stones, and soil. This Guardian offers the qualities of resilience, prosperity, and protection, helping practitioners to stay grounded and centered in their practice. When calling upon the North, Wiccans honor the earth beneath their feet, the stability of roots, and the quiet wisdom of the land.

In ritual, the Guardian of the North may be invoked to provide grounding energy, to foster growth, or to protect the space from negative influences. Wiccans often place a representation of Earth in the northern part of the circle, such as a stone, salt, or soil, as an offering and symbol of respect. This Guardian is particularly helpful in rituals for prosperity, healing, and manifestation, guiding practitioners to align with the slow, steady rhythms of the earth. When the energy of North is present, it brings a sense of calm and security, a reminder of the ancient, unwavering strength of the earth.

The **Guardian of the East** represents the element of Air, embodying clarity, intellect, and the breath of life. East is the direction of new beginnings, inspiration, and the dawning of ideas, connected to the wind that sweeps away old energy and brings freshness and insight. This Guardian is associated with the sky, birds, clouds, and the movement of air. When calling upon the Guardian of the East, Wiccans invite mental clarity, inspiration, and open communication, allowing the spirit of Air to bring new perspectives and to clear away mental fog.

In ritual, the Guardian of the East is invoked to enhance intuition, communication, and the flow of ideas. Wiccans often place a feather, incense, or another symbol of Air in the eastern part of the circle to honor this Guardian. The Guardian of the East is particularly beneficial for spells or meditations focused on creativity, insight, and wisdom. By connecting with this energy, practitioners are reminded of the importance of openness, curiosity, and the power of breath as a bridge between body and spirit. The presence of the Guardian of the East brings a sense of expansion, a feeling of limitless possibility and mental freedom.

The **Guardian of the South** is the representative of Fire, symbolizing transformation, passion, and the raw energy of creation. South is associated with warmth, courage, and vitality, embodying the spark that ignites change and drives the will forward. The Guardian of the South is connected to the sun, flames, and the heat of life itself, bringing a dynamic and vibrant energy to ritual work. When calling upon the South, Wiccans invoke the powers of strength, courage, and the inner fire that fuels creativity and action.

In ritual, the Guardian of the South may be honored with the lighting of a candle or by placing a symbol of Fire, such as a red stone or match, in the southern part of the circle. This Guardian is called upon to instill courage, to break through obstacles, and to inspire transformation. The energy of the South is particularly powerful in rituals that require strength, change, and the pursuit of one's goals. Through the Guardian of the South, Wiccans connect to the fiery spirit within themselves, finding the willpower and inspiration to move forward and to bring their intentions to life. This Guardian's presence fills the space with warmth and light, a reminder of the power that lies in embracing one's passion and drive.

The **Guardian of the West** embodies the element of Water, representing intuition, emotion, and the mysteries of the subconscious. West is the direction of dusk, of the setting sun, and of introspection. The Guardian of the West is connected to rivers, lakes, oceans, and rain, bringing the qualities of compassion, healing, and emotional depth. When Wiccans call upon the West, they seek connection to their own inner world, to the flow of emotions and the wisdom that comes from reflection and acceptance.

In ritual, the Guardian of the West is often represented by a bowl of water, a seashell, or another symbol of Water placed in the western part of the circle. This Guardian is particularly helpful in rituals for healing, emotional release, and dream work, allowing practitioners to explore their inner realms and to release what no longer serves them. The energy of the West encourages practitioners to listen to their intuition, to embrace their emotions, and to find peace within themselves. The presence of the Guardian of the West brings a sense of fluidity, openness, and compassion, helping Wiccans to navigate their own emotional landscapes with grace and understanding.

The **Guardian of the Center** (or Spirit) is invoked in some Wiccan practices to represent unity, balance, and the divine essence that binds all things. Spirit is often seen as the fifth element, transcending and connecting the energies of Earth, Air, Fire, and Water. The Guardian of Spirit is not limited by direction but resides within the center of the circle, embodying the sacred unity of all creation. When Wiccans call upon this Guardian, they seek connection with the divine source, with the inner truth that exists beyond form and identity.

The presence of Spirit as a Guardian brings wholeness, aligning the practitioner with the interconnectedness of all life. In some rituals, Spirit is represented by a white candle or an item that holds personal spiritual significance. The Guardian of Spirit offers guidance in moments of stillness, inviting practitioners to experience their own divine essence and to understand their place within the vast web of existence. Spirit teaches unity, compassion, and the truth that all beings are connected through the same sacred force.

When all four Guardians—or five, including Spirit—are present, they create a balanced, harmonious space for ritual work. This alignment strengthens the energy within the circle, providing protection, focus, and a profound sense of connection. The Guardians are more than energies; they are ancient allies, beings who watch over the sacred space, who lend their strength and wisdom, and who guide the practitioner in aligning with the elements. By inviting these Guardians into their rituals, Wiccans recognize their place within the natural world and their responsibility to walk in harmony with the forces that sustain it.

The act of **thanking and releasing** the Spirit Guardians is a vital part of Wiccan practice. When the ritual concludes, each Guardian is respectfully released back to their direction, thanked for their guidance and protection. This act of gratitude reinforces the sacred relationship between the practitioner and the Guardians, acknowledging the support they provide and honoring their presence. Releasing the Guardians helps to close the ritual space, returning the practitioner to ordinary consciousness and grounding the energy raised during the ritual.

Working with Spirit Guardians teaches Wiccans the values of respect, balance, and the interconnectedness of life. Each Guardian holds unique qualities and gifts, reminding practitioners of the diverse energies within themselves and within the world around them. By aligning with these energies, Wiccans find balance, strength, and guidance, learning to live in harmony with the elements and the directions.

In honoring the Spirit Guardians, Wiccans embrace the mysteries of nature, the wisdom of the elements, and the sacredness of each direction. The Guardians are protectors, guides, and teachers, offering a path to deeper understanding and a means to connect with the energies that shape existence. Through them, practitioners learn that life is woven from countless threads, each one a reflection of the divine, and that by honoring these threads, they honor the very essence of the Wiccan path.

Chapter 17
Protective Circle

The casting of a protective circle is one of the most essential and revered practices in Wicca, serving as both a boundary and a sanctuary. This sacred space creates a sphere of protection, a veil that shields practitioners from external energies while containing and amplifying their own. Within this circle, Wiccans step into a place of spiritual safety and heightened awareness, where they can commune with the divine, work magic, and explore the inner realms without interference. The protective circle is more than just a boundary; it is a space that reflects the unity of life, embodying the Wiccan belief in harmony, balance, and interconnectedness.

The circle itself is not limited by physical dimensions but is instead a boundary defined by intention and energy. When a Wiccan casts a circle, they are creating an energetic field that surrounds and encompasses their sacred space, establishing a container for ritual work. This field acts as a shield, keeping out any unwanted influences and creating an environment in which energy can flow freely, enhancing the focus and depth of the practitioner's work. Casting a protective circle is one of the first skills taught to those new to Wicca, as it provides the foundation for safe and effective ritual practice.

To cast a circle, Wiccans often begin by **cleansing the space**. This preparatory step clears away any lingering energies, ensuring that the area is neutral and ready to hold sacred intention. Cleansing can be done with smoke from sage, lavender, or other sacred herbs, or by sprinkling saltwater around the perimeter. Some Wiccans use sound, such as bells, chimes, or chanting, to purify the space. This cleansing process not only prepares the physical area but also prepares the practitioner's mind and spirit, creating a calm, focused atmosphere.

Once the space is cleansed, the practitioner stands at the **starting point**, traditionally in the East, where they begin casting the circle. With a ritual tool, often an athame, wand, or simply an outstretched hand, the Wiccan walks clockwise, or "deosil," around the space. This movement follows the path of the sun and aligns with the energies of creation, growth, and manifestation. As they walk, they visualize energy flowing from their tool or hand, creating an unbroken line of light that encircles the space. This line becomes the boundary of the circle, a visible or imagined barrier that separates the sacred from the mundane.

The visualization of the circle is an important aspect of the process. Many Wiccans envision the circle as a glowing sphere of light, extending above and below them, forming a complete sphere rather than a flat circle. This visualization helps the practitioner to feel fully protected and enveloped in sacred energy, as though they are stepping into a different realm. The light may appear in different colors depending on the intention of the ritual—white for purity, blue for protection, or gold for empowerment. This visualized energy is a manifestation of the practitioner's will, an extension of their power and focus.

After casting the circle, Wiccans **call upon the four elements and directions**—Earth in the North, Air in the East, Fire in the South, and Water in the West. By inviting these elemental forces, practitioners balance the energy within the circle, creating harmony and drawing strength from each element's unique qualities. These elements serve as both protectors and guides, their presence enhancing the sacred space and connecting the practitioner to the natural world. The invocation of the elements is often done with words or gestures, each direction greeted and welcomed in turn, filling the circle with stability, insight, passion, and fluidity.

In some Wiccan traditions, after invoking the four elements, practitioners also **invoke Spirit** as the fifth element, aligning the circle with the divine unity that binds all things. Spirit is seen as the essence of life itself, the thread that connects all beings, and its presence completes the circle, creating a space that is whole and balanced. By acknowledging Spirit, Wiccans affirm their connection to the divine and to the deeper mysteries that guide their path.

With the circle cast and the elements present, the practitioner can now fully engage in their ritual or magical work. Inside the circle, time feels suspended, creating a sense of timelessness and stillness. This focused, sacred space allows for meditation, invocation, and spellwork with heightened awareness and concentration. Within the circle, Wiccans feel protected and supported, free to express their intentions, connect with the divine, and explore the inner realms without distraction or interference. The circle becomes a container for energy, holding and amplifying the power generated by the practitioner's will and intention.

As the ritual progresses, the **energy within the circle intensifies**, building with each word, gesture, and focus of intent. This energy is carefully guided and shaped by the practitioner, directed toward a specific purpose or goal. The circle not only contains this energy but enhances it, allowing it to reach its peak before being released. For Wiccans, this contained energy acts as a beacon, reaching out to the spirit world, to deities, or to the forces of nature, connecting the practitioner's intentions with the wider universe.

When the ritual or magical work is complete, the practitioner must **release the energy** and **take down the circle**. This step is as crucial as casting the circle itself, as it allows the energy that has been raised to dissipate or be directed toward its intended purpose. To take down the circle, Wiccans return to the starting point and walk counterclockwise, or "widdershins," around the perimeter. This direction symbolizes the closing and grounding of energy, a reversal of the creative motion that cast the circle. As they walk, they may visualize the light of the circle dissolving or being absorbed back into the earth, bringing the space back to its ordinary state.

Just as they thanked the elements upon inviting them, Wiccans **formally release and express gratitude to each of the elemental forces** at this stage. Moving in reverse order from West to North, they bid farewell to Water, Fire, Air, and Earth, thanking each element for its presence and assistance. This respectful closure ensures that the connection is ended gracefully, leaving no residual energies within the space. This act of gratitude reinforces the practitioner's relationship with the elements, recognizing the support and guidance they provide.

With the circle dissolved and the energy grounded, Wiccans take a moment to **center themselves**, returning to ordinary consciousness. This step helps to reintegrate the practitioner's mind and body, bringing them back into the everyday world with a sense of calm and completion. The closing of the circle is not an ending but a transformation, a gentle return to the ordinary world after having touched the divine.

The protective circle serves many purposes in Wiccan practice. It is a **space of transformation**, a place where the practitioner can shed old energies and open to new insights. The circle is also a **sanctuary**, offering safety and focus, especially in powerful rituals where intense energy is raised. It serves as a **mirror** of the practitioner's inner self, a reflection of their intent, focus, and alignment with the natural world. Each circle is unique, shaped by the practitioner's energy, the purpose of the ritual, and the energies they invite into the space.

For those new to Wicca, learning to cast a circle can be an empowering experience, offering a sense of agency and connection to the energies that surround and support all life. It is a practice that deepens with time, each circle cast becoming a little more intuitive, a little more powerful, as the practitioner's skill and confidence grow. Over time, casting a circle becomes second nature, a grounding ritual that brings focus and clarity to the Wiccan path.

The act of casting a circle also instills a sense of **responsibility and respect** for the sacred. In Wicca, all life is seen as interconnected, and the circle serves as a reminder of this unity. It encourages practitioners to approach their work with humility, to honor the forces they invoke, and to treat the natural world with reverence. By casting a circle, Wiccans reaffirm their commitment to walk a path of respect, balance, and harmony with the earth.

In essence, the protective circle is both a **vessel of magic and a reflection of the sacred within**. It represents the practitioner's will, their intention to engage with the divine, and their desire to live in harmony with the elemental forces. Within its boundaries, Wiccans find a space of peace, empowerment, and connection, a place where they can explore their inner worlds and connect with the mysteries that lie beyond the everyday.

Each time a Wiccan casts a circle, they participate in an ancient tradition, a timeless ritual that honors the cycles of life, the balance of nature, and the interconnectedness of all beings. The circle is more than a ritual structure; it is a symbol of the practitioner's journey, a place where magic, intention, and the sacred meet. Through the protective circle, Wiccans connect with the world around them and the world within, finding strength, guidance, and a profound sense of belonging in the dance of life.

Chapter 18
Power of Colors

In Wiccan tradition, color holds deep symbolic power, a language through which practitioners communicate intentions, evoke energies, and align with the natural world. Each color vibrates with its own frequency, embodying specific qualities, emotions, and spiritual resonances. By understanding the meanings and uses of colors, Wiccans harness this subtle energy to enhance rituals, spells, and daily life. The power of colors is not limited to objects or clothing; it permeates nature itself, from the red glow of a sunset to the green of spring's first leaves. To work with color is to connect with these energies, allowing them to influence and empower one's intentions.

Color in Wiccan practice is a tool of **focus and amplification**. Each color brings a unique quality to ritual work, assisting practitioners in channeling specific intentions or feelings. For instance, green may be chosen to draw the energy of growth and prosperity, while purple is used to invite wisdom and spiritual insight. Whether through candles, stones, clothing, or altar decor, color serves as a bridge between intention and manifestation, allowing the practitioner's desires to resonate with the world's natural energies.

White is often seen as the color of purity, protection, and clarity. In Wicca, it is associated with Spirit, divine energy, and the presence of the Goddess in her aspect as Maiden. White reflects all colors and is therefore seen as all-encompassing, able to substitute for any other color in ritual when needed. It is frequently used for purification, cleansing spaces, and invoking protective energies. A white candle can be lit to create a clean slate, free from unwanted influences, or to call upon the energy of peace and unity. For Wiccans, white symbolizes spiritual wholeness, clarity, and the openness needed to connect with the higher realms.

Black holds a different kind of power, embodying protection, grounding, and the mysteries of the unseen. Contrary to common misconceptions, black is not a negative color in Wicca; rather, it is a symbol of transformation, representing the deep, fertile darkness from which all things grow. Black is used to banish negativity, to protect against harm, and to seal a ritual space. It absorbs energy, grounding and containing it, which is especially useful in protective or banishing spells. Black candles, stones, or clothing are often used in rituals that require a strong sense of boundary and protection, invoking the Crone aspect of the Goddess and the Horned God in his guardian form.

Red is the color of passion, courage, and life force. It resonates with the element of Fire, symbolizing strength, willpower, and the energy of the body. Red is frequently used in love spells, to kindle desire, or in rituals focused on courage and vitality. It carries the fierce energy of Mars, the planet associated with action and determination, and serves as a powerful tool for instilling motivation and confidence. A red candle or crystal, such as garnet, can be used to boost inner strength, to face challenges, or to ignite the spark of a new project or relationship. Red reminds practitioners of the primal force of life itself, the dynamic and unstoppable energy that fuels change.

Green is the color of growth, fertility, and prosperity, deeply connected with the element of Earth. It symbolizes nature's abundance, the healing energy of plants, and the nurturing quality of the Mother aspect of the Goddess. Green is used in spells for financial success, fertility, and physical well-being. When a Wiccan seeks grounding or stability, green is chosen to invoke the presence of the Earth, encouraging patience, balance, and harmony. Placing green stones like jade or aventurine on the altar enhances rituals for healing and prosperity, drawing on the grounding energy of nature. Green reminds practitioners of the steady growth of the earth, the patient unfolding of life in all its forms.

Blue embodies tranquility, healing, and emotional depth, resonating with the element of Water. It represents peace, intuition, and the flow of life, often used in spells for emotional healing, calm, and spiritual insight. In Wicca, blue is also associated with the divine energy of the Goddess in her aspect as healer and nurturer. Blue candles or stones like lapis lazuli and aquamarine are chosen to deepen one's intuition, to bring peace during stressful times, and to enhance connection with one's inner self. Blue reminds Wiccans of the boundless expanse of the sky and sea, the calming and transformative qualities of Water, and the wisdom found in stillness and reflection.

Purple is the color of spiritual insight, psychic awareness, and transformation. Aligned with the energy of Spirit, purple is frequently used in meditation, divination, and rituals that seek to connect with higher wisdom. Purple embodies mystery and power, associated with deities of wisdom and magic, and is a popular color for those who seek to expand their consciousness or deepen their spiritual practice. In Wiccan rituals, purple candles and amethyst crystals are often employed to enhance intuition, to protect the aura, or to seek guidance from the divine. Purple teaches practitioners to trust in the unseen, to honor the mystery of the unknown, and to find strength in their spiritual journey.

Yellow is the color of intellect, clarity, and joy, aligned with the element of Air. It represents mental energy, creativity, and the brightness of the mind. Yellow is frequently used in spells to stimulate learning, to bring insight, or to encourage self-expression. It is a color of positivity and communication, helping practitioners to speak their truth and to connect with the world around them. In rituals, yellow candles or stones like citrine are used to invoke clarity, to brighten one's mood, and to enhance mental focus. Yellow symbolizes the light of understanding, the curiosity of the Maiden aspect of the Goddess, and the warmth of the sun as it illuminates the world.

Pink embodies love, compassion, and emotional healing, often associated with the gentle aspects of the Goddess. It is a softer form of red, resonating with the energy of love and harmony rather than passion and intensity. Pink is commonly used in spells for self-love, friendship, and reconciliation, fostering a sense of connection and understanding. It brings a nurturing energy, helping to heal emotional wounds and to promote inner peace. Pink candles, rose quartz, or pink flowers can be placed on the altar to enhance feelings of affection, to mend relationships, or to bring comfort to the heart. Pink reminds Wiccans of the beauty of gentleness, compassion, and the power of unconditional love.

Orange is the color of enthusiasm, creativity, and strength, embodying the warmth and vitality of Fire with an added touch of joy and spontaneity. It is used to spark creativity, to bring excitement to new ventures, and to encourage social connections. Orange is ideal for rituals focused on success, personal empowerment, or adventurous spirit, helping practitioners to break free from stagnation and to embrace new possibilities. An orange candle or carnelian stone can be used to instill confidence, to attract opportunity, or to invigorate one's spirit. Orange reflects the zest for life, the courage to pursue dreams, and the beauty of living with passion and purpose.

Gold represents the Sun, abundance, and success, resonating with the energy of prosperity and divine masculine power. Gold is often used in rituals for wealth, success, and high achievement, embodying the radiant energy of the Sun God and the blessings of abundance. A gold candle or a piece of jewelry worn during ritual can amplify prosperity work, attract financial gain, or bring a sense of joy and optimism. Gold is a color of confidence and self-worth, reminding practitioners of their own inner light and the unlimited potential that lies within.

Silver is connected with the Moon, intuition, and the divine feminine, a color of mystery and reflection. Silver is used in rituals that seek to enhance psychic abilities, to connect with lunar energies, and to honor the Goddess. It embodies the gentle illumination of the moon, a light that reveals the hidden and brings calm in the darkness. Silver items, such as candles, jewelry, or moonstone crystals, are used to deepen one's intuition, to heighten spiritual awareness, or to honor the cycles of the moon. Silver teaches Wiccans to trust in their inner voice, to honor the cycles of life, and to find beauty in quiet reflection.

Brown is the color of the earth, grounding, and stability, reflecting the nurturing aspect of nature itself. It is associated with security, endurance, and resilience, used in rituals for home protection, stability, and animal blessings. Brown stones, candles, or other natural objects are used to create a grounded, balanced energy, helping practitioners connect with the earth and find strength within themselves. Brown reminds Wiccans of the sacredness of the land, the stability found in nature, and the strength that lies in patience and rootedness.

In Wicca, color is more than an aesthetic choice; it is a powerful tool that amplifies intention, shapes energy, and aligns the practitioner with the forces of nature. Each color holds its own vibration, an energy that resonates with specific emotions, desires, and spiritual principles. Through the thoughtful use of color, Wiccans bring depth and clarity to their rituals, enhancing their ability to connect with the divine, to manifest intentions, and to walk in harmony with the world around them.

The power of colors invites practitioners to see the world as a canvas of energy, where every shade carries meaning and purpose. In working with colors, Wiccans learn to attune themselves to these vibrations, recognizing the beauty of each hue and the way it reflects the cycles of nature and the divine within. Through the magic of color, Wiccans find a language that speaks to the soul, a path that brings beauty, balance, and purpose to their journey.

Chapter 19
Magical Herbs

Herbs have held a sacred place in Wiccan tradition since ancient times, revered for their natural powers, healing properties, and mystical energies. Known as the "green allies" of the craft, herbs connect Wiccans to the earth and embody the lifeforce of nature, each plant carrying its own unique magic. Whether used in spells, rituals, medicine, or daily life, magical herbs serve as potent allies, lending their energies to the intentions of the practitioner. The practice of herbology in Wicca is not merely about knowledge but about cultivating a relationship with the living world, honoring the spirit within each plant and respecting its role in the natural web of life.

Herbs are chosen based on their specific qualities, associations, and planetary correspondences, which align with certain aspects of Wiccan beliefs. Many herbs are tied to particular elements, deities, or energies, making them suitable for a wide variety of uses in magic and healing. When selecting an herb for ritual, a Wiccan might consider the plant's color, scent, folklore, and the season in which it grows, all of which contribute to its magical properties. By understanding the attributes of different herbs, Wiccans are able to align their magical work with the forces of nature, using the energy of the plants to enhance, protect, or transform.

One of the most versatile and widely used herbs in Wicca is **sage**. Known for its cleansing and purifying qualities, sage is often burned as incense to clear negative energies from a space, a person, or an object. This ancient practice, known as smudging, uses the smoke to cleanse and protect, allowing fresh, positive energy to fill the space. Sage is aligned with the element of Air and the Sun, bringing warmth, clarity, and a sense of spiritual protection. Wiccans often burn sage before rituals, meditations, or any time they feel the need to cleanse their environment. The pungent, earthy scent of sage is a reminder of the sacred, helping practitioners connect with their intentions and focus their mind.

Rosemary is another cherished herb in Wiccan tradition, valued for its protective and healing properties. Often associated with the element of Fire and the Sun, rosemary carries a vibrant, uplifting energy that is said to ward off negativity and enhance memory. In rituals, rosemary is used to cleanse, to promote clarity, and to provide protection for the home or personal space. A sprig of rosemary placed on the altar can also enhance focus and mental clarity, aiding in meditation and concentration. Rosemary is often included in spells for love, healing, and remembrance, its resilient nature symbolizing loyalty, strength, and the power of memory.

Lavender, with its calming fragrance and gentle energy, is a powerful herb for healing, peace, and sleep. Associated with the element of Air and the planet Mercury, lavender promotes relaxation, enhances intuition, and invites a sense of tranquility. Wiccans use lavender in rituals to soothe emotions, to ease anxiety, and to bring harmony to the mind and spirit. Its purple flowers reflect the color of spiritual insight, and lavender is often included in spells or sachets for restful sleep, dream work, and emotional healing. By placing dried lavender in a sachet or burning it as incense, Wiccans can draw upon its calming, restorative energy, creating a space of peace and clarity.

Thyme is valued in Wicca for its courage-enhancing properties and connection to purification. Associated with the element of Water and the planet Venus, thyme has a fresh, green scent that embodies resilience, growth, and renewal. In spellwork, thyme is used to banish fear, to promote self-confidence, and to protect against harmful influences. It is also used to cleanse ritual tools or spaces, creating a foundation of purity and strength for magical work. A sprig of thyme can be carried as an amulet for courage or placed on the altar to boost the practitioner's resolve, reminding them of the strength that lies within.

Basil, known for its associations with prosperity and protection, is a vibrant, aromatic herb often used in spells for abundance and love. Aligned with the element of Fire and the planet Mars, basil brings a warm, energetic quality that supports the manifestation of goals and intentions. In Wiccan practice, basil is used in rituals to attract wealth, to provide protection for the home, and to bring harmony to relationships. Wiccans may place basil leaves in a wallet, plant it near the front door, or sprinkle it around their home as a charm for prosperity and good fortune. The herb's rich green color reflects the abundance it invites, symbolizing growth and the generosity of nature.

Mint, with its refreshing scent and invigorating energy, is associated with healing, clarity, and renewal. Connected to the element of Air and the planet Mercury, mint is used in spells to stimulate mental clarity, to promote physical healing, and to enhance communication. Mint leaves can be placed in a bath for purification, burned as incense for focus, or added to a sachet for prosperity and success. Its cooling energy is particularly useful in rituals for calming and emotional healing, helping Wiccans to clear away mental or emotional blocks and to create space for new ideas and growth. Mint's crisp, revitalizing scent brings clarity, focus, and a renewed sense of purpose.

Mugwort is highly regarded for its ability to enhance psychic abilities, dream work, and spiritual vision. Known as a "witch's herb," mugwort is associated with the Moon and the element of Earth, resonating with the energies of intuition and mystery. Wiccans use mugwort in rituals for divination, scrying, and connecting with the subconscious. Its leaves are often placed under pillows to encourage vivid dreams or burned as incense to aid in meditation and trance work. Mugwort opens the door to inner wisdom, allowing practitioners to journey into their own depths and to explore the mysteries of spirit.

Chamomile is cherished for its calming, healing, and protective qualities. Aligned with the element of Water and the Sun, chamomile is often used to bring peace, to ease emotional distress, and to attract good fortune. Chamomile flowers are included in charm bags, bath rituals, or sachets to bring blessings and to protect against harm. The sweet, golden blossoms of chamomile symbolize hope, optimism, and the lightness of spirit, making it a powerful ally for those seeking comfort and protection. Chamomile is also used in spells to attract luck, its gentle energy fostering an atmosphere of joy and abundance.

In Wiccan practice, each herb has its own **ritual of preparation**, as Wiccans believe in honoring the spirit within each plant. Herbs are often gathered with respect, ideally during specific times that enhance their energy, such as dawn for renewal or dusk for introspection. A simple phrase of thanks may be spoken to honor the plant's spirit and to acknowledge its role in the practitioner's work. Once gathered, the herbs are dried, stored, and sometimes ground or brewed to release their energy. Through this process, the herb becomes more than a tool; it becomes a partner, an active participant in the spell or ritual.

Herbs can be incorporated into **various forms of magical work**. In charm bags or sachets, they are combined to enhance their effects, their energies blending to support a specific intention. Wiccans might create a protection sachet by combining rosemary, sage, and thyme, each herb adding its own protective quality. Herbs are also added to baths, infusions, oils, or even culinary recipes, bringing their magic into the body and spirit. When used as incense, herbs connect the practitioner with the element of Air, their smoke carrying intentions to the spiritual realms. Each method of use allows the herbs to contribute their power to the practitioner's work, transforming intentions into reality.

The **creation of herbal amulets and talismans** is a common practice in Wicca, with herbs carefully chosen, combined, and charged to serve a specific purpose. For example, a healing amulet may include lavender, chamomile, and mint, each herb resonating with the energies of peace, restoration, and renewal. These amulets are often carried or placed on the altar, serving as constant sources of energy and support. By working with these herbal creations, Wiccans align themselves with nature's wisdom, finding strength, comfort, and guidance in the plant kingdom.

Wiccans also use herbs in **seasonal rituals** that align with the Wheel of the Year. During Imbolc, they might burn rosemary or basil to celebrate the renewal of life and the first stirrings of spring. At Beltane, flowers like hawthorn and rose may be used to honor fertility and love, bringing warmth and vitality to the ritual space. Each herb is chosen not only for its properties but also for its connection to the changing seasons, the cycles of growth and decay that mirror the Wiccan path.

Working with herbs teaches Wiccans to see the **interconnectedness of life** and to honor the power of nature in its most intimate forms. By forming a relationship with the green allies of the earth, Wiccans learn to listen to the wisdom of plants, to respect their cycles, and to recognize their power. The use of magical herbs is not just about achieving an outcome; it is a practice of reverence, an acknowledgment of the sacred energy that flows through all things.

In the end, herbs are more than simple ingredients; they are living beings with their own wisdom, energy, and spirit. Through the careful and respectful use of herbs, Wiccans find a way to deepen their connection with nature, to honor the cycles of growth and decay, and to work in harmony with the earth's energy. Each herb is a teacher, a healer, and a guide, offering support and insight on the spiritual path. In the practice of herbology, Wiccans see the magic of life itself, the sacred essence of the natural world, and the interconnectedness that binds all beings in a web of vibrant, living energy.

Chapter 20
Precious Stones

In Wiccan practice, precious stones and crystals are revered as gifts from the earth, each possessing unique energies that resonate with the cycles of nature and the inner realms of spirit. These stones are not merely beautiful objects; they are potent symbols of the earth's strength, resilience, and memory. Each stone vibrates with its own energy, offering qualities of healing, protection, intuition, or grounding. For Wiccans, working with precious stones is a way to tap into the earth's wisdom, to align with the energies of specific intentions, and to deepen their connection with the natural and spiritual worlds.

Precious stones are chosen based on their color, texture, and energetic qualities, each one holding a specific frequency that complements different types of magical work. Some stones carry gentle, calming energies, while others resonate with intensity and transformation. When Wiccans select a stone for ritual or daily use, they do so with care and respect, seeking to form a bond with the stone's unique essence. The relationship between practitioner and stone is a subtle yet powerful one, grounded in the belief that the stone's energy can harmonize with the practitioner's intentions, guiding, supporting, and amplifying their work.

Clear Quartz is one of the most versatile and widely used stones in Wicca, often regarded as the "Master Healer." Its translucent clarity and high vibration make it ideal for amplifying energy, intentions, and the effects of other stones. Clear quartz is associated with clarity, focus, and alignment, helping practitioners to see through illusions and to connect with their inner truth. Its energy is both gentle and powerful, assisting in healing, meditation, and all forms of magical work. Clear quartz can be used to cleanse and purify an environment, to enhance meditation, or to channel and amplify intentions in spellwork. Its clear, balanced energy resonates with all chakras, making it a universal ally in Wiccan practice.

Amethyst, with its soothing purple hue, is a stone of intuition, spiritual growth, and protection. It is often associated with the element of Water and the planet Neptune, and is revered for its calming and clarifying qualities. Amethyst is a powerful aid in meditation and psychic development, helping practitioners to open their third eye and connect with their inner wisdom. It is used in rituals for dream work, intuition, and spiritual insight, bringing a sense of peace and heightened awareness. Many Wiccans keep amethyst near their beds to encourage restful sleep and vivid dreams, believing that it opens the door to the subconscious and the mysteries of spirit. In times of stress or inner turmoil, amethyst offers comfort, helping to soothe emotions and clear the mind.

Rose Quartz is the stone of unconditional love, compassion, and emotional healing, often associated with the Goddess in her nurturing aspect. Its gentle pink color resonates with the heart, encouraging self-love, empathy, and forgiveness. Rose quartz is used in spells and rituals to attract love, to heal emotional wounds, or to promote harmony in relationships. It brings a soft, comforting energy that helps to heal the heart, allowing for acceptance and compassion both for oneself and others. Many Wiccans place rose quartz on their altars or wear it as a talisman for love, peace, and emotional healing. Rose quartz is a reminder of the beauty of kindness, a gentle ally in the journey of self-discovery and love.

Citrine is a radiant yellow stone associated with abundance, joy, and manifestation. Known as the "Merchant's Stone," citrine carries the energy of prosperity, confidence, and creative inspiration. Its bright, sunny energy resonates with the Solar Plexus chakra, empowering practitioners to pursue their goals and manifest their dreams. In Wiccan practice, citrine is often used in rituals for success, wealth, and personal empowerment. It is a powerful stone for those seeking to overcome fear, to find motivation, or to bring a sense of optimism to their lives. Citrine's energy encourages self-worth and confidence, helping practitioners to trust in their abilities and to draw abundance into their lives.

Black Tourmaline is a protective stone, valued for its grounding and shielding qualities. Associated with the element of Earth, it is used in Wiccan practice to ward off negativity, to protect against psychic attacks, and to purify energy. Black tourmaline is often placed at the boundaries of a sacred space to create a protective barrier or carried as a personal talisman for grounding and protection. Its energy is dense and stabilizing, helping to dispel fear and anxiety, and it is commonly used in rituals that require a strong sense of boundary and security. By working with black tourmaline, practitioners find a sense of stability and resilience, feeling rooted and supported by the earth's strength.

Lapis Lazuli is a deep blue stone associated with wisdom, truth, and spiritual insight. This stone, often flecked with gold, has been prized for centuries by cultures around the world as a symbol of royalty, divinity, and enlightenment. In Wiccan practice, lapis lazuli is used in rituals for inner vision, communication, and connection with higher wisdom. It is especially helpful for those seeking to enhance their psychic abilities or to deepen their meditation practice. Lapis lazuli aligns with the Third Eye and Throat chakras, aiding in self-expression and the pursuit of knowledge. Many Wiccans keep this stone on their altars or carry it as a reminder of the importance of truth, integrity, and the search for wisdom.

Carnelian is a warm, vibrant stone that embodies courage, vitality, and creative energy. Its reddish-orange color is connected to the element of Fire and resonates with the Sacral chakra, the center of passion, creativity, and personal power. Carnelian is often used in rituals for courage, motivation, and the pursuit of goals, helping practitioners to overcome fear and self-doubt. It is also a powerful stone for grounding, as its earthy energy connects one to the physical realm. Carnelian is a favored stone for Wiccans seeking to ignite their inner fire, to enhance their creativity, or to pursue their ambitions with confidence. It serves as a reminder of the beauty of life's passion and the strength found in authenticity.

Selenite is a translucent, milky stone that carries a high vibrational energy associated with clarity, purity, and spiritual connection. Known as the "Stone of the Moon," selenite resonates with lunar energies and is used to cleanse and elevate the spirit. It is commonly used in Wiccan practices to purify spaces, to clear other stones, and to enhance meditation and spiritual awareness. Selenite's gentle energy helps to connect practitioners with their higher selves and with the divine, offering a sense of calm and alignment. Many Wiccans place selenite on their altars to keep their space clear of unwanted energies, or they use it in meditation to foster a sense of peace and clarity.

Hematite is a metallic, grounding stone associated with the element of Earth and used for protection, stability, and resilience. Its reflective surface is believed to ward off negativity, and it is often used in rituals for strength, courage, and boundary-setting. Hematite resonates with the Root chakra, providing a sense of balance and helping practitioners stay centered. In Wiccan practice, hematite is used to ground energy after rituals, to anchor one's intentions, or to protect against harmful influences. Its weight and density make it a powerful tool for grounding, helping practitioners feel rooted and aligned with the strength of the earth.

To **prepare stones for magical work**, Wiccans often cleanse and charge them to align with specific intentions. Cleansing can be done with sunlight, moonlight, smoke, or water, each method chosen to suit the stone's natural qualities. For instance, a stone intended for protection might be placed under the light of the full moon, drawing on the moon's strength to amplify the stone's energy. After cleansing, Wiccans often hold the stone and speak an intention or visualize the energy they wish the stone to carry. This ritual dedication transforms the stone into a sacred object, attuned to the practitioner's own energy and purpose.

Stones in ritual can be placed on the altar, held during meditation, or arranged in grids to amplify energy. When placed on the body, stones can help balance energy centers, clear blockages, or support healing. For example, placing amethyst on the Third Eye during meditation may enhance intuition, while holding rose quartz over the heart invites compassion and emotional healing. Stones are often combined with herbs, candles, or symbols to create a powerful focal point in rituals, each element enhancing and supporting the other.

Wiccans also use **stone amulets and talismans**, carrying them throughout the day as a source of constant support and protection. A stone worn as a pendant, carried in a pocket, or placed in a charm bag becomes a close ally, its energy influencing the practitioner's state of mind and emotional well-being. These amulets serve as reminders of the earth's strength, the stability of nature, and the practitioner's own intentions.

Through the use of precious stones, Wiccans find a way to **connect with the deeper mysteries of the earth** and to work in harmony with the natural energies that shape life. Each stone is a piece of the earth's memory, a reflection of time and transformation, and a reminder of the sacredness found in all things. Stones offer stability, guidance, and comfort, helping practitioners align with the energy of their intentions and to walk their path with strength, purpose, and respect for the natural world.

In working with precious stones, Wiccans discover the beauty of life's rhythms, the wisdom of nature's cycles, and the interconnectedness of all things. The stones serve as guides, teachers, and allies, their energies resonating with the practitioner's spirit and intentions. Through these crystals, Wiccans find a profound connection to the earth, drawing on the ancient power of the stones to bring balance, healing, and magic into their lives.

Chapter 21
Natural Meditation

Natural meditation in Wiccan practice is a way of aligning oneself with the rhythms and energies of the natural world, creating a sacred connection between the inner and outer realms. Wiccans view meditation as an essential spiritual tool that enables them to calm the mind, open the heart, and deepen their awareness of the earth's cycles. Natural meditation differs from other forms of meditation in that it is rooted in observing, sensing, and merging with the natural elements, seasons, and phases that govern life itself. Through this practice, Wiccans experience the interconnectedness of all beings, drawing strength, wisdom, and peace from the world around them.

In natural meditation, Wiccans are encouraged to see the earth as a living temple and to regard each element—Earth, Air, Fire, and Water—as a guide. Rather than retreating from the world, natural meditation involves a process of blending into it, attuning oneself to the presence of life in its many forms. This form of meditation is often practiced outdoors, though it can be done anywhere by visualizing natural settings and embodying their qualities. Wiccans meditate not just to find inner peace, but to harmonize with the world's cycles, connecting with the same forces that govern the changing seasons and the movement of the stars.

The first approach to natural meditation is to **connect with the elements**. Each element provides a doorway to different states of awareness and offers a unique type of guidance. By focusing on one element at a time, practitioners learn to embody its energy and to develop a deeper relationship with its qualities. This connection can be fostered through outdoor meditation in natural settings that correspond to each element, or through visualization exercises that bring the essence of the element into the mind and heart.

To meditate with the **element of Earth**, Wiccans may sit on the ground, feeling the soil or grass beneath them, and focus on the sensations of grounding and stability. Earth meditation is about connecting with the physical body and the land, experiencing the strength, patience, and resilience that the earth embodies. Practitioners may visualize themselves as a tree with deep roots, drawing strength and nourishment from the earth. This form of meditation fosters a sense of stability and support, helping practitioners to ground themselves and to cultivate inner strength. Earth meditation is especially beneficial when one feels scattered or anxious, as it brings a sense of calm and rootedness.

When working with the **element of Air** in meditation, Wiccans often seek places where they can feel the wind or breathe in fresh air, allowing their senses to focus on the movement and clarity that Air brings. Air is associated with thoughts, clarity, and inspiration, and in meditation, it helps practitioners release stagnant mental energy and find new perspectives. By focusing on the breath, practitioners attune themselves to the rhythm of life, feeling each inhalation and exhalation as a reminder of their connection to the world around them. Air meditation encourages openness, curiosity, and flexibility, making it ideal for times when one seeks clarity or inspiration, or needs to release mental clutter.

Meditating with the **element of Fire** can involve sitting near a candle, a bonfire, or even the sun. Fire represents transformation, passion, and the spark of creation. In Fire meditation, Wiccans focus on the warmth and light, visualizing the flames as symbols of personal power, inner strength, and change. Practitioners might imagine themselves as a flame, burning brightly, releasing fear or limitations, and embodying courage. Fire meditation is energizing and purifying, encouraging practitioners to connect with their passions and to ignite the inner fire that drives them forward. This meditation is especially useful when one seeks motivation, strength, or the courage to overcome obstacles.

The **element of Water** is best experienced near rivers, lakes, or the ocean, where practitioners can attune to the fluidity and depth of Water's energy. Water meditation is calming, healing, and associated with emotions, intuition, and the subconscious. Practitioners focus on the sound and movement of water, allowing its flow to wash over them, soothing the mind and bringing a sense of peace. Water meditation teaches adaptability, emotional release, and the acceptance of life's ebb and flow. It is ideal for times when one feels overwhelmed or needs emotional healing, as it encourages practitioners to let go and to trust in the natural currents of life.

Seasonal meditation is another profound approach in natural meditation, aligning one's awareness with the cycles of the seasons as they turn through the Wheel of the Year. Each season brings unique energies and lessons, which Wiccans honor through meditation. This practice enables them to deepen their relationship with nature, to attune to the changes of the earth, and to align their intentions with the current phase of the year. Each season offers specific qualities to explore, providing guidance for growth, reflection, and renewal.

Spring represents renewal, growth, and the awakening of life. In spring meditation, practitioners focus on the energy of new beginnings, envisioning themselves blossoming like flowers, opening to new possibilities. They may sit in a garden or green space, breathing in the scent of fresh earth and observing the delicate colors of emerging plants. Spring meditation encourages hope, resilience, and the joy of life's potential, helping practitioners plant the seeds of their intentions and nurture them as they grow.

Summer is the season of vitality, abundance, and the fullness of life. In summer meditation, Wiccans focus on the sun's warmth, the energy of growth, and the spirit of celebration. They may meditate outside under the sunlight, feeling the life-giving force of the sun on their skin, or envisioning their own lives in full bloom. Summer meditation is about embracing one's power, celebrating achievements, and basking in the joy of the present. This practice teaches confidence, gratitude, and the strength that comes from embracing one's own radiance.

Autumn brings the energies of harvest, reflection, and release. During autumn meditation, practitioners focus on gratitude for what has been achieved and on letting go of what no longer serves them. This season is associated with wisdom and preparation for the quieter winter months. Wiccans may meditate in nature, surrounded by the colors of falling leaves, or visualize themselves releasing burdens as the trees let go of their leaves. Autumn meditation teaches acceptance, transformation, and the beauty of letting go, making space for new growth to come.

Winter is the season of rest, introspection, and inner stillness. Winter meditation is often done indoors, in candlelight, or near a fire, focusing on the quiet, dark energy that encourages contemplation and renewal. This meditation invites practitioners to turn inward, to listen to the wisdom of silence, and to honor the cycle of rest. Wiccans may visualize themselves as seeds beneath the snow, gathering strength for the coming spring. Winter meditation is a time for deep reflection, healing, and preparation, offering practitioners a sense of peace and inner alignment.

Natural meditation can also be **enhanced with visualization techniques**, which allow Wiccans to create mental landscapes that reflect the beauty of nature and the qualities of the elements. Visualization is a powerful tool in meditation, enabling practitioners to connect with distant places, to embody symbolic images, or to bring the energies of nature into their personal space. Through visualization, Wiccans journey inward, creating images of forests, rivers, mountains, or starry skies, each one resonating with their spirit and intention. This practice deepens meditation, allowing the practitioner to feel surrounded by the energies of the natural world, even if they are indoors or far from wild landscapes.

The use of **natural sounds** further enhances meditation, as sounds evoke the essence of the earth and the elements. The sound of ocean waves, wind rustling through trees, or birds singing at dawn transports practitioners into nature's embrace, grounding them in the rhythms of life. Many Wiccans meditate to recordings of natural sounds or listen to these sounds directly in nature, allowing them to immerse fully in the experience. Sound deepens awareness and encourages a sense of calm and connectedness, bringing the spirit of the natural world into the meditation.

In addition to these practices, **grounding meditations** are integral to natural meditation, helping practitioners anchor their energy and return to a state of balance. Grounding meditation typically involves visualizing roots extending from the body into the earth, drawing strength, stability, and peace. This practice is especially helpful after intense ritual work or emotional experiences, as it restores equilibrium and prevents energy from becoming scattered. Grounding teaches Wiccans to feel centered, resilient, and connected to the support of the earth.

Natural meditation encourages Wiccans to live with an awareness of their place within the world, to feel the pulse of life that flows through all beings, and to approach each moment with reverence. It is a reminder that meditation is not an escape from the world, but a way of stepping into a deeper communion with it. Through these practices, Wiccans honor the earth's rhythms, attune to the elements, and cultivate inner harmony. Natural meditation opens the heart to nature's wisdom, fostering a connection that guides practitioners on their spiritual journey, offering clarity, healing, and the beauty of a life lived in balance with the natural world.

In every meditation, Wiccans find the presence of the divine, a reminder that the sacred is within and around them, woven into every leaf, every stone, and every breath of air. Through the practice of natural meditation, practitioners come to see the world as a living, breathing temple, filled with guidance, wonder, and the wisdom of the ages. It is a path that deepens the connection to self, to nature, and to the eternal cycles of existence, bringing peace, purpose, and a profound sense of belonging to the Wiccan path.

Chapter 22
Creative Visualization

Creative visualization is a core practice in Wiccan spirituality, a method of shaping one's thoughts, intentions, and imagination to create tangible change in the world. Through visualization, Wiccans use the mind's natural ability to form mental images, transforming abstract desires into vivid, energetic blueprints. This skill is foundational to magical work, as it harnesses the practitioner's focus and intent, bridging the inner and outer worlds. By envisioning their goals and intentions with clarity and conviction, Wiccans send their wishes into the universe, setting energies in motion to bring their desires into reality.

In Wicca, visualization is not seen as a passive exercise but as an active, potent method of aligning oneself with universal energies. Visualization engages both the conscious and subconscious mind, awakening hidden potentials and making the invisible visible. It allows Wiccans to tune into the vibrations of their intentions, connecting deeply with the forces they wish to manifest. Whether used in spellwork, healing, or personal growth, visualization empowers practitioners to become co-creators of their own lives, working in harmony with nature's rhythms and the energies of the cosmos.

The process of creative visualization in Wicca typically begins with **setting a clear intention**. This intention serves as the guiding force of the visualization, a focused goal that the practitioner wishes to manifest. Clear intentions are essential, as they allow the mind to direct energy without distraction or ambiguity. For example, if the goal is to bring healing energy to a loved one, the intention should be specific, with a clear understanding of what healing means in that context. Defining the intention brings focus, helping the practitioner visualize a detailed outcome that aligns with their true desires.

Once the intention is set, the practitioner enters a **state of relaxation** to quiet the mind and prepare for visualization. A calm and centered mind allows for deeper focus and a clearer mental image, enhancing the potency of the practice. Wiccans often use breathing exercises or a brief meditation to release tension and center their thoughts. By focusing on the breath and clearing away distractions, practitioners create a mental space that is receptive to the energy of visualization, allowing them to step fully into the imagery they create.

With the mind calm and the intention clear, the next step is to **build the mental image**. The practitioner visualizes the desired outcome as vividly as possible, incorporating all senses—sight, sound, touch, taste, and smell—to make the scene feel real and tangible. If visualizing a peaceful forest, for example, they might imagine the earthy scent of pine, the cool touch of moss underfoot, the gentle rustling of leaves in the wind, and the warm, dappled sunlight filtering through the trees. By engaging all the senses, practitioners bring the visualization to life, making it more than a thought but an experience that resonates deeply in the mind and spirit.

In Wiccan practice, **symbolic imagery** is often used to deepen the power of visualization. Symbols serve as archetypes, resonating with the subconscious mind and representing universal forces. For instance, visualizing a radiant sun for confidence, a growing tree for healing, or a protective circle of light for safety connects the practitioner with the essence of those energies. Wiccans may visualize themselves holding a glowing crystal, a blossoming flower, or a vibrant flame—each image carefully chosen to align with the desired outcome. By working with these symbols, practitioners tap into the ancient language of the soul, amplifying their intentions and directing energy with purpose and clarity.

Color is another powerful tool in creative visualization, each hue carrying its own energetic resonance that can shape and enhance intentions. For instance, blue might be visualized to promote calm and peace, red for vitality and courage, green for growth and healing, and white for purity and protection. Practitioners often infuse their visualizations with these colors, imagining their intention surrounded by an aura or glow that aligns with their goal. Color not only intensifies the image but also reinforces the energy of the intention, allowing the practitioner's vision to resonate with the frequencies of their desired outcome.

A crucial aspect of creative visualization in Wicca is the **emotional engagement** with the imagery. Emotion fuels the visualization, infusing it with the energy needed to manifest. Wiccans are taught to feel the joy, excitement, peace, or relief that comes with achieving their goal, to experience it as if it has already come to pass. This emotional connection strengthens the visualization, transforming it from a mental picture into a lived experience. For example, if visualizing success, the practitioner might feel the satisfaction and pride of accomplishment, or if visualizing protection, they might feel enveloped in warmth, safety, and comfort.

Many Wiccans use **guided visualizations** as a way to deepen their practice. Guided visualizations are journeys led by a teacher, recording, or script that provides a framework for the imagination, leading the practitioner through specific scenes or symbols. These visualizations might take practitioners to enchanted forests, serene lakes, or magical temples, each landscape designed to foster relaxation, clarity, or healing. Guided visualizations are especially helpful for those new to visualization, providing structure and support while allowing the imagination to flourish. Over time, practitioners often develop their own guided journeys, creating personal visualizations that resonate with their unique intentions.

Another powerful technique in Wicca is **future self-visualization**, where practitioners imagine themselves in the future, having already achieved their goal. This practice fosters confidence and belief, allowing practitioners to align with the energy of success and to see themselves as capable of manifesting their desires. For example, if a practitioner seeks to deepen their spiritual practice, they might visualize themselves as an experienced and wise Wiccan years from now, feeling fulfilled and connected to their path. This type of visualization helps bridge the gap between the present and the desired future, creating a sense of certainty and empowering the practitioner to take steps toward that vision.

Wiccans often integrate creative visualization with **breathwork**, using the breath to intensify focus and to guide energy through the body. Inhale and exhale patterns can be used to "charge" the visualization, inhaling to gather energy and exhaling to project it outward. For example, when visualizing healing energy, a Wiccan might inhale while visualizing a glowing ball of light at the center of their being, then exhale to send that light toward a loved one in need of healing. Breath becomes a conduit, directing the visualized energy to where it is needed and reinforcing the practitioner's focus.

To deepen their visualization practice, Wiccans sometimes create **vision boards or sacred drawings** that depict their intentions in symbolic or literal form. These visual aids serve as physical representations of their goals, providing a constant reminder of their desires and helping to anchor the energy of their intentions. A vision board might include images of nature, symbols, or keywords, while a sacred drawing could be an intricate mandala or a personal sigil. By engaging in this creative process, practitioners externalize their intentions, giving their visualizations a tangible form that continually reinforces their focus and aligns their energy.

One final but essential step in creative visualization is **releasing the vision** into the universe. Once the visualization is complete, Wiccans let go of their attachment to the outcome, trusting that the energy will flow and manifest as it should. This step is crucial, as attachment can create energetic blockages that hinder manifestation. Wiccans often conclude their visualization with a phrase like, "As I will, so mote it be," releasing their intention and allowing it to take form without interference. This act of release reflects the trust that Wiccans place in the universe, understanding that what is meant to be will come to pass in its own time and way.

Creative visualization is also a tool for **self-exploration and healing** in Wiccan practice. By visualizing aspects of themselves—such as their inner child, shadow self, or higher self—practitioners confront their own fears, discover hidden strengths, and find acceptance within. For example, a Wiccan might visualize a safe space where they can communicate with their shadow self, asking it questions, listening to its fears, and offering it compassion. This inner journey fosters self-knowledge, allowing practitioners to heal, grow, and become more aligned with their true selves.

Through creative visualization, Wiccans find a way to become active participants in their own lives, taking responsibility for their intentions and working to bring their goals to fruition. The practice reveals the vast potential of the mind, the magic of imagination, and the transformative power of belief. Visualization allows Wiccans to bridge the inner and outer worlds, to see their desires as attainable, and to embrace their role as co-creators in the universe.

In the Wiccan tradition, creative visualization is a reminder that the world itself is filled with possibilities, shaped by intention and fueled by spirit. The practice encourages Wiccans to dream boldly, to trust in their visions, and to step forward with confidence on their path. Through the power of visualization, Wiccans learn to harness their own light, to align with the forces of nature, and to bring beauty, purpose, and magic into their lives.

Chapter 23
Sacred Chants

In Wiccan practice, sacred chants are powerful tools for raising energy, focusing intent, and connecting with the divine. Chanting is an ancient form of vocal magic, a method of weaving sound and intention into a resonant force that supports rituals, meditation, and personal transformation. When Wiccans chant, they infuse words with energy, allowing their voices to become conduits for their desires, beliefs, and spiritual intentions. This form of vocal expression serves not only to enhance personal focus but also to harmonize the energy of a group, creating a shared field of power that magnifies each individual's intent.

Sacred chants in Wicca often include phrases that invoke deities, honor the elements, or reflect the natural cycles of life. Each chant is a mantra, an affirmation, or a prayer, and as it is repeated, the words take on a life of their own, creating a rhythm that invites the practitioner into a deeper, more connected state. Whether spoken alone or with others, chanting is a form of invocation, an act of calling forth the energies, qualities, or beings that Wiccans wish to engage. Through the repetition of sacred sounds, Wiccans find both inner peace and a sense of unity with the world around them.

The essence of chanting lies in the **power of sound**. Each word and tone vibrates with energy, resonating within the body and extending outward. In Wiccan belief, sound is one of the primal forces of creation, a manifestation of the divine that brings spirit into form. When Wiccans chant, they tap into this creative power, using sound to align their inner energy with their desired outcome. A chant's rhythm and tone shape its energy, allowing practitioners to create vibrations that heal, protect, or transform. The act of chanting transforms mere words into magical instruments, turning voice and breath into vessels of intention.

Chants are often used to **invoke specific deities or spirits**, calling upon their qualities to aid in ritual or to deepen the practitioner's connection to the divine. Each deity has traditional chants associated with their name and attributes, which can be either simple affirmations or longer invocations. For example, a chant to honor the Triple Goddess might include phrases that celebrate her as Maiden, Mother, and Crone, each aspect evoked to bring wisdom, nurturing, or transformation. A chant to the Horned God may focus on his strength, his protection, or his guidance through life's mysteries. By repeating these names with reverence, Wiccans strengthen their bond with the divine, inviting the presence of the deity into their sacred space.

Many Wiccans use chants to **raise energy within a ritual**. This process, known as "raising the cone of power," involves chanting or drumming in a focused, rhythmic way, building energy until it reaches a peak. This energy is then directed toward a specific goal, whether it be for healing, protection, or manifestation. Group chanting is especially powerful for this purpose, as each voice contributes to the growing energy, amplifying it with each repetition. In these moments, the boundaries between individual voices dissolve, creating a unified sound that resonates with intention and purpose. The chant becomes a living entity, a shared energy that Wiccans direct toward their collective aim.

In addition to formal chants, Wiccans often use **simple affirmations** or **rhymed couplets** in daily life to bring focus to their intentions. These chants may be short, such as "As above, so below," or "Earth my body, water my blood," repeated to align with natural forces. Such affirmations act as grounding tools, reminding Wiccans of their place within the world and reinforcing their intentions. Rhymed chants are easy to remember, their rhythm making them effective tools for focus and concentration. In moments of doubt or distraction, a simple chant can bring the practitioner back to their center, restoring clarity and purpose.

Chants also play a significant role in **seasonal and lunar rituals**, aligning practitioners with the cycles of the moon and the Wheel of the Year. For instance, during the full moon, Wiccans may chant to honor the Goddess in her fullness, drawing upon the moon's energy to amplify their intentions. Common full moon chants include phrases like "Mother Moon, shine bright tonight, bless us with your silver light." At seasonal celebrations, chants reflect the qualities of the season—chants for Beltane celebrate fertility and growth, while those for Samhain honor ancestors and the mysteries of death and rebirth. Through these seasonal chants, Wiccans connect with the rhythms of nature, expressing gratitude and reverence for the gifts each season brings.

Wiccans also **create personal chants** that reflect their unique beliefs, desires, or spiritual journey. These personalized chants can be crafted to address specific intentions or to express an individual's relationship with the divine. When creating a personal chant, Wiccans choose words that resonate with their heart and soul, shaping each phrase to reflect their inner truth. The process of writing a chant is itself a sacred act, a way of focusing one's thoughts and desires into a single, powerful affirmation. Personal chants may include names of deities, elements, or personal symbols, creating a unique invocation that aligns with the practitioner's energy.

Chants are often combined with **rhythmic movement** or **hand gestures**, adding layers of intention and focus. Simple hand movements, such as raising hands skyward to invoke divine energy or placing hands over the heart to center oneself, reinforce the chant's meaning. In some group rituals, practitioners may join hands, sway, or move in a circle while chanting, synchronizing their movements with the rhythm of the chant. This physical engagement helps to ground the energy, making the experience more embodied and dynamic. When combined with movement, chanting becomes a full-body expression of intent, blending voice, gesture, and spirit into a harmonious whole.

The **breath** is another vital component in chanting, as it fuels the sound and helps the practitioner to stay focused and relaxed. By synchronizing breath with rhythm, Wiccans can sustain a chant for extended periods without strain, allowing the energy to build gradually. Slow, deep breathing creates a meditative effect, while rapid breathing can increase excitement and intensity. In moments of release—such as when concluding a chant—practitioners exhale fully, letting go of their intentions and allowing the energy to flow outward. The breath transforms the chant from words into energy, each exhale releasing vibrations into the world.

Many traditional Wiccan chants have been passed down through generations, each one carrying the **wisdom of the craft** and the energies of those who came before. Chants like "We all come from the Goddess" or "The Earth, the Air, the Fire, the Water" have become woven into the fabric of Wiccan ritual, serving as touchstones for practitioners. These chants offer a sense of continuity, connecting Wiccans to the collective energy of their tradition. Each repetition of a traditional chant strengthens the practitioner's bond with their heritage, uniting them with the energy of the past, present, and future.

In addition to spoken chants, **toning** and **humming** are often used in meditation and ritual, allowing practitioners to feel the sound resonating within their body. Toning involves holding a single sound, such as "Om" or "Ah," which vibrates through the chest, throat, and head, creating a physical sensation of energy flow. This practice calms the mind, centers the spirit, and helps practitioners tune into their inner energy. Toning is often used at the beginning of rituals to create a peaceful, focused atmosphere, helping Wiccans to shift from ordinary awareness into a sacred state of mind.

For those who practice alone, chanting can be an **intimate and transformative experience**. Solitary chanting allows practitioners to connect with their inner voice, to express their desires freely, and to build confidence in their own power. In private, Wiccans may experiment with different chants, tones, and rhythms, finding what resonates most deeply with their spirit. Solo chanting becomes a personal journey, a way of connecting with the divine without distraction, allowing one's voice to become a direct expression of their innermost self.

At the conclusion of a chant, **silence** is often observed, allowing the energy to settle and the mind to rest. This moment of quiet is an essential part of chanting, as it brings a sense of completion and integration. After raising energy, silence allows practitioners to listen inwardly, to feel the effects of the chant resonating within, and to connect with the stillness that lies beyond sound. In this silence, Wiccans find a sense of peace, a reminder that magic is both in the sound and in the space that holds it.

For Wiccans, chanting is a way to **honor the sacredness of sound** and to embrace their own voice as a source of power. Through chant, practitioners find a language for the soul, a way of expressing their connection to the divine, to nature, and to each other. Each chant is an offering, a gesture of gratitude, and a call to the mysteries of the universe. In these sacred sounds, Wiccans discover the magic of resonance, the beauty of harmony, and the transformative power of intention.

In the practice of sacred chants, Wiccans learn that every sound is an expression of the divine, that each voice has the power to shape energy, and that through chanting, they become one with the forces they honor. Chanting transforms the everyday into the sacred, allowing practitioners to walk their path with a sense of purpose, unity, and reverence for the vibrational magic of life. Through their voices, Wiccans sing the sacred into being, celebrating the mystery, the power, and the beauty of their path.

Chapter 24
Ritual Dances

In Wiccan tradition, ritual dances are expressions of sacred movement, a way for practitioners to engage with the rhythms of nature and channel their energy through the body. These dances are more than just motions—they are embodiments of intention, gestures that harmonize the spirit, mind, and body in a single flow. By moving to the rhythms of chants, drums, or even the silence within, Wiccans align themselves with the primal forces that shape life, celebrating their connection to the divine, to the elements, and to each other. Ritual dances create a sacred space of movement and freedom, allowing practitioners to let go, to transform, and to experience the sacred through the language of their bodies.

Dancing in ritual is an ancient practice found in many cultures, where it is often used to celebrate the turning of the seasons, to honor deities, or to call forth specific energies. In Wicca, these dances serve to raise energy, to attune to natural cycles, and to bring focus to the ritual's purpose. Each dance is unique, shaped by the practitioner's intention, the setting, and the energies they wish to engage. Through rhythmic movements, Wiccans embody their intentions, turning them into expressions that flow from the body, creating a living spell that resonates with the forces they wish to invoke.

Ritual dances begin with **grounding and centering**, a process that prepares the practitioner's mind and body for sacred movement. By taking a few moments to breathe deeply, to feel the earth beneath their feet, and to visualize themselves as balanced and centered, practitioners open themselves to the flow of energy. Grounding is essential, as it ensures that each step and gesture is rooted in presence, allowing practitioners to focus fully on the dance and to move with purpose. This connection to the earth is crucial, as it provides stability, anchoring the dancer's energy and connecting them to the natural forces they seek to honor.

Many Wiccan dances are designed to **honor the elements**, with each movement reflecting the qualities of Earth, Air, Fire, or Water. An Earth dance might involve slow, deliberate steps, movements that evoke the grounded, steady qualities of soil and stone. In contrast, an Air dance might include graceful, swirling motions that mimic the wind, light and free, symbolizing thoughts and inspiration. A Fire dance often features bold, quick movements, a representation of passion and transformation, while a Water dance may flow smoothly, capturing the fluid, gentle qualities of rivers and seas. By embodying these elements, practitioners align with the essence of each force, experiencing their power and wisdom in an intimate, physical way.

One of the most common uses of ritual dance in Wicca is **raising the cone of power**. In this practice, dancers move in a circle, often in a clockwise direction (deosil), building energy with each step, turn, or clap. The movement, combined with chanting or drumming, generates a shared field of power that grows in intensity with each cycle. As the energy peaks, practitioners direct it toward a specific goal, such as healing, protection, or manifestation. This dance is often performed in groups, with each person contributing to the energy raised, creating a sense of unity and shared intention. The cone of power rises like an invisible vortex, shaped by the dance, the rhythm, and the focus of each participant.

Seasonal dances are an integral part of Wiccan celebrations, aligning practitioners with the cycles of the Wheel of the Year. Each Sabbat has its own energy, and the dances performed during these festivals reflect the qualities of the season. For example, during Beltane, a time of fertility and growth,

Wiccans often perform joyful, exuberant dances that celebrate life and abundance. These may include the weaving of the Maypole, where dancers hold ribbons and move around a central pole, creating patterns that represent the weaving of life's energies. In contrast, Samhain dances may be slower, more introspective, honoring ancestors and the cycle of death and rebirth. Seasonal dances connect practitioners with the earth's natural rhythms, grounding them in the changing tides of life.

In many Wiccan traditions, **spiral dances** are performed to honor the interconnectedness of life and the eternal cycle of birth, death, and rebirth. In a spiral dance, participants form a line, often holding hands, and move in a spiraling pattern that winds inward and then outward, symbolizing the journey into the self and back into the world. This dance is especially popular at Samhain, a time when the veil between worlds is thin and spirits are honored. The spiral movement reflects the journey of the soul, the passage through life's mysteries, and the interconnectedness of all beings. Through this dance, Wiccans feel their connection to their ancestors, to the earth, and to the cycles that bind all things.

The **ecstatic dance** is a freer, more spontaneous form of movement, where practitioners allow themselves to be guided by intuition rather than structured steps. In ecstatic dance, Wiccans move without self-consciousness, letting the music or rhythm lead them. This dance is a way to release inhibitions, to express emotions, and to connect with the divine through pure, unfiltered movement. Practitioners may find that they embody different energies or archetypes, feeling themselves as both grounded and free, powerful and open. Ecstatic dance is often used in rituals focused on liberation, healing, or connection with the divine, as it allows the dancer to move beyond the mind and experience the sacred directly.

Drumming and rhythmic clapping are often combined with ritual dance to create a shared pulse that unifies the group and guides the dancers' movements. The steady beat of a drum provides a foundation for the dance, its resonance felt in the bones and the heart. The rhythm of the drum is seen as the heartbeat of the earth, a pulse that grounds and connects each dancer to the natural world. In group dances, participants may clap or drum in unison, creating a sense of unity that amplifies the energy. The rhythm becomes a sacred language, a vibration that transcends words, connecting each person to the dance, to each other, and to the divine.

In addition to group dances, **solitary dances** are practiced by many Wiccans, allowing individuals to explore their inner landscapes through movement. A solitary dance may be performed in silence or with music, in a natural setting or a private indoor space. These dances are deeply personal, each movement reflecting the practitioner's emotions, intentions, or connection with the sacred. Solitary dance offers Wiccans a way to engage in self-discovery, to express gratitude, or to honor a personal connection with a deity. In the privacy of solitary dance, practitioners find freedom, healing, and a sense of inner peace.

For those new to ritual dance, **intuitive movement** serves as a gentle introduction. Practitioners are encouraged to let go of self-judgment, to allow their bodies to move naturally, and to explore how each movement feels. This intuitive approach removes the need for formal steps or choreography, creating a space where the dancer can connect with their body's wisdom. Each movement becomes an expression of intent, a way to feel energy moving through the body, grounding and centering the practitioner. Through intuitive dance, Wiccans learn to trust their own rhythm, to listen to the body, and to discover the sacred within each gesture.

The **clothing and adornments** chosen for ritual dance can enhance the experience, as they help to set the tone and to focus the practitioner's mind. Flowing garments, scarves, or robes allow freedom of movement and create a sense of grace and fluidity, while jewelry, bells, or sashes may be worn to add texture and sound to the dance. These garments and adornments become part of the ritual, amplifying the energy of the dance and transforming the dancer's appearance to reflect their inner state. In this way, the clothing itself becomes a part of the spell, an expression of the sacred energy being invoked.

Concluding a ritual dance is an important step, as it allows the energy to settle and the practitioner to return to a grounded state. Dancers may slow their movements, bringing their focus back to their breath and feeling the earth beneath their feet. This grounding process helps to integrate the energy raised, allowing it to flow within and around the dancer. In group settings, participants may join hands, forming a circle to share a moment of silence or gratitude, honoring the energy created together. By closing the dance with intention, practitioners complete the ritual, bringing their focus back to the present while carrying the dance's energy within.

For Wiccans, ritual dance is a way to **celebrate life's cycles, to honor the body, and to connect with the divine** through movement. It is a practice that transcends words, allowing practitioners to express their intentions in a language as old as time. Each dance is a journey, a moment of communion with the earth, the elements, and the energies that shape existence. Through dance, Wiccans find balance, joy, and a sense of belonging, embracing the beauty and magic of life's rhythms.

Ritual dance is both a celebration and a prayer, a movement that brings practitioners closer to the world's natural flow and to their own inner truths. In the circle of dance, Wiccans discover the power of unity, the strength of community, and the sacredness of every step taken with intention and love. Through this art of movement, they honor the spirit within, the world around, and the mysteries that lie beyond, dancing as one with the heartbeat of life itself.

Chapter 25
Waxing Moon

In Wiccan practice, each phase of the moon holds distinct energies and meanings, guiding practitioners in aligning their intentions with the natural rhythms of the earth and cosmos. The waxing moon, the period from the new moon to the full moon, is a time of growth, expansion, and building energy. As the moon's light increases, it mirrors the process of manifestation, a gradual unfolding of intention into reality. The waxing moon is the perfect phase for planting seeds—both literal and metaphorical—and for focusing on intentions that require growth, development, or attraction.

The symbolism of the waxing moon in Wicca is one of **beginnings, potential, and upward movement**. This phase reflects the energy of the Maiden aspect of the Goddess, who embodies youth, curiosity, and the promise of new possibilities. The Maiden's spirit, vibrant and forward-looking, resonates with the waxing moon's pull toward new achievements, whether they are spiritual, emotional, or practical in nature. Wiccans attune to this energy by embracing curiosity, optimism, and the excitement of starting fresh. During the waxing moon, practitioners find the courage to set forth on new paths, trusting in the potential of their visions and dreams.

Working with the waxing moon begins with **setting clear intentions**. This phase is ideal for starting projects, initiating changes, or drawing in energies that will support the manifestation of goals. Before beginning any ritual, Wiccans take time to clarify their purpose, identifying what they wish to bring into their lives and how this intention aligns with their path. This clarity provides the foundation for their work, allowing each step in the ritual to amplify their goals. Whether it's for love, success, healing, or creativity, intentions set under the waxing moon are fueled by the moon's increasing light, growing stronger each day until the full moon.

Candle magic is particularly powerful during the waxing moon, as the flame symbolizes the spark of intention growing into full strength. Practitioners often choose a candle color that aligns with their goal—green for prosperity, pink for love, blue for health—and inscribe it with symbols or words that represent their desires. As the candle burns, they visualize their intention growing brighter and stronger, the flame carrying their desires to the universe. Some Wiccans light the candle each night during the waxing phase, watching it burn a little longer each day as a reminder of their intention building toward fulfillment. Candle magic during the waxing moon teaches patience and focus, as practitioners commit to nurturing their desires with care and consistency.

Crystal work also aligns well with the waxing moon's energy, as crystals act as amplifiers of intention. Stones like citrine, carnelian, and clear quartz resonate with the energies of growth, confidence, and manifestation, supporting the practitioner's work to attract positive outcomes. Wiccans may place these stones on their altar or carry them as talismans, keeping their intentions close as they move through each day. Charging these crystals under the waxing moonlight adds potency to their energy, enhancing their ability to support the practitioner's goals. Each night, as the moon grows brighter, practitioners reconnect with their stones, reaffirming their intentions and reinforcing their commitment to growth.

The waxing moon phase is also a time for **visualization exercises**, where practitioners use the power of their imagination to see their intentions coming to life. By creating a vivid mental image of the desired outcome, they send a powerful message to the universe, directing energy toward manifestation. Visualization may involve creating a mental picture of success, love, or healing, seeing oneself in a future where the goal has been achieved. This exercise is done with conviction, as if the vision were already a reality. Through visualization, Wiccans not only align with the energy of growth but also strengthen their belief in their ability to bring their dreams into the world.

In group settings, Wiccans may perform **circle rituals to honor the waxing moon**, combining their energies to magnify each other's intentions. Circle rituals often begin with a focus on gratitude for what has already been accomplished, followed by a sharing of personal goals for the coming weeks. By sharing these intentions within the circle, practitioners lend their support to one another, creating a collective force that enhances each individual's energy. As the group chants or raises energy together, the combined power is directed toward each person's goals, amplifying the energy of growth. This collective ritual is both empowering and unifying, reminding practitioners of the strength found in community.

Nature itself provides many **symbols and signs during the waxing moon** that Wiccans use in their practices. Budding trees, sprouting seeds, and lengthening days reflect the energy of growth, serving as reminders of the waxing moon's potential. Practitioners often incorporate natural elements into their rituals, using seeds, flowers, or branches to represent their goals. Planting a seed during the waxing moon, for instance, is a symbolic act of manifestation, representing the slow and steady growth of intention into reality. As the plant grows, so does the practitioner's goal, creating a living symbol of their connection to the natural cycles and their ability to nurture life.

The waxing moon is also an ideal time for **affirmations and personal growth practices**. Affirmations, or positive statements that reinforce self-belief, are particularly effective during this phase, as they help to build confidence and focus on what one wishes to attract. Wiccans may create affirmations that align with their goals, such as "I am worthy of love and abundance," or "I am capable of achieving my dreams." By repeating these affirmations each day, practitioners strengthen their sense of purpose and align their thoughts with their intentions. This practice reinforces the idea that thoughts and words carry power, helping practitioners to stay focused on their path.

Working with the waxing moon teaches Wiccans the **importance of patience and gradual growth**. Unlike rapid results, which may not endure, the waxing moon emphasizes the beauty of steady progress. Just as the moon's light increases night by night, so too do intentions develop over time. Practitioners learn to nurture their desires with care, celebrating each small step as a victory on the path to fulfillment. This perspective encourages resilience, as practitioners come to understand that true growth requires dedication and trust in the process. By honoring each phase of development, Wiccans cultivate a sense of gratitude for the journey itself, rather than only for the outcome.

For those seeking to attract love or strengthen relationships, the waxing moon offers a potent opportunity for **love and attraction spells**. These rituals may include roses, pink candles, or rose quartz to symbolize love and harmony. Practitioners focus on opening their hearts, setting intentions for self-love or attracting a kindred spirit. These spells are done with respect for free will, aiming to invite compatible energy rather than to control. In this way, Wiccans align with the waxing moon's energy of attraction, allowing love to blossom naturally, free from force or manipulation.

For Wiccans who work with **career or financial goals**, the waxing moon provides a time to focus on abundance, opportunity, and prosperity. Rituals for prosperity often include green candles, coins, or symbols of wealth, such as grains or herbs associated with abundance, like basil or mint. Practitioners may visualize themselves achieving financial stability, success in their endeavors, or attracting opportunities. As they perform these rituals, they infuse their intentions with confidence, seeing the waxing moon's energy as a source of support for their goals. Through these practices, they reinforce their belief in their ability to achieve abundance, attracting what they need through the power of focused intent.

For those who wish to connect more deeply with the **spiritual aspect of the waxing moon**, meditation and journaling are effective tools. Meditation during this phase may involve sitting in moonlight, feeling the energy of growth and expansion, and reflecting on one's spiritual path. Journaling offers a space for self-exploration, where practitioners can write about their goals, their hopes, and the steps they plan to take to reach them. By recording these thoughts, they create a map of their journey, one they can revisit to see how far they have come. This reflective practice enhances their connection with the waxing moon's energy of self-discovery, helping them to align with their higher purpose.

In the final days of the waxing moon, as the full moon approaches, Wiccans begin to **shift their focus from growth to celebration**, preparing to honor the culmination of their intentions. They may revisit the intentions they set at the new moon, assessing how their goals have developed and giving thanks for any progress made. This transition serves as a reminder that every phase has its place, and that the efforts of the waxing moon ultimately lead to fulfillment at the full moon. This period of reflection brings a sense of closure to the waxing phase, honoring the journey that has unfolded and the power of intention nurtured through each step.

The waxing moon teaches Wiccans the value of **faith in their own abilities**, the power of patience, and the beauty of gradual unfolding. By working in harmony with this phase, practitioners align themselves with the energies of growth, manifesting their desires in a way that is organic, respectful, and grounded in the natural cycles. The waxing moon is a time of empowerment, a reminder that each small step contributes to a larger whole, and that through dedication and trust, anything is possible.

In honoring the waxing moon, Wiccans celebrate the magic of potential, the joy of watching dreams take root, and the strength found in nurturing growth. Each ritual, each visualization, and each moment of focus becomes a part of this journey, a testament to the power of intention and the beauty of becoming. Through the waxing moon, Wiccans find a partner in the universe, a guiding light that inspires them to dream, to build, and to create, trusting in the rhythms that connect them to the divine flow of life.

Chapter 26
Full Moon

The full moon holds a place of profound reverence in Wiccan practice, representing the peak of the lunar cycle and the culmination of the moon's energy. As the moon reaches its fullest, it shines with a powerful, magnetic light, amplifying intentions, emotions, and spiritual awareness. In Wicca, the full moon is seen as a time of celebration, gratitude, and connection with the divine. It is when the Goddess is viewed as her most radiant, embodying the Mother aspect in her fullness, her nurturing, protective energy at its height. The full moon is a time to honor both the completion of past intentions and the abundance present in life.

The full moon, often called the Esbat in Wiccan tradition, is celebrated with rituals that connect practitioners to their higher selves, their guides, and the forces of nature. Unlike Sabbats, which align with seasonal festivals, Esbats are lunar ceremonies held each month, giving Wiccans a chance to honor the cycles of the moon and to align themselves with its energies. The full moon is a time of heightened intuition, magic, and insight, a sacred moment when the veil between the spiritual and material worlds is thinner, making it ideal for divination, manifestation, and communion with the divine.

Preparing for a full moon ritual begins with clearing one's space and mind, creating an environment that is conducive to focus and reverence. Many Wiccans cleanse their ritual space with sage or other herbs, lighting candles to create a calm atmosphere and placing objects of significance on their altar.

These objects may include crystals, symbols of the elements, flowers, or representations of deities. The altar itself serves as a focal point for the ritual, a sacred space where the practitioner can center their intentions and channel the moon's energy. By preparing both space and mind, practitioners step into a state of readiness, honoring the full moon's energy with mindfulness and respect.

Setting intentions of gratitude and completion is a central aspect of the full moon ritual. Wiccans often begin by reflecting on the goals they set during the waxing moon phase, acknowledging any progress made, and giving thanks for the lessons and growth they have experienced. This time of reflection fosters a sense of closure, allowing practitioners to release what no longer serves them. For instance, if they set an intention for healing, they might express gratitude for the healing journey they have begun, even if it is still unfolding. By honoring both progress and challenges, Wiccans align with the natural cycle of beginnings and endings, cultivating a mindset of appreciation.

The **casting of the circle** during a full moon ritual holds special significance, as the energy raised within the circle is amplified by the lunar phase. The circle acts as a container, holding the power of the ritual and protecting it from outside influences. To cast a circle, practitioners may walk clockwise with an athame or wand, visualizing a boundary of light that surrounds the ritual space. This act of casting creates a sacred sphere where energy can build, a place outside of ordinary time where the practitioner is free to connect with the divine. Within this protected space, the energies of the full moon are welcomed and honored.

Many Wiccans choose to perform **full moon meditations** as part of their ritual, opening themselves to the moon's guidance and wisdom. In meditation, practitioners visualize the full moon's light filling their bodies, purifying their energy, and illuminating hidden aspects of themselves. This meditation often brings insights, clarity, and a sense of inner peace, as the moon's gentle yet powerful energy reveals truths that were previously obscured.

By meditating with the full moon, Wiccans find a moment of stillness, a time to listen to the soul's whisper and to gain perspective on their lives and spiritual paths.

A practice deeply connected to the full moon is **charging crystals and tools** in moonlight. The full moon's energy is believed to cleanse and energize, infusing objects with its power. Wiccans place crystals, wands, and other ritual tools outside or on a windowsill where they can absorb the moon's light. This charging process purifies the tools, renewing their energy and aligning them with the current lunar phase. Practitioners may set intentions for each object, visualizing the full moon's energy imbuing them with purpose, protection, or clarity. Charged by the moon, these objects hold a heightened resonance, ready to support the practitioner's magical work in the coming weeks.

Full moon rituals often include offerings to the Goddess or other deities, expressing gratitude for guidance, protection, and abundance. These offerings may take the form of flowers, food, herbs, or personal items left on the altar or in nature. Wiccans see these offerings as acts of reciprocity, a way of honoring the divine and acknowledging the blessings in their lives. By giving something of value, practitioners open a flow of energy, reinforcing their connection with the Goddess and the natural world. The offering itself becomes a symbol of devotion, a gesture of respect and humility that deepens the practitioner's relationship with the divine.

Divination is particularly powerful during the full moon, as the heightened energy sharpens intuition and enhances the clarity of readings. Wiccans may use tarot cards, runes, or pendulums to seek guidance or gain insight into specific areas of their lives. Full moon divination is often approached with the intention of gaining wisdom or understanding hidden aspects of a situation, as the full moon's light is said to reveal what was previously unseen. This practice allows practitioners to connect with their inner knowledge, to ask questions of the universe, and to receive messages that guide their spiritual journey.

Another significant aspect of the full moon ritual is **releasing and letting go** of anything that no longer serves the practitioner. The full moon represents the completion of a cycle, making it an ideal time to release habits, beliefs, or emotions that hinder growth. Wiccans often write down what they wish to release on small pieces of paper and then burn them in a fire-safe dish or cauldron, watching as the flames transform the paper into ash. This symbolic act of release clears space for new intentions, helping practitioners to move forward unburdened by old energies. The act of letting go at the full moon teaches resilience and renewal, fostering a willingness to embrace change.

Moon water is a popular practice during the full moon, where water is left outside to absorb the moon's energy and then used for various magical and healing purposes. Practitioners place a glass or bowl of water under the full moon, often surrounded by crystals, flowers, or herbs to enhance its properties. This water, charged with lunar energy, can be used for anointing, cleansing, or as a base for spells. Moon water carries the essence of the full moon's light, holding its energy long after the night has passed. This elixir serves as a reminder of the moon's influence and as a source of magic that can be drawn upon throughout the month.

Full moon rituals also often include **chanting or singing**, as sound resonates powerfully under the full moon's light. Wiccans may chant names of the Goddess, recite invocations, or sing sacred songs that honor the moon's beauty and strength. These chants create a vibrational field that enhances the ritual, each word and note carrying the practitioner's energy into the cosmos. Chanting becomes a bridge between the physical and spiritual realms, a form of vocal magic that connects Wiccans with the divine and aligns them with the full moon's energy. The voice, empowered by intention and devotion, transforms sound into a sacred offering.

As the full moon ritual concludes, Wiccans **express gratitude** for the energy, guidance, and insights received. Practitioners may thank the Goddess, the elements, or any deities or guides they invited into the ritual. Closing the circle is done with care, reversing the steps of casting and visualizing the sacred boundary dissolving. This final act brings the practitioner back to ordinary consciousness, grounding the energy raised and honoring the space. Gratitude reinforces the bond between the practitioner and the divine, acknowledging the gifts received and the magic of the moment.

The full moon invites Wiccans to **celebrate the cycles of completion and wholeness**, to honor the journey of intention that began with the new moon. It teaches that life is a continuous dance of creation, growth, fulfillment, and release, each phase flowing into the next. By honoring the full moon, Wiccans embrace this natural rhythm, finding peace in both growth and letting go. The full moon reminds practitioners of their own inner light, their power to manifest, and the beauty of life's ebb and flow.

In the light of the full moon, Wiccans connect with the divine presence that guides them, feeling the blessings of the Goddess in her fullest expression. This moment of communion is both grounding and uplifting, a time when the soul feels both seen and supported. Through the full moon, Wiccans find a sacred mirror, reflecting the wholeness of their journey, the beauty of their spirit, and the timeless dance of the earth and sky.

Chapter 27
Waning Moon

The waning moon is a time of reflection, release, and transition in Wiccan practice, embodying the energies of letting go and making space for renewal. As the moon's light gradually diminishes after the fullness of the full moon, it symbolizes a winding down, a retreat from intensity toward calm. This lunar phase represents the final stages of a cycle, inviting practitioners to shed what they no longer need, to clear away obstacles, and to prepare for new beginnings. In Wicca, the waning moon is seen as a sacred period for healing, introspection, and spiritual cleansing, a time to align with the natural rhythms of decrease and return to center.

The symbolism of the waning moon is often associated with the Crone aspect of the Goddess, who embodies wisdom, closure, and transformation. The Crone represents the deep knowledge that comes with experience, the understanding of life's cycles, and the courage to let go. Her energy is one of acceptance and surrender, a reminder that release is as important as growth in the spiritual journey. During the waning moon, practitioners turn inward, seeking to uncover hidden patterns, to confront fears, and to honor the wisdom found in endings. The Crone's presence teaches the value of patience and self-reflection, guiding Wiccans through the subtle power of transformation.

The work of the waning moon begins with **self-reflection** and the acknowledgment of areas in life that need release or change. Wiccans often take time to examine their goals, intentions, and emotions, identifying anything that may be holding them back. This reflection is done with compassion and honesty, allowing practitioners to see their own strengths and weaknesses without judgment. By understanding what no longer serves their path, they can prepare to let go with grace, freeing themselves from old patterns and embracing the potential for renewal.

Banishing rituals are particularly suited to the waning moon, as this phase supports the removal of negative influences, habits, or energies. Wiccans may use banishing spells to release fears, unwanted attachments, or negative thoughts, creating space for healing and growth. These rituals often involve symbols of release, such as black candles, salt, or herbs like sage and rosemary. Practitioners focus their intentions on dispelling unwanted energies, visualizing these energies dissolving or transforming into light. By performing banishing rituals, Wiccans take an active role in clearing away obstacles, empowering themselves to move forward without the burdens of the past.

Cord-cutting ceremonies are also powerful practices during the waning moon, particularly for releasing emotional ties that are no longer healthy. In a cord-cutting ritual, practitioners visualize a symbolic cord connecting them to a person, situation, or memory they wish to release. With intention, they imagine this cord being severed, freeing both themselves and the other party from any lingering attachments. Wiccans often use an athame, scissors, or even their hands to physically represent the act of cutting, making the release tangible. This ritual brings closure and healing, allowing practitioners to honor the connection and let it go without resentment or regret.

The waning moon is also a time for **cleansing and purification**, both of the physical and energetic space. Wiccans often cleanse their homes, altars, and ritual tools during this phase, using sage, salt, or sacred water to remove any residual energy that may have accumulated. This cleansing process reflects the inner work of release, symbolizing the clearing away of emotional or spiritual clutter. By creating a purified environment, practitioners feel a sense of renewal and readiness, aligning their space with the calm, reflective energy of the waning moon. Cleansing during this phase helps to bring closure to the previous cycle, making way for fresh energy as the new moon approaches.

For many Wiccans, **shadow work** is a significant part of the waning moon phase. Shadow work involves exploring the hidden, often unconscious parts of oneself—those aspects that are repressed, denied, or feared. This introspective practice allows practitioners to confront unresolved emotions, fears, and beliefs, fostering greater self-awareness and integration. The waning moon provides a safe, supportive energy for this exploration, encouraging honesty and acceptance. Through shadow work, Wiccans come to understand their whole selves, recognizing that light and dark are both essential parts of the human experience. This practice of self-acceptance cultivates compassion, resilience, and inner harmony.

Another important aspect of the waning moon is **forgiveness and emotional release**. This phase encourages practitioners to let go of resentment, anger, or guilt, creating space for healing and peace. Wiccans may write letters expressing their emotions, acknowledging the hurt or disappointment, and then burn these letters as a symbolic act of release. This ritual transforms emotional energy into smoke, allowing it to rise and dissipate. Forgiveness becomes an act of self-liberation, a way of releasing the emotional weight that may have lingered. By embracing forgiveness, practitioners find freedom, compassion, and a deeper sense of inner calm.

Meditation during the waning moon is often focused on letting go, centering, and grounding. Practitioners sit in quiet reflection, visualizing the moon's waning light as a soothing, calming force that helps them to release stress, tension, and lingering worries. In this meditation, they may imagine their burdens as leaves falling from a tree, gently drifting away, or as waves washing away on the shore. This visualization allows them to surrender fully, feeling the lightness that comes with release. Meditation during the waning moon is both restful and restorative, aligning practitioners with the earth's cycles of ebb and flow.

Wiccans may also engage in **protection spells** during the waning moon, reinforcing their boundaries and guarding against negative influences. These spells are often performed with black candles, protective crystals like obsidian or tourmaline, and herbs such as basil, garlic, or thyme. Practitioners create a protective boundary around themselves, their home, or loved ones, visualizing this shield as a barrier of light that repels negativity. The waning moon's energy supports these protective measures, helping to seal the ritual's effects and to fortify one's personal space. Protection spells during this phase bring peace of mind, reinforcing the strength of one's boundaries and sense of security.

Journaling is a valuable tool during the waning moon, offering a way to process emotions, reflect on lessons, and track personal growth. Wiccans use this time to write about their experiences, the insights gained from their inner work, and the areas where they have let go. Journaling becomes a record of transformation, a way to honor each step of the journey. Practitioners may also write down their intentions for release, acknowledging the aspects they wish to leave behind. This act of writing brings clarity, helping to crystallize intentions and to affirm the commitment to self-growth.

The waning moon also invites Wiccans to **connect with nature's cycles of decay and renewal**. Practitioners may spend time in natural settings, observing the changes in plants, animals, and landscapes as they transition toward a quieter phase. Fallen leaves, bare branches, and resting soil are all symbols of release, reminding Wiccans that life is a cycle of growth and retreat. By attuning to these rhythms, practitioners find solace in nature's wisdom, understanding that letting go is a necessary step in making way for new growth. This connection to nature deepens their appreciation for the balance of life, encouraging them to embrace both light and shadow.

As the waning moon approaches the new moon, Wiccans begin to **shift their focus toward rest and introspection**, preparing for the quiet, reflective energy of the dark moon. They honor the journey they have taken through the lunar cycle, recognizing the transformations that have occurred. This transition is a time of patience and acceptance, a reminder that not every phase requires action; sometimes, simply being and allowing oneself to rest is the most powerful choice. The waning moon encourages this return to self, a gentle pulling inward that nurtures the soul and restores balance.

The **closing ritual of the waning moon** often involves a final act of gratitude and grounding. Practitioners thank the moon for its guidance and support, honoring the lessons of release and transformation. They may light a single candle or sit in silence, grounding themselves by focusing on their breath and the earth beneath them. This closing ritual brings a sense of peace, helping Wiccans feel complete as they conclude the lunar cycle. In this moment, they let go of their intentions with trust, knowing that they are aligned with the natural flow of life.

Through the waning moon, Wiccans learn the **value of release, surrender, and quiet strength**. This phase teaches that endings are not losses but transformations, steps in the journey that bring wisdom and peace. By embracing the process of letting go, practitioners find freedom, clarity, and resilience, recognizing that every cycle is a chance to grow. The waning moon is a teacher of patience, acceptance, and the beauty found in silence, reminding Wiccans that life is a balance of creation and release.

In honoring the waning moon, Wiccans celebrate the sacredness of life's ebb and flow, finding meaning in every stage of the journey. Through the rituals, meditations, and introspections of this phase, practitioners come to know themselves more deeply, to trust in the process of transformation, and to walk in harmony with the cycles that shape existence. The waning moon offers both closure and renewal, a time to pause, to reflect, and to prepare for the new beginnings that await with the dark moon.

Chapter 28
New Moon

The new moon is a time of introspection, renewal, and setting intentions in Wiccan practice. As the moon turns dark, disappearing from sight, it symbolizes a fresh start, an empty space ripe for planting new seeds. This phase is often associated with beginnings, spiritual cleansing, and self-discovery. For Wiccans, the new moon represents the Maiden aspect of the Goddess, who embodies potential, creativity, and the promise of what is to come. It is a time of quiet yet potent energy, an invitation to go within, to release what has passed, and to envision new possibilities.

The new moon phase marks the start of the lunar cycle and serves as a **foundation for the month ahead**. In this darkness, Wiccans find an opportunity to connect with their deepest desires and to set intentions aligned with their true selves. This phase invites a pause, a retreat from outward action to look inward and listen to the whispers of the soul. The new moon is often celebrated with rituals that focus on clarity, purification, and vision, creating a sacred space for practitioners to align with their personal path and the cycles of nature.

Before beginning a new moon ritual, Wiccans often spend time in **cleansing and preparation**, both of their space and their spirit. This might involve smudging with sage, cedar, or other purifying herbs, bathing in water infused with sea salt or herbs, or simply taking a few deep breaths to center the mind. Cleansing prepares the practitioner for the new cycle, clearing away lingering energies and helping them enter the ritual with a sense of purity and openness. By creating a fresh, clean environment, practitioners honor the energy of the new moon, allowing themselves to start anew.

The **setting of intentions** is central to new moon rituals. These intentions act as seeds, thoughts, and desires planted in the dark soil of potential, which will grow throughout the month. Wiccans approach this step with clarity and focus, reflecting on what they truly wish to bring into their lives. Some may write down these intentions in a journal, while others speak them aloud, visualizing each intention taking root within them. Whether it's a goal for personal growth, healing, prosperity, or creativity, each intention is treated as a sacred promise to oneself and the universe, a declaration of purpose and direction.

Journaling during the new moon is a powerful way to reflect on intentions and to explore one's inner landscape. Many Wiccans use this time to write freely about their goals, feelings, and dreams, allowing their thoughts to flow without censorship. This journaling practice deepens self-awareness and creates a record of intentions that can be revisited at the full moon or later. Writing during the new moon offers practitioners a space to examine their lives, to connect with their intuition, and to bring hidden desires to light. The journal becomes a mirror, reflecting the journey of self-discovery and the unfolding of the soul's path.

Visualization is another important component of new moon rituals, helping practitioners **see their intentions as already fulfilled**. Through visualization, Wiccans imagine their goals coming to life, feeling the emotions, and experiencing the sensations associated with their success. This mental image serves as a blueprint for the energy they wish to create, sending a clear signal to the universe. Some practitioners visualize a garden where each intention is planted as a seed, watching it grow and flourish in their mind's eye. By engaging fully with this vision, Wiccans strengthen their connection to their goals and increase the likelihood of manifestation.

The new moon is also an ideal time for **quiet, meditative rituals** that focus on spiritual growth and inner peace.

Practitioners may choose to meditate in darkness or by candlelight, connecting with the energy of the dark moon and the stillness it brings. This meditation encourages a journey inward, an exploration of the self that is both grounding and expansive. Wiccans may visualize themselves sinking into the earth, feeling the support of the soil and connecting with the heartbeat of the earth. This inward focus is calming, helping practitioners to feel centered and aligned with their true nature.

In group rituals, the new moon is often celebrated with **circle ceremonies** that allow participants to share their intentions and support each other's journeys. Within the circle, practitioners speak their goals aloud or hold silent space for each other, creating a collective energy that amplifies each person's intentions. This shared experience fosters a sense of community and mutual support, reinforcing each individual's commitment to their path. Group new moon rituals may also include chanting, drumming, or lighting candles, each element contributing to the energy of new beginnings and shared purpose.

Symbolic actions such as lighting a single candle or planting a seed can add depth to new moon rituals. A candle, for example, symbolizes the spark of new intentions, its flame representing hope and potential. As the candle burns, practitioners focus on their intentions, seeing the light as a beacon for what they wish to attract. Planting seeds in soil is another meaningful action, a tangible reminder of growth and patience. Each time the practitioner waters the seed, they reaffirm their commitment to nurturing their goals, watching as life emerges from the darkness, just as intentions grow from the depths of the soul.

During the new moon, Wiccans may also work with **crystals that support clarity, intuition, and new beginnings**. Stones such as moonstone, clear quartz, and labradorite resonate with the energies of the new moon, enhancing focus and intuitive insight. Practitioners may meditate with these stones, place them on their altar, or carry them as talismans throughout the lunar cycle. By working with crystals during this phase, Wiccans amplify their intentions and align with the moon's subtle energies, creating a stronger connection to their own inner wisdom and to the cycles of the cosmos.

Affirmations are often used to reinforce intentions set during the new moon, offering positive, focused statements that guide the mind and spirit. Wiccans may choose affirmations that reflect their desires and repeat them daily as a reminder of their commitment. For example, "I am open to new opportunities and growth" or "I am grounded, focused, and ready for change." By repeating these affirmations, practitioners internalize their goals, aligning their thoughts and actions with the energy of the new moon. This practice strengthens their resolve, helping to maintain focus and momentum as the month unfolds.

Dream work is another practice that aligns well with the new moon's energy, as this phase often brings heightened intuition and deeper insights from the subconscious. Wiccans may keep a dream journal by their bedside, noting any symbols, feelings, or messages that arise during this phase. Dreams during the new moon can provide guidance, reveal hidden desires, or clarify the path forward. By paying attention to dreams, practitioners deepen their understanding of themselves and gain insight into the energies that surround their intentions. Dream work during the new moon opens the door to inner wisdom, helping Wiccans to navigate their journey with intuition and trust.

In addition to setting personal goals, the new moon is a time to **seek guidance from spirit guides, ancestors, or deities**. Wiccans may call upon these beings during ritual, asking for wisdom, protection, and support as they begin a new cycle. This connection is often established through quiet meditation or prayer, with practitioners opening themselves to receive guidance. Spirit guides are seen as allies on the path, offering insights that may clarify intentions or reveal new perspectives. By honoring these relationships, Wiccans build a foundation of trust and support, feeling held by the unseen forces that guide their spiritual journey.

The new moon also encourages practitioners to **honor the balance of light and dark** within themselves. This phase is a reminder that both aspects are essential, that darkness is not an absence of light but a space of potential, a place where new life takes root. By embracing the mystery of the new moon, Wiccans learn to trust the unknown, to find strength in uncertainty, and to appreciate the beauty of beginnings that emerge from silence. This perspective fosters resilience, teaching that growth requires both stillness and movement, both reflection and action.

As the new moon ritual concludes, Wiccans may take a moment for **gratitude and grounding**. Practitioners give thanks for the insights, support, and energy they have received, honoring the moon and the divine for their presence. Grounding is often done through deep breathing, focusing on the earth beneath, or holding grounding stones like hematite or black tourmaline. This practice helps practitioners to center their energy and to feel anchored, bringing a sense of peace and readiness for the cycle ahead. Closing the ritual with gratitude reinforces a connection to the earth and to the rhythms that sustain all life.

Through the new moon, Wiccans learn the importance of **intentional beginnings, inner listening, and trust in the unfolding journey**. This phase reminds practitioners that every goal, every dream, starts with a single seed of intention, nurtured through patience and dedication. By working with the new moon, Wiccans honor the power of potential, the beauty of empty space, and the mystery that surrounds creation. The new moon offers a sacred pause, a moment of alignment with the universe, inviting each practitioner to walk their path with clarity, purpose, and hope.

In the darkness of the new moon, Wiccans find a place of peace, a reminder that even in stillness, there is life, growth, and transformation. By honoring this phase, they embrace the cycles of becoming, finding strength in silence, purpose in vision, and magic in the possibilities that await in the unfolding light.

Chapter 29
Harvest Festivals

In Wiccan tradition, the harvest festivals of Lughnasadh and Mabon mark two pivotal moments in the Wheel of the Year, honoring the abundance of the earth and the cycles of growth and gathering. These festivals, celebrated in late summer and early autumn, are times of gratitude, reflection, and community. As the earth's bounty reaches its peak, Wiccans gather to celebrate the gifts of the land, to recognize the effort that has brought them to this moment, and to prepare for the gradual turn toward winter. The harvest festivals are both a celebration of life's abundance and a reminder of the balance between receiving and giving, life and death, light and darkness.

Lughnasadh, also known as Lammas, is celebrated around August 1st and is the first of the harvest festivals. Named after the Celtic god Lugh, a deity of light, skill, and craftsmanship, this festival honors the initial gathering of grains and the promise of a bountiful harvest. Traditionally, Lughnasadh is a time for giving thanks for the growth of the year, acknowledging both the earth's fertility and the hard work required to bring forth sustenance. As the first grains are cut and gathered, Wiccans focus on themes of abundance, gratitude, and the interconnectedness of all beings, honoring the life that sustains them.

At the core of Lughnasadh celebrations is the theme of **gratitude and sacrifice**. In ancient times, this festival was marked by offerings of the first harvest, a way of giving thanks to the deities and the earth for their generosity. Today, Wiccans may celebrate this tradition by baking bread, a symbol of transformation and sustenance, using grains from the current harvest. The act of baking bread represents a union of human effort and natural abundance, a way of honoring the cycle of life and death that allows new life to flourish. This bread is often shared with family, friends, or the community, reinforcing the bonds that sustain the collective spirit.

Lughnasadh rituals frequently include **outdoor feasts, games, and offerings**, mirroring the ancient festivals that honored the earth's bounty. Wiccans may gather in fields, forests, or gardens to celebrate, bringing together food, flowers, and handmade crafts. Some practitioners hold symbolic games or contests in honor of Lugh, who was a god of skills and talents, and use this time to celebrate their own strengths and achievements. Offerings are often left in nature—bread, fruit, or flowers—serving as gifts to the earth in thanks for her abundance. These outdoor gatherings foster a sense of unity with nature and community, reflecting the gratitude that defines this festival.

During Lughnasadh, **harvest altars** are often decorated with symbols of abundance: grains, corn, sunflowers, and fruits like apples and berries. Each item represents the fruits of the earth and the rewards of hard work. Practitioners may arrange these items on their altar as a focal point for rituals, using them to express gratitude and honor the cycle of growth. As they meditate on these symbols, Wiccans connect with the energy of harvest, grounding themselves in the knowledge that all of life is a cycle of planting, nurturing, and reaping. The altar becomes a space of celebration, a reminder of the year's journey and the blessings received.

Lughnasadh is also a time for **personal reflection on goals and achievements**. Wiccans often use this period to assess their progress, to recognize what they have "harvested" in their own lives, and to give thanks for the fruits of their efforts. Practitioners may journal about their experiences, acknowledging the lessons they have learned and the areas where they have grown. This reflection is a way of honoring one's journey, celebrating the accomplishments and the growth that each person has cultivated within themselves. By recognizing these inner harvests, Wiccans find a sense of fulfillment and gratitude, preparing to move forward with wisdom and clarity.

Mabon, the second harvest festival, is celebrated around the autumn equinox in late September. This festival marks the point of balance between light and dark, as day and night are equal in length, symbolizing harmony, reflection, and the gradual transition toward the darker months. Mabon is a time of thanksgiving and completion, honoring the last fruits of the harvest and the fullness of the earth before winter's rest. Named after the Welsh god Mabon, a symbol of youth, beauty, and rebirth, this festival invites Wiccans to celebrate the cycles of life, to reflect on the gifts of the year, and to prepare for the coming introspection of winter.

The **balance of light and dark** is central to Mabon's symbolism, reminding Wiccans of the cyclical nature of life. As the days grow shorter, practitioners reflect on the balance between activity and rest, outward achievement and inner reflection. Mabon rituals often include meditations on balance, harmony, and the need to find equilibrium within oneself. This focus encourages Wiccans to honor both light and shadow, recognizing that each has its place in the cycle of growth. By embracing this balance, practitioners prepare to welcome the quiet introspection that winter will bring, understanding that rest is as essential as action in the wheel of life.

Mabon altars are adorned with the colors and symbols of autumn: apples, pumpkins, squash, nuts, and colorful leaves. These items represent the **last harvest**, the earth's final gift before it turns inward for winter. Wiccans may decorate their altar with candles in warm, autumnal colors—reds, oranges, and yellows—to evoke the fading light and the warmth of community. Apples are a particularly sacred symbol at Mabon, representing wisdom, abundance, and the life-giving force of nature. Many Wiccans cut apples crosswise to reveal the five-pointed star at the core, a symbol of the elements and spirit united in balance.

Sharing food and drink is a key part of Mabon celebrations, symbolizing the gratitude and connection that arise from the harvest. Wiccans may prepare a feast with seasonal foods like apples, grains, wine, and root vegetables, each dish a tribute to the earth's gifts. This meal is often shared with loved ones, reinforcing the bonds of community and mutual support. During Mabon feasts, practitioners may offer toasts of gratitude, expressing thanks for the blessings of the year, for the strength of friendships, and for the wisdom gained through life's challenges. Each bite, each sip, becomes an act of reverence for the earth and the cycles of life.

Mabon is also an ideal time for **acts of generosity and community service**, reflecting the spirit of thanksgiving and abundance. Wiccans may donate food to those in need, volunteer, or give offerings to the earth. These acts of kindness and reciprocity honor the understanding that abundance is a shared blessing, one that is enriched when it is given freely. By sharing their harvest, whether it is food, time, or energy, practitioners embody the essence of Mabon, reinforcing the connections that sustain the web of life.

As Mabon marks the **end of the harvest season**, it is also a time of introspection, a period for reflecting on what has been gathered and what may need to be released. Wiccans often meditate on their own "inner harvest," taking stock of personal growth, lessons learned, and any lingering burdens that they wish to leave behind. This introspective practice allows practitioners to appreciate their journey and to let go of any energies that no longer serve them. By doing so, they prepare themselves for the quieter, more reflective time of year, ready to enter the dark half of the year with clarity and peace.

The **gratitude and reflection** associated with Mabon help practitioners to see the interconnectedness of all things, recognizing that each season, each moment, contributes to the whole. By honoring the cycles of the harvest, Wiccans embrace the beauty of change, the wisdom of nature, and the endless flow of life and death, growth and release. This celebration reinforces the understanding that all of life is woven together, that each blessing is a gift from the earth, and that gratitude is the thread that binds the cycle of abundance.

As Mabon draws to a close, Wiccans give thanks to the Goddess and God, the elements, and the earth itself for the gifts of the season. They acknowledge the balance of light and dark within themselves, preparing for the journey inward that winter will bring. In this closing moment, practitioners feel a profound sense of connection to the land, to each other, and to the sacred cycles that guide their lives.

Through the harvest festivals of Lughnasadh and Mabon, Wiccans find a way to honor the earth's generosity, to celebrate the fruits of their labor, and to embrace the cycles of change. These festivals are times of community, reflection, and celebration, reminders of the strength found in both giving and receiving. By participating in the harvest, Wiccans deepen their connection to the earth, to each other, and to the divine, walking in harmony with the rhythms that sustain all life.

In honoring the harvest, Wiccans embrace the full circle of existence, the joy of abundance, and the wisdom of letting go. The festivals of Lughnasadh and Mabon are celebrations of life's gifts and lessons, expressions of gratitude for the journey, and preparations for the transformation that lies ahead. Through these sacred gatherings, Wiccans reaffirm their place within the wheel of life, finding peace, purpose, and magic in the beauty of the harvest.

Chapter 30
Light Festivals

In Wiccan tradition, the light festivals of Yule and Imbolc celebrate the return and strengthening of light in the darker months of the year. These festivals, falling at the winter solstice and early February, are times of renewal, hope, and anticipation. As the days gradually grow longer, Wiccans honor the rebirth of the sun and the life force it brings, marking a sacred shift in the cycle of the year. Yule and Imbolc are seen as symbols of endurance, reminding practitioners that even in the deepest darkness, light is born anew, carrying with it the promise of warmth, growth, and renewal.

Yule, the winter solstice, is celebrated around December 21st and is one of the most important Sabbats in the Wiccan Wheel of the Year. Yule marks the longest night and the rebirth of the sun, symbolizing hope, resilience, and the triumph of light over darkness. In Wiccan lore, the Goddess gives birth to the Sun God at Yule, bringing light back into the world and signaling the slow return of spring. This festival is a time of quiet joy, reflection, and connection with family and community, honoring the endurance of life through winter's darkness.

Central to Yule is the **symbol of the Yule log**, an ancient tradition that celebrates the light and warmth of the sun. Traditionally, a log of oak or pine is chosen, decorated with holly, pine cones, and other evergreens, and placed on the hearth. The Yule log is then lit, symbolizing the rebirth of the sun and the promise of returning light. In some Wiccan traditions, a piece of the previous year's Yule log is saved and used to kindle the new one, connecting past celebrations with the present and future. Modern Wiccans who may not have fireplaces can adapt this tradition with a candlelit Yule log centerpiece or symbolic candle lighting, honoring the spirit of renewal.

Yule altars are adorned with **evergreens, pine cones, and winter berries**, reflecting the resilience of nature even in the coldest months. Symbols like holly and ivy represent eternal life, while mistletoe is regarded as a sacred plant that bridges the worlds of earth and sky. Wiccans may also add candles in colors of red, green, white, and gold, each representing the strength of the returning sun and the warmth of community. These decorations serve as reminders of nature's endurance and the cyclical nature of life, filling the space with symbols of hope and protection.

Another important tradition during Yule is **gift-giving and acts of kindness**, symbolizing the blessings of the season and the spirit of generosity. Wiccans often exchange handmade gifts, candles, or objects with personal meaning, fostering a sense of connection and gratitude. For some, this is also a time to donate to those in need or to offer acts of service, spreading light and warmth beyond their immediate circle. Gift-giving at Yule is more than an exchange of items; it is an offering of joy, friendship, and goodwill, a way of honoring the abundance that exists even in times of scarcity.

Yule is also a time for **reflection and introspection**, as the longest night encourages practitioners to look within and honor their inner light. Many Wiccans use this time for journaling, meditation, or quiet contemplation, reviewing the past year and setting intentions for the new one. This reflection fosters a sense of closure, helping practitioners let go of what no longer serves them and make space for new growth. The stillness of Yule invites a connection with the soul's wisdom, guiding practitioners as they prepare to move forward with hope and clarity.

At Yule, **feasting and gathering** are joyful expressions of life's resilience. Traditional foods like nuts, apples, mulled wine, and hearty winter stews are shared in celebration, each dish symbolizing warmth, nourishment, and abundance. These gatherings bring family, friends, and community together, reinforcing the bonds of love and support that sustain the spirit through winter's darkness. Each shared meal and warm toast becomes a tribute to the light within each person and the collective strength that carries everyone through challenging times.

Imbolc, celebrated around February 1st or 2nd, marks the midway point between the winter solstice and the spring equinox. Known as the "festival of light," Imbolc celebrates the first signs of spring's approach, honoring the stirrings of new life beneath the earth. This festival is dedicated to Brigid, the Celtic goddess of fire, healing, and creativity, whose presence brings warmth, inspiration, and the promise of renewal. Imbolc is a time of cleansing, preparation, and the rekindling of hope, as Wiccans honor the gradual awakening of the land and the spark of life returning.

The **symbolism of fire** is central to Imbolc, representing both the sun's growing strength and the inner fire of creativity and inspiration. Wiccans may light candles or small bonfires in Brigid's honor, calling upon her energy to illuminate their path and ignite their own inner fire. This act of lighting candles is a symbolic gesture, a way of bringing light to the darkness and affirming faith in the return of life. Each flame represents potential and growth, a spark that reminds practitioners of their power to create and transform.

Imbolc altars are decorated with **white and red candles, snowdrops, and early spring flowers**, celebrating the purity and promise of new beginnings. White symbolizes the light returning, while red represents the fire of Brigid and the warmth she brings. Wiccans may also place symbols of Brigid on their altars, such as crosses made of straw or wheat, or small figures representing the goddess. Milk and honey are

Chapter 31
Life Festivals

The life festivals of Ostara and Beltane mark two vibrant points on the Wiccan Wheel of the Year, celebrating the forces of renewal, growth, and vitality. These festivals, observed at the spring equinox and in early May, embody the energies of rebirth and fertility, encouraging Wiccans to embrace the abundant life that awakens with the coming of spring. Ostara and Beltane honor the blossoming of nature and the creative energies within each person, inspiring practitioners to nurture both the seeds planted in the earth and the intentions set in their hearts. These festivals invite Wiccans to celebrate their connection to the cycles of life, fertility, and renewal, honoring the beauty and power of life itself.

Ostara, celebrated around March 20th at the spring equinox, marks the balance between light and darkness, day and night. Named after Eostre, a Germanic goddess of dawn and fertility, Ostara is a festival of new beginnings, growth, and the promise of warmth and abundance. As the days lengthen and the earth begins to bloom, Wiccans celebrate this turning point in the year, a time when life emerges from the quiet depths of winter. Ostara is a celebration of balance and potential, a reminder of the cycles of death and rebirth that sustain life.

The symbolism of **balance and equilibrium** is central to Ostara, as the equal length of day and night represents harmony between opposing forces. Wiccans often take this opportunity to seek balance in their own lives, reflecting on areas where they may need to create harmony or to align more fully with their true selves. Rituals may focus on releasing the remnants of winter—

such as stagnant energy or outdated habits—and embracing the fresh, optimistic energy of spring. By honoring this balance, Wiccans align with the natural rhythms of the earth, finding peace in the harmony of the season's transitions.

Ostara altars are often adorned with **flowers, eggs, and green foliage**, representing the fertility of the earth and the renewal of life. Eggs, in particular, are powerful symbols of potential and new beginnings, as they embody the mystery of life waiting to unfold. Some Wiccans may decorate eggs with symbols or colors that represent their intentions for the coming months, blessing them in a ritual of creativity and hope. Green candles and crystals like moss agate or aventurine are also commonly used on the Ostara altar, enhancing the themes of growth, healing, and abundance.

Planting seeds is a cherished practice at Ostara, a symbolic act that mirrors the intentions and goals practitioners wish to cultivate. Whether planting actual seeds in a garden or placing symbolic representations of intentions on their altar, Wiccans use this act to connect with the energy of new life. As the seeds grow and blossom, they serve as living reminders of the goals set at Ostara, reflecting the nurturing and commitment required to bring intentions to fruition. This simple act of planting teaches patience and dedication, reminding Wiccans that growth requires both care and time.

In many Wiccan traditions, **egg hunts and feasts** are held to celebrate Ostara, bringing family and community together in joyful activities. Egg hunts reflect the playful spirit of the season, encouraging participants to embrace wonder and discovery. The feast table is often filled with fresh greens, eggs, breads, and dairy products, symbolizing the nourishing gifts of the earth and the return of plenty. By sharing food and laughter, Wiccans celebrate the abundance of life, embracing the spirit of renewal that defines Ostara. These gatherings foster a sense of community and unity, reinforcing the bonds that sustain each person through the cycles of the year.

Meditation on rebirth and personal growth is a valuable part of Ostara rituals. Practitioners may take time to sit quietly, visualizing themselves as seeds breaking through the soil, opening to the light and warmth of the sun. This meditation focuses on the beauty of potential, allowing Wiccans to feel themselves awakening, expanding, and connecting with their goals and dreams. Through this practice, they draw upon the energy of the season to renew their own sense of purpose, opening to the opportunities that lie ahead. This meditation serves as both a grounding and an inspiring moment, aligning practitioners with the natural flow of life's renewal.

Following Ostara on the Wheel of the Year is **Beltane**, celebrated on May 1st, a festival that marks the height of spring and the beginning of summer's warmth and vitality. Beltane is one of the most exuberant and joyous festivals in Wiccan tradition, celebrating fertility, love, and the union of masculine and feminine energies. The earth is alive with blooming flowers, lush greenery, and the promise of fruitful harvests, and Wiccans honor this abundance with rituals that emphasize passion, creativity, and connection. Beltane is a celebration of life in its fullest expression, a tribute to the forces of creation that sustain the world.

Central to Beltane is the **symbol of the Maypole**, a tall pole decorated with colorful ribbons, flowers, and greenery. Dancers weave around the Maypole, holding ribbons that they intertwine in a circular dance, symbolizing the union of opposites and the weaving of life's energies. This traditional dance is both joyful and sacred, a celebration of the interconnectedness of all beings and the creative forces that animate life. The Maypole dance embodies the spirit of Beltane, honoring both community and the beauty of life's cycles. The woven ribbons represent the merging of paths, a symbol of unity, harmony, and the blessings of the season.

Fire plays a significant role in Beltane rituals, symbolizing the sun's growing power and the warmth of love and passion. Bonfires are lit as part of the celebration, and in ancient times, people and animals would jump over or pass between two fires for purification, blessing, and fertility. Today, Wiccans often light small fires or candles to honor the strength of the sun and the life-giving warmth it brings. This fire symbolizes transformation, the spark of creation, and the energy that fuels growth. Beltane fire rituals encourage Wiccans to connect with their own inner fire, to embrace their passions and dreams, and to celebrate life's joy.

Beltane is also associated with **fertility and union**, both in nature and within the self. Wiccans honor the sacred union of the Goddess and the God, a joining that brings forth the abundance of the earth and the fullness of life. This union is symbolic of balance, creativity, and the harmonious blending of energies, a force that supports all growth and transformation. Beltane is an ideal time for love spells, blessings for partnerships, and rituals that celebrate creativity and personal empowerment. These practices honor the divine within relationships, fostering harmony, respect, and mutual support.

Decorating altars with flowers, ribbons, and greenery reflects the vibrant energy of Beltane. Flowers like roses, daisies, and hawthorn represent beauty, fertility, and abundance, while ribbons in bright colors bring an element of joy and playfulness. Wiccans may also place symbols of the sun and earth on their altar, recognizing the sacred relationship between these forces. This colorful display honors the season's vitality and serves as a focal point for Beltane rituals, a space where practitioners can connect with the earth's creative energy and celebrate their own connection to the cycles of life.

Beltane is also a time for **community feasts, music, and dancing**, a celebration of life that brings people together in joy and shared purpose. Feasts are filled with seasonal foods such as fresh berries, honey, bread, and wine, each dish a tribute to the abundance of the earth. Music and dancing are central to the festivities, allowing practitioners to express their gratitude, joy, and vitality through movement and song. These gatherings strengthen the bonds between people and reinforce the connections that nurture the spirit. Beltane's joyous spirit reminds Wiccans that life is to be celebrated, that love and community are gifts to be cherished.

For many, Beltane is a time to **reflect on desires and creativity**, setting intentions for personal growth, love, and self-expression. Practitioners may spend time in meditation or journaling, exploring the dreams and passions they wish to pursue. This introspection encourages a deeper connection with one's inner desires and with the creative energy that Beltane represents. By focusing on these intentions, Wiccans align themselves with the season's energy of growth and expansion, opening to the life-affirming power of the natural world. This reflection honors both the spirit of Beltane and the individual's journey toward fulfillment and joy.

In closing Beltane rituals, Wiccans often express **gratitude for the season's blessings**, giving thanks for the earth's beauty, the bonds of community, and the opportunities for growth and love. Practitioners may offer flowers, bread, or wine to the earth as a token of their appreciation, honoring the balance of giving and receiving. This moment of gratitude grounds the energy raised during the ritual, fostering a sense of peace, unity, and reverence for life's cycles.

Through the life festivals of Ostara and Beltane, Wiccans celebrate the richness of existence, the magic of creation, and the beauty of renewal. These festivals honor both the earth's physical abundance and the spiritual vitality that flows through all beings, reminding practitioners of the joy, purpose, and wonder found in each phase of life. By participating in these sacred celebrations, Wiccans reaffirm their connection to nature, to one another, and to the divine, embracing the dance of life in all its forms.

In honoring Ostara and Beltane, Wiccans find renewal, inspiration, and the courage to live fully, with hearts open to the beauty and mystery of the world. The life festivals are celebrations of hope, growth, and connection, an affirmation of life's enduring magic and the endless cycles of creation and rebirth. Through these rituals, Wiccans walk in harmony with the earth, the seasons, and the life force that sustains all things, finding meaning, joy, and sacred purpose in the journey of life.

Chapter 32
Transformation Festivals

In Wiccan tradition, the transformation festivals of Litha and Samhain are pivotal moments in the Wheel of the Year, symbolizing the cycles of life, death, and rebirth. These festivals, celebrated at the summer solstice and the end of October, embody both the light's peak and the shadow's descent, reflecting the dual nature of existence. Litha celebrates the sun at its zenith, a festival of abundance, joy, and outward energy, while Samhain marks the end of the harvest, a time for honoring ancestors, introspection, and embracing the mysteries of life and death. Together, these festivals teach Wiccans to honor both growth and release, to celebrate life's fullness, and to find wisdom in its transitions.

Litha, the summer solstice, is celebrated around June 21st and marks the longest day and shortest night of the year. This festival, also known as Midsummer, is a celebration of light, vitality, and the full power of the sun. At Litha, the sun is at its peak, symbolizing life at its most vibrant and abundant. Wiccans celebrate Litha by honoring the earth's fertility, the joy of growth, and the energy of creativity and expression. This festival is a time to embrace life's fullness, to connect with the earth's beauty, and to express gratitude for the abundance that summer brings.

The **symbol of fire** is central to Litha, representing the strength and warmth of the sun, as well as the fire of transformation and passion. Bonfires are often lit during Litha celebrations, symbolizing the sun's power and inviting practitioners to connect with their own inner fire. These fires serve as focal points for ritual, dancing, and song, each flame a tribute to the energy and potential that life holds. By lighting fires, Wiccans honor the sun's life-giving force, celebrating the earth's beauty and the vibrant energy that fills the world during the summer months.

Litha altars are adorned with **sun symbols, flowers, and bright colors** such as gold, yellow, and orange. Flowers like sunflowers, roses, and lavender are often placed on the altar, representing the peak of growth and the abundance of nature. Herbs such as St. John's wort, chamomile, and mugwort are also used, each associated with protection, vitality, and magic. These symbols create a visual celebration of life's beauty, filling the ritual space with the colors and scents of summer. By decorating their altars in this way, Wiccans connect with the energy of the season, grounding their intentions in the earth's vibrancy.

One of the most cherished rituals of Litha is **dancing around the bonfire or maypole**, an act of joy and celebration that embodies the festival's spirit of vitality. These dances are often lively and rhythmic, inviting participants to feel the energy of life within their own bodies. Dancers may weave ribbons around a maypole or join hands in a circle, each movement a tribute to the interconnectedness of life. These dances express gratitude for the earth's bounty and honor the light within each person, a reflection of the sun's warmth and generosity.

Feasting on seasonal foods is another important aspect of Litha, as this festival celebrates the abundance of the earth. Wiccans often prepare feasts with fresh fruits, vegetables, honey, and wine, each dish a tribute to the gifts of summer. Sharing food with family, friends, and community fosters a sense of unity and gratitude, reinforcing the bonds that sustain life. By feasting together, Wiccans honor the earth's abundance, celebrating the fullness of life and the blessings of connection and community.

Litha is also a time for **reflection on personal growth and achievements**, a moment to recognize the goals that have come to fruition and to celebrate progress made. Practitioners may journal about their accomplishments, expressing gratitude for the steps they have taken on their journey. This reflection allows Wiccans to pause and appreciate their growth, to celebrate their efforts, and to feel empowered by the progress they have made. By acknowledging these achievements, they ground themselves in the energy of success, drawing strength from their journey as they prepare for the next steps.

Following Litha on the Wheel of the Year is **Samhain**, celebrated on October 31st, one of the most sacred festivals in Wiccan tradition. Samhain marks the end of the harvest and the beginning of winter, a time when the veil between the worlds is thin and spirits are close. Known as the Wiccan New Year, Samhain is a time for honoring ancestors, reflecting on the cycles of life and death, and embracing the mysteries of the unseen. This festival is a solemn, introspective celebration, honoring both the gifts of the past year and the wisdom found in endings.

Ancestor veneration is a central part of Samhain rituals, as Wiccans honor those who have come before and seek to connect with the wisdom of the departed. Practitioners may set up an ancestor altar, placing photographs, mementos, and offerings such as candles, flowers, or food for those who have passed. This altar becomes a sacred space of remembrance and connection, allowing Wiccans to honor their lineage and to express gratitude for the guidance and love of their ancestors. Through this ritual, practitioners feel the presence of those who have shaped their lives, drawing strength from the connection and acknowledging the continuity of spirit.

Samhain altars are often decorated with **symbols of death, harvest, and protection**, such as skulls, pumpkins, corn, and black candles. Each item represents the mysteries of the season and the cycle of life and death. Apples are particularly sacred at Samhain, symbolizing knowledge, the soul, and the promise of rebirth. Some Wiccans cut apples crosswise to reveal the five-pointed star within, a symbol of the elements and spirit. These altar items serve as reminders of the season's themes, grounding practitioners in the reality of change, the beauty of endings, and the potential for renewal.

Divination practices are especially potent during Samhain, as the thinning veil between worlds enhances intuition and spiritual insight. Wiccans may use tarot cards, runes, scrying mirrors, or pendulums to seek guidance for the coming year, to connect with the spirit realm, or to explore hidden aspects of themselves. Divination at Samhain is often approached with reverence, seen as a way to receive messages from the other side and to deepen one's understanding of life's mysteries. This practice encourages practitioners to embrace the unknown, to trust their inner wisdom, and to find peace in the mysteries of existence.

Another important Samhain ritual is **the dumb supper**, a silent meal shared with both the living and the spirits of the departed. During this meal, a place is set for loved ones who have passed, and participants eat in silence, reflecting on memories and inviting the presence of the spirits. The dumb supper is both a ritual of remembrance and a form of communion with the unseen, honoring those who have shaped one's life and recognizing the continued connection between realms. Through this act, Wiccans offer respect, gratitude, and love to those who have journeyed beyond, bridging the worlds in a moment of quiet reverence.

Samhain is also a time for **inner reflection and release**, as the festival marks both an ending and a new beginning. Practitioners may meditate on the past year, recognizing both the achievements and the lessons learned. This introspective practice encourages Wiccans to let go of any lingering energies, fears, or regrets, creating space for renewal. Rituals of release, such as burning written intentions or symbolically burying objects, help to mark the transition, allowing practitioners to move forward with clarity and peace. This act of release fosters resilience, teaching that transformation often requires letting go.

Lighting candles or lanterns to guide the spirits is a common tradition at Samhain, symbolizing both remembrance and protection. These lights are placed in windows or outside the home, serving as beacons for wandering spirits and as symbols of the enduring light within each soul. By lighting these candles,

Wiccans honor the spirits of the dead, creating a welcoming space for connection and remembrance. These flames also represent hope, a reminder that even in the darkest times, light and life persist.

In closing Samhain rituals, Wiccans give thanks for the gifts of the past year, for the lessons learned, and for the presence of loved ones, both living and departed. This closing is often done in a spirit of gratitude and humility, acknowledging the cycles that shape existence. Practitioners may offer final blessings to the earth, to their ancestors, and to the spirits, affirming the sacred bonds that connect all beings. This moment of gratitude grounds the ritual, bringing a sense of peace and acceptance as the Wheel of the Year turns once more.

Through the transformation festivals of Litha and Samhain, Wiccans embrace both the light and shadow aspects of life, celebrating the joys of growth and the wisdom of endings. These festivals remind practitioners that all life is a cycle, that every peak is followed by a valley, and that each ending holds the seeds of new beginnings. By honoring both the height of summer and the depths of autumn, Wiccans find balance, resilience, and peace, walking in harmony with the ever-turning Wheel of the Year.

In celebrating Litha and Samhain, Wiccans affirm their place within the natural cycles, embracing the beauty of transformation and the power of renewal. These festivals are sacred pauses in the journey, opportunities to honor both the fire of life and the quiet mystery of death. Through the rituals of Litha and Samhain, practitioners connect with the depths of existence, finding strength, wisdom, and grace in each stage of the journey, and embracing the sacred truth that all life, in its endless transformations, is a gift.

Chapter 33
Candle Magic

Candle magic is one of the most accessible and versatile forms of magic in Wiccan practice, a method of harnessing fire's transformative power to bring focus, clarity, and energy to an intention. In Wiccan belief, fire symbolizes change, passion, and the divine spark that fuels all creation. The flame of a candle is a direct representation of this sacred force, bridging the visible and invisible worlds, carrying the practitioner's wishes, dreams, and goals into the realm of spirit. Candle magic is used for a wide range of purposes—love, protection, healing, prosperity, or personal growth—each spell tailored to the practitioner's intention and the energy they wish to direct.

The **fundamental principle of candle magic** is that focused intention, when combined with the element of fire, becomes a powerful agent of transformation. The flame serves as both a focus for the mind and a conduit for energy, enhancing the practitioner's ability to connect with their inner self and with the forces around them. Wiccans believe that each candle flame holds the potential to carry a message, a prayer, or a desire into the universe, amplifying it as it burns and releasing that intention into the spiritual realms. Through candle magic, Wiccans connect with the sacred fire within, aligning their energy with the flame's ability to create, cleanse, and transform.

Choosing the right candle is an important first step in candle magic, as each color carries its own unique vibration and resonance, adding layers of meaning to the ritual. In Wiccan practice, specific colors are associated with different energies:

white for purification and spiritual work, red for strength and passion, green for prosperity and health, blue for calm and healing, and pink for love and friendship. By selecting a candle in the color that corresponds to their goal, practitioners align their spell with the color's energy, reinforcing their intention on multiple levels. Many Wiccans also use natural beeswax or unscented candles, believing that the purity of these candles enhances the spell's focus and effectiveness.

Cleansing and consecrating the candle is a crucial part of preparing for candle magic. Practitioners often cleanse their candles to remove any residual energies from previous handling or environments, ensuring that the candle is clear and receptive to their specific intention. This cleansing can be done by anointing the candle with oils, such as rosemary for purification or frankincense for spiritual power, or by passing it through incense smoke. Some Wiccans also inscribe symbols, words, or runes into the candle's surface, engraving their intention directly into the wax. This act of consecration infuses the candle with personal meaning, transforming it from a simple object into a tool of magic.

Once the candle is prepared, Wiccans focus on **charging the candle with their intention**. This process involves holding the candle, closing one's eyes, and visualizing the desired outcome as if it has already come to pass. Practitioners may feel the warmth of the goal as if it were already achieved, seeing the candle as a beacon of that future reality. This visualization charges the candle with focused energy, aligning the practitioner's mind, heart, and spirit with their intention. Through this focused visualization, the candle becomes a vessel for the practitioner's desire, holding their energy within until it is released by the flame.

Anointing the candle with oils is another way to personalize and empower the spell. Certain oils correspond with specific intentions, each chosen to complement the goal of the magic. Lavender or rose oil is often used for love spells, eucalyptus for healing, and cedar for grounding and protection.

To anoint the candle, Wiccans typically dip their fingers in the oil and stroke it along the candle's surface, either from top to bottom (for releasing or banishing spells) or from bottom to top (for attraction and growth spells). This anointing process binds the practitioner's intention with the oil's properties, enhancing the spell's potency and aligning it with the chosen energy.

Once the candle is lit, **the flame becomes the focus of the spell**, representing the transformation of thought into action, spirit into matter. Practitioners may watch the flame closely, allowing their gaze to soften as they connect with its energy. They visualize the flame carrying their desire, each flicker a step toward manifestation. Some Wiccans meditate on the flame, seeing it as a doorway to higher consciousness, a direct link to the spiritual realms. This process deepens the practitioner's connection with the magic, anchoring their intention and creating a clear, focused channel for energy to flow.

Releasing the energy of the spell is a pivotal part of candle magic, as it is through release that transformation can occur. Once the candle has burned for the appropriate amount of time, practitioners may either extinguish it (if the spell will continue across multiple sessions) or allow it to burn completely. If they choose to extinguish it, this is typically done with a candle snuffer, as blowing out the candle is believed to scatter the energy. When the candle is allowed to burn down completely, the spell's energy is fully released, a final act that sends the practitioner's intention into the universe, carried by the flame's last embers and smoke.

The **remnants of the candle spell**—wax, ashes, or candle stubs—can be used in various ways to reinforce the spell's effects or to mark the conclusion of the ritual. Some Wiccans choose to bury the remnants in the earth, particularly if the spell was for grounding, growth, or healing. Others may scatter the remains in flowing water to release the energy or keep them on the altar as a reminder of the intention set. These remnants hold the residual energy of the spell, and by mindfully disposing of or keeping them, practitioners honor the magic's journey and its impact on their path.

Candle magic is often performed with **mantras or affirmations**, repeating phrases that affirm the intention. For example, a practitioner working for self-confidence may say, "I am strong, worthy, and whole," while focusing on the candle's flame. This repetition aligns the mind and spirit, amplifying the spell's focus and clarity. By repeating these words, practitioners infuse the flame with their belief, creating a rhythm that supports the spell's unfolding. Each affirmation is a step closer to manifestation, an act of bringing thought into form through the power of word and fire.

In addition to single-candle spells, some Wiccans practice **multi-candle spells** for more complex intentions or layered goals. Each candle in a multi-candle spell may represent a different aspect of the intention or a specific energy that the practitioner wishes to invoke. For instance, a love and healing spell might involve a pink candle for love, a green candle for healing, and a white candle for purity and protection. These candles are lit in sequence, creating a layered effect that builds a cohesive energy. Multi-candle spells are often used in complex workings, where different energies must harmonize to achieve the desired outcome.

The **timing of candle magic** can further enhance its effectiveness, aligning the spell with specific lunar phases or days of the week. In Wiccan practice, the waxing moon is ideal for attraction and growth spells, while the waning moon is suited to banishing and release. Each day of the week also has its own correspondences—Friday for love and beauty, Saturday for protection and transformation, Sunday for success and vitality. By aligning the timing of the spell with these energies, practitioners reinforce the spell's focus, synchronizing their intention with the natural flow of the cosmos.

Color magic and candle shape are additional elements that practitioners use to tailor their spells. In addition to choosing a candle color that aligns with the intention, Wiccans may use candles in different shapes—such as figure candles representing individuals or animals to symbolize certain energies. For example, a green candle shaped like a leaf or tree might be used for growth and healing, while a red heart-shaped candle could enhance a love spell. These shapes create a visual link to the spell's intention, adding another layer of resonance to the ritual.

Recording and reflecting on candle magic is an important practice, as it allows Wiccans to observe the effects of their work and to learn from each experience. Many practitioners keep a Book of Shadows or a magical journal where they record the details of each candle spell—color, timing, intention, and any insights or outcomes. This record provides a map of the practitioner's journey, a guide to their growth and evolution. Reflecting on past spells helps Wiccans understand the impact of their intentions, to refine their practice, and to honor the lessons learned.

Through candle magic, Wiccans connect deeply with the elemental power of fire, embracing its capacity to create, transform, and renew. The flame is both a physical and spiritual tool, a source of inspiration that brings clarity and strength to the practitioner's goals. Each candle spell is an affirmation of the Wiccan's role as a co-creator with the universe, a reminder that thoughts, words, and actions have the power to shape reality. Candle magic, though simple, is profound, revealing the magic that lies in focus, intention, and the courage to act.

In the warm glow of candlelight, Wiccans find a way to bring their desires into the world, to align with the sacred rhythms of fire, and to honor the transformative power within themselves. Candle magic teaches patience, focus, and the beauty of small, intentional acts. Each candle becomes a journey, a symbol of hope, and a testament to the resilience of the spirit, guiding practitioners as they walk their path with purpose and light.

Chapter 34
Knot Magic

Knot magic, also known as cord magic or binding magic, is a form of spellcraft that uses the symbolic power of knots to bind, release, protect, or connect energies. This ancient form of magic weaves intention into tangible form, each knot securing the practitioner's desires within the fibers of a cord. Knot magic is both subtle and potent, its simplicity hiding a deep wisdom and elegance. In Wiccan practice, knots can symbolize unity, containment, or liberation, depending on the intention behind them. This versatile form of magic is used for protection, love, health, prosperity, and even to remove unwanted influences.

In Wiccan tradition, knot magic is valued for its adaptability and directness. The act of tying and untying knots allows practitioners to create a physical representation of their intention, each twist and loop embodying their energy. Knot magic aligns with the principle that actions, thoughts, and words carry energy that can be directed and contained within physical form. By working with cords, Wiccans find a way to take hold of their desires, infuse them with purpose, and bind them into a manifestation that is both seen and felt.

Selecting the cord or thread is the first step in knot magic, as the material itself becomes an integral part of the spell. Cords of natural fibers like cotton, wool, or silk are often chosen, as these materials connect the spell to the energies of the earth and allow for the free flow of intention. The color of the cord is also significant, with each hue resonating with specific types of energy: red for passion, blue for healing, green for prosperity, and black for protection or banishing. Practitioners may choose one or more cords, each representing a unique layer of the spell, weaving these together to create a more intricate and potent binding.

Once the cord is chosen, practitioners **begin by clearing and consecrating it**, a process that prepares the cord to carry their intention. Cleansing can be done by passing the cord through incense smoke, sprinkling it with blessed water, or holding it in the light of the sun or moon. This cleansing removes any residual energies, ensuring that the cord is receptive to the practitioner's intent. Consecrating the cord, whether through a spoken blessing or silent meditation, aligns it with the desired energy, transforming it from a simple material into a sacred tool of magic.

The **act of knotting** holds symbolic power, each knot created with focused intent. Wiccans often recite a phrase, chant, or affirmation with each knot, infusing it with the energy of their words. For example, a protection spell might involve tying nine knots, each with a statement like, "With this knot, I bind protection." The repetitive, rhythmic act of tying and speaking focuses the mind, anchoring the intention in each knot and strengthening the spell's energy. Each knot becomes a seal of intention, a point where the practitioner's energy converges, binding thought into matter.

In traditional knot magic, **nine knots** are commonly used, as nine is a sacred number symbolizing completion, fulfillment, and spiritual attainment. A simple spell may involve tying nine knots along a single cord, each one corresponding to a specific goal or desire. The final knot serves as the closure, securing all previous intentions and completing the spell. Some Wiccans choose to tie knots at intervals along the cord, creating a pattern that represents their journey or progression toward their goal. This pattern adds layers of meaning, with each knot a step along the path to manifestation.

Intentional untying of knots is another powerful practice, especially in spells designed for release, freedom, or banishing. Untying a knot can symbolize the act of letting go, freeing oneself from limiting beliefs, habits, or influences. Practitioners may set an intention as they undo each knot, visualizing the release of obstacles or negativity. This untying process can be done all at once or gradually, with each knot untied as progress is made toward a goal. By untying knots with intention, Wiccans transform the act into a ritual of liberation, creating space for new energies and experiences.

Knot magic is also used in **binding spells**, a practice that seeks to contain or restrict specific energies. Binding spells are often used to neutralize harmful influences, to prevent negative behavior, or to protect oneself or others from unwanted attention. For instance, a practitioner may tie a knot while visualizing a disruptive influence being contained, reciting a phrase like, "With this knot, I bind harm." Binding spells are always approached with caution and respect for free will, as Wiccans understand the importance of ethical considerations in magic. The purpose of a binding spell is not to control, but to create protective boundaries that prevent harm.

One of the most beloved forms of knot magic in Wiccan practice is **love knot magic**, a gentle and nurturing form of magic focused on connection, harmony, and affection. Practitioners may use a pink or red cord to represent love, tying knots that symbolize unity, attraction, or the strengthening of bonds. Love knot magic can be used to deepen existing relationships, to attract harmonious connections, or to foster self-love and acceptance. Each knot holds an intention for love, whether it be romantic, platonic, or self-directed, anchoring the practitioner's desires in a tangible form. This form of knot magic is gentle yet powerful, a reminder of love's ability to heal and connect.

In addition to cords, **other materials** can be incorporated into knot magic to enhance its potency. Practitioners may weave herbs, charms, or small crystals into the cord, each chosen for its unique properties. Rosemary may be added for protection, rose petals for love, or amethyst for spiritual insight. These materials bring additional energy to the spell, reinforcing the intentions set with each knot. By combining natural elements with the power of knotting, Wiccans create a multi-layered spell that draws on the properties of earth, air, fire, and water, harmonizing these forces within the cord.

Sealing the spell is the final step in knot magic, ensuring that the energy contained within the knots is secure. Some Wiccans may anoint the completed cord with a few drops of oil, sealing it with a protective or empowering essence. Others may pass it through incense smoke, visualizing the knots being charged and protected. Sealing the spell brings closure, affirming that the energy has been contained and that the intention is ready to manifest. This act also prevents any unintentional release of energy, keeping the spell intact until the goal is achieved or the cord is intentionally untied.

In some cases, Wiccans choose to **keep the knotted cord on their person** or in a special place, such as an altar or a sacred box, where it can continue to work. Keeping the cord close allows practitioners to maintain a connection with the spell's energy, serving as a constant reminder of their intention. For protection or love spells, practitioners may carry the cord as a talisman, its knots a physical anchor for the energy they wish to attract or maintain. By keeping the cord nearby, they reinforce the spell's influence in their daily life, drawing strength from the energy bound within each knot.

Timing and lunar phases can enhance the potency of knot magic, aligning the spell with the natural rhythms of growth and release. The waxing moon is ideal for attraction spells, such as drawing love or prosperity, while the waning moon supports banishing or release spells. By timing the spell according to the moon's phase, Wiccans attune their energy to the ebb and flow of nature, amplifying the spell's effectiveness. Knot magic performed during specific days of the week or astrological influences can also be aligned with the energies of planets, bringing additional resonance to the work.

Recording the spell is an essential part of knot magic, as each cord becomes a chapter in the practitioner's journey. Wiccans often document the details of their knot magic in a Book of Shadows, noting the materials used, the number and placement of knots, and the intentions set. Reflecting on these spells over time helps practitioners to understand the impact of their work, to refine their techniques, and to deepen their connection to their path. Each entry serves as a record of growth, a map of the soul's journey, and a testament to the power of focused intention.

Through knot magic, Wiccans find a way to blend intention with action, to create physical symbols of their desires and dreams. Each knot, tied with care and focus, becomes a vessel for energy, a point where spirit and matter meet. Knot magic teaches the importance of patience, commitment, and the beauty of small acts imbued with meaning. In the practice of tying and untying knots, practitioners engage with the cycles of connection and release, binding and letting go, aligning themselves with the rhythms of the universe.

In the woven threads of knot magic, Wiccans discover a powerful tool for transformation, a path of magic that is both humble and profound. Each cord becomes a journey, each knot a milestone, guiding practitioners as they walk their path with intention, integrity, and a deep connection to the forces that shape their lives. Knot magic is an art that honors the interconnectedness of all things, a reminder that with each knot, we hold the power to create, transform, and release, weaving the fabric of our own reality.

Chapter 35
Mirror Magic

Mirror magic is a form of reflective and introspective spellwork within Wiccan practice, using the symbolic and energetic properties of mirrors to focus on self-awareness, manifestation, protection, and even divination. Mirrors, as objects that reflect and reveal, are thought to hold a unique power to bridge the physical and spiritual realms. They reflect not only physical images but also energy, thoughts, and intentions, making them powerful tools for those who seek to look inward, to connect with unseen forces, or to amplify their desires. Wiccans use mirror magic as a means of self-discovery and to project and direct energy in ways that align with their personal growth and magical path.

The mirror's **dual nature of reflection and portal** makes it a versatile instrument in magic. Mirrors can show the practitioner both what is present and what may lie hidden, allowing them to connect with their deeper self or with the energies surrounding them. Mirror magic can be as simple as using one's own reflection to focus an intention or as complex as crafting a portal for scrying or exploring other realms. Through the mirror, practitioners can gaze into their own consciousness, examine their emotions and motives, or peer into the mysteries of the universe.

Selecting and preparing a mirror for magic is an intentional process, as each mirror becomes a specific tool dedicated to its unique purpose. Many Wiccans choose small hand mirrors for personal introspective work or larger mirrors for rituals involving manifestation or protection. Some practitioners also work with black mirrors, specially crafted for scrying, as the dark surface allows for deeper concentration and clearer visions. Preparing the mirror may involve cleansing it with moonlight, saltwater, or sage smoke to remove any residual energies. By consecrating the mirror with a specific intent, the practitioner establishes a connection to the tool, transforming it from an everyday object into a sacred instrument.

Mirror scrying, or gazing into a reflective surface for visions and insights, is one of the most traditional uses of mirror magic. In Wiccan practice, scrying is often used for divination, seeking answers from the unconscious mind or the spirit realm. Practitioners may dim the lights, place a candle near the mirror, and gaze into it with a soft focus, allowing the mind to relax and open to impressions or images that may arise. The act of scrying in a mirror allows the practitioner to go beyond ordinary sight, to see with the "inner eye" or intuitive vision. Through scrying, Wiccans may gain insight into future events, receive messages from spirit guides, or explore aspects of themselves they may not have been consciously aware of.

The mirror's capacity to **reflect energy** makes it a powerful tool for protective magic, as it can repel negativity or harmful intentions. In mirror protection spells, practitioners place a mirror facing outward, reflecting any negative energy back to its source. This is done with the intent to neutralize harmful influences, not to harm anyone, creating a shield of reflective energy around the practitioner's space. Small mirrors can be placed in windows, entryways, or around the home as wards, creating an energetic barrier that repels unwanted influences. The mirror's ability to deflect energy in this way brings peace and security, allowing the practitioner to feel protected and at ease.

Self-reflection rituals using mirrors are a profound way for practitioners to connect with their inner selves, to see beyond the surface and into the heart of their being. In these rituals, Wiccans may sit in front of a mirror, gazing at their own reflection with compassion and openness. This practice allows them to explore their own feelings, strengths, fears, and goals, a form of self-examination that fosters greater self-awareness. Some practitioners speak affirmations or intentions while looking into the mirror, anchoring their words in the reflected image. This act of reflection, literally and symbolically, helps Wiccans see themselves clearly, embrace their inner truth, and deepen their self-love.

Mirror portals are used in Wiccan practice for connecting with other realms, spirit guides, or energies beyond the ordinary world. By setting an intention to open a mirror as a portal, practitioners create a space through which communication can flow. This practice requires grounding, focus, and protective measures, as it opens a channel to energies beyond the physical. Practitioners often cast a protective circle around themselves, cleanse the mirror, and call upon spirit guides or deities for support before engaging with a portal. Mirror portals are used for meditation, exploring spiritual guidance, or journeying into the subconscious, bringing insights from realms beyond ordinary perception.

For those seeking to manifest specific goals, **mirror manifestation rituals** focus on projecting the practitioner's desires into the mirror, as if the reflection holds the potential reality. Practitioners may visualize themselves as already having achieved their goal while gazing into the mirror, seeing this future self clearly within the reflective surface. By speaking intentions aloud or writing affirmations on the mirror's surface, Wiccans strengthen their connection to this vision, aligning their energy with the outcome they wish to manifest. This type of mirror magic acts as a powerful affirmation, a way of projecting one's intentions into the universe with clarity and conviction.

Breaking an unwanted connection is another application of mirror magic, often performed to remove unhealthy or draining ties to people, habits, or past events. In this ritual, practitioners may use a mirror to represent the connection, visualizing the bond reflected within it. They then cleanse the mirror or place a barrier over it, symbolically breaking or shielding the connection. This process allows the practitioner to release attachments without harboring negativity, as the mirror acts as a safe container for the energy being severed. Through this ritual, Wiccans free themselves from influences that no longer serve their growth, creating space for healthier connections.

Beauty and self-empowerment spells are another popular use of mirror magic, focusing on self-confidence, self-love, and inner strength. Practitioners may stand before a mirror, repeating affirmations or visualizing themselves embodying the qualities they wish to enhance. This ritual can be empowering, as it aligns the practitioner with their own inner beauty and strength, reinforcing a positive self-image. By gazing into the mirror and affirming their worth, practitioners create a transformative experience, a moment of honoring their true self. Mirror magic in this form fosters self-love, self-respect, and an alignment with one's highest potential.

In some Wiccan traditions, mirrors are used in **ancestral and spirit communication**, serving as a medium for connecting with loved ones who have passed on. Practitioners may create a sacred space with a mirror, candles, and offerings to invite the presence of their ancestors or guides. By gazing softly into the mirror, they open themselves to receive messages, signs, or impressions from those on the other side. This practice is done with reverence, honoring the spirits invited to connect, and with gratitude for the guidance and support they may offer. Mirror magic for ancestral work strengthens the bond between worlds, bringing comfort, wisdom, and a sense of continuity.

As with all powerful tools, **cleansing and closing the mirror** after a ritual is essential, ensuring that any residual energy is respectfully released. Practitioners may cleanse the mirror with water, salt, or smoke, visualizing it as clear and neutral once again. Closing the mirror is especially important after portal work, as it protects the practitioner's space and seals the mirror from uninvited influences. This act of closure honors the magic worked, bringing the ritual to a peaceful end and leaving the mirror ready for future use. Through this process, Wiccans maintain the integrity of their practice, ensuring that the mirror remains a safe and effective tool.

In addition to physical mirrors, Wiccans may also work with **reflective surfaces in nature**—such as still water, polished stones, or even dewdrops—for mirror magic. These natural mirrors hold a different energy, connecting the practitioner to the earth's wisdom and cycles. Reflecting upon these surfaces invites a unique form of connection, one that is rooted in the natural world and aligned with the rhythm of nature. This form of mirror magic can be deeply grounding, allowing practitioners to draw strength from the earth and to find balance within the beauty of natural reflections.

Documenting mirror magic experiences in a Book of Shadows allows practitioners to reflect on their progress and the insights gained through each ritual. By recording details of the ritual—such as the mirror used, the intention set, and any visions or feelings that arose—Wiccans build a map of their journey, a record of their evolution and growth. Reviewing these entries over time reveals patterns, helps refine techniques, and deepens the practitioner's understanding of their path. Each entry becomes a testament to the power of self-reflection, a mirror of the soul's journey.

Through mirror magic, Wiccans engage with the reflective and transformative power of this ancient tool, finding a partner in their search for insight, growth, and connection. The mirror, in all its forms, becomes a bridge between worlds, a window into the self, and a channel for intention. Each ritual brings the practitioner closer to their own truth, inviting them to see themselves clearly, to honor the depths within, and to trust in the unfolding journey.

In the practice of mirror magic, Wiccans find a way to gaze into the heart of reality, to see the invisible connections that shape their lives, and to honor both the light and shadow within. Mirror magic reveals the beauty of reflection, the wisdom of looking within, and the power of aligning with one's true self. Each ritual is an affirmation of the magic that lies in perception, a reminder that with focus, intention, and courage, Wiccans can transform their reflection into a mirror of their highest potential.

Chapter 36
Sigil Magic

Sigil magic is a powerful and symbolic form of spellwork within Wiccan practice, using drawn or inscribed symbols to encapsulate a specific intention or desire. Sigils, which are unique and personally crafted symbols, serve as conduits of energy, distilling complex intentions into a single, potent image. In Wicca, sigil magic is valued for its simplicity, versatility, and effectiveness, allowing practitioners to focus their intent into a visual form that bypasses conscious barriers. Sigils transform desire into an abstract yet deeply personal symbol, empowering practitioners to bring their goals into the world through the focused creation and activation of a sacred design.

The practice of sigil magic combines both **intention and creative expression**, encouraging Wiccans to craft symbols that reflect their deepest desires. The beauty of sigil magic lies in its flexibility; each sigil is unique to the practitioner's intent, making it a deeply personal and private form of magic. Sigils can be used for protection, love, prosperity, healing, confidence, and nearly any other purpose, making them one of the most adaptable forms of magical practice. As each symbol is created, it becomes a visual affirmation of the practitioner's will, charged with their energy and ready to manifest change.

The first step in sigil magic is to **formulate a clear and focused intention**. This intention should be positive, specific, and stated in the present tense as if the desired outcome has already occurred. For instance, rather than saying, "I will find inner peace," a practitioner might state, "I am at peace within." This wording anchors the intention in the present moment, empowering the practitioner to resonate with the energy of their goal. By setting a clear intention, the Wiccan aligns their mind, heart, and spirit, preparing to channel this focus into the sigil.

Designing the sigil is an intuitive process, one that allows for creative freedom and personal expression. There are several traditional methods for creating sigils, each involving the transformation of letters, words, or phrases into a unique symbol. One common approach is to write out the intention, remove duplicate letters, and then merge the remaining letters into a single cohesive design. Another method involves simplifying the intention into key letters or shapes, connecting and overlapping these elements until a visually appealing and meaningful symbol emerges. The goal is to create a symbol that resonates with the practitioner on a deep level, one that visually encapsulates the essence of the intention.

Creating sigils from magical alphabets is another popular technique among Wiccans, particularly for those who feel a connection to specific alphabets such as Theban, Ogham, or Norse runes. By crafting a sigil from letters in a magical script, practitioners draw upon the ancient power and symbolism of these alphabets, adding layers of resonance to the sigil. Each symbol from these alphabets carries its own associations and energies, which can be woven into the intention, amplifying its impact. This practice aligns the sigil with the traditions of the craft, infusing the symbol with both personal and historical significance.

Once the sigil is designed, **charging the sigil** is the next step, imbuing it with the energy of the practitioner's intent. Charging can be done through meditation, breathwork, chanting, or visualization, each method focusing energy into the symbol. Practitioners may hold the sigil in their hands, close their eyes, and visualize it glowing with light, radiating the energy of their intention. They might repeat affirmations or the intention itself, feeling the sigil absorb this energy. This process infuses the sigil with power, transforming it from a mere drawing into a living symbol charged with purpose.

Activating the sigil is an essential part of the process, as it releases the sigil's energy into the universe to work toward the desired outcome. There are many ways to activate a sigil, depending on the practitioner's intention and preference. Some Wiccans choose to burn the sigil, allowing the smoke to carry their intent into the spiritual realm. Others bury it in the earth, symbolizing the planting of their desire, or place it in flowing water to let their intention merge with the natural flow of energy. Each method represents a release of energy, a moment of surrender where the practitioner lets go, trusting the universe to bring their desire to fruition.

Incorporating the sigil into daily life can also strengthen the spell, making the symbol a subtle, constant reminder of the intention. Some practitioners draw their sigil on a piece of paper and carry it with them, while others may carve it into a candle, a piece of jewelry, or even their altar. By surrounding themselves with the symbol, Wiccans maintain a connection to the energy of their goal, reinforcing their focus and commitment. This integration into daily life makes the sigil a living part of the practitioner's reality, infusing their world with the energy of the desired outcome.

Disposing of the sigil is a step that symbolizes the completion and release of the intention, as the spell now takes its course independently. For practitioners who choose not to keep the sigil after charging, disposal can be done by burning, burying, or casting it into water, with each method representing a full release of energy. Burning symbolizes transformation, returning the sigil's energy to the spiritual realm. Burying places the intention in the earth's care, grounding it in physical reality, while water allows the intention to flow into the universal current. By letting go, practitioners demonstrate their trust in the magic, freeing the sigil to work on their behalf.

The **timing of sigil magic** can enhance its potency, as certain lunar phases, days, or astrological influences may align with the practitioner's goal. The new moon is ideal for beginnings and attraction spells, while the full moon amplifies manifestations and clarity. Specific days of the week are also associated with different energies—such as Sunday for success, Tuesday for courage, or Thursday for abundance. Aligning sigil magic with these natural rhythms adds a layer of harmony to the practice, grounding the intention within the cycles of nature and enhancing the sigil's effectiveness.

Sigils as personal talismans are commonly used in Wicca, turning the symbol into a protective or empowering charm. Practitioners may draw or carve the sigil onto an object, such as a stone, pendant, or piece of wood, and carry it as a constant source of energy. When worn or kept close, the sigil becomes a focal point for the practitioner's will, an enduring source of support and alignment with their intention. This talismanic use of sigils reinforces the intention within the practitioner's energy field, creating a personal connection to the spell and strengthening its effect over time.

In addition to personal talismans, **sigils for sacred spaces** can be used to infuse specific areas with protection, peace, or creativity. Practitioners may draw or inscribe sigils onto their altar, walls, or even doorways, dedicating these spaces to their intended purpose. A sigil for protection might be drawn on the doorframe, while one for peace could be placed in the living room. By marking these spaces with sigils, Wiccans align their environment with their intentions, creating a home or workspace that resonates with supportive energy.

Documenting sigil magic in a Book of Shadows allows practitioners to reflect on the process and track the outcomes of each spell. Wiccans often record the details of the sigil's creation, charging, and activation, noting any insights or results. This record becomes a valuable resource for learning, showing patterns in the effectiveness of different methods and providing a personal history of growth. Reviewing past sigils helps practitioners understand their journey, refine their techniques, and deepen their connection with their path. Each entry is a testament to the power of will, focus, and the magic of intention.

Through sigil magic, Wiccans engage with a profound and personal form of spellwork, creating symbols that are both magical tools and reflections of their inner desires. Each sigil becomes a bridge between thought and manifestation, a visual expression of the practitioner's will. This form of magic teaches the power of simplicity, focus, and creativity, revealing that true magic often lies in the ability to concentrate one's intentions into a single, clear vision.

In the art of crafting sigils, Wiccans find a pathway to align with their highest goals, to bring their dreams into the world, and to transform their inner vision into reality. Sigil magic is a practice that embodies the essence of Wicca—the union of intention, energy, and creativity. Through each carefully crafted symbol, practitioners honor the power within, trusting in the universe to transform desire into being, and walking their path with purpose, confidence, and magical clarity.

Chapter 37
Sacred Ogham

The Ogham, often called the Celtic Tree Alphabet, is a sacred system of symbols deeply rooted in Celtic tradition and revered in Wiccan practice as a powerful tool for divination, connection with nature, and understanding the cycles of life. Consisting of twenty primary symbols, each representing a specific tree or plant with unique spiritual qualities, the Ogham holds a complex and timeless wisdom. Wiccans see the Ogham as more than an alphabet—it is a gateway to the mysteries of the natural world, each symbol offering insights into both the physical and spiritual realms. Through the Ogham, practitioners deepen their connection to the earth, attune to the rhythms of nature, and explore the guidance these symbols provide for their journey.

The **origins of the Ogham** are steeped in myth and lore, often associated with the ancient Druids who were said to have used this alphabet as both a means of communication and a system of divination. Each Ogham symbol, or "fid," is linked to a specific tree or plant, each of which held a sacred role in Celtic culture. Trees were believed to embody spiritual qualities, holding wisdom and energy that could guide and protect those who sought them. The Ogham alphabet reflects this relationship with nature, each symbol a connection to the energy and essence of the tree it represents. By learning the Ogham, Wiccans embrace this ancient wisdom, bringing its insights into their spiritual practice.

The **structure of the Ogham alphabet** consists of twenty primary symbols, each represented by a series of lines along a central stem, traditionally carved on stones or pieces of wood. Each symbol, when inscribed or drawn, carries the energy of its corresponding tree, creating a physical and spiritual link to the qualities associated with that tree. The Ogham is typically divided into four groups, called "aicme," with five symbols in each group. These groups are thought to correspond to different energies or aspects of life, from physical well-being to spiritual growth. Understanding the structure of the Ogham enhances the practitioner's connection to each symbol, grounding their knowledge in both its mystical and practical aspects.

Using Ogham for divination is a revered practice in Wicca, allowing practitioners to seek guidance, insight, and clarity on their spiritual path. Similar to rune casting, practitioners may draw one or several Ogham symbols at random, interpreting their meanings in relation to the question or situation at hand. Each symbol offers specific insights, drawn from the characteristics of the tree or plant it represents. For instance, the symbol for Birch (Beith) represents new beginnings, growth, and purity, making it a positive sign for fresh starts. The symbol for Oak (Duir), associated with strength and wisdom, may suggest resilience and grounding in times of challenge. By interpreting these symbols, Wiccans gain deeper insights into their own lives and the natural cycles that guide them.

To begin an Ogham divination session, practitioners often **create a sacred space**, invoking the energies of the trees and the natural world. This can be done by setting up an altar with symbols of the forest—leaves, branches, stones, or representations of the specific trees associated with the Ogham. Practitioners may call upon tree spirits or the Celtic deities associated with nature to bless the reading, seeking guidance and clarity. This preparation grounds the divination, aligning it with the energies of the earth and enhancing the practitioner's connection to the symbols. By opening themselves to the wisdom of the trees, Wiccans allow the Ogham to speak through them, guiding their path with the timeless knowledge of nature.

Creating a set of Ogham staves or cards is a personal and sacred process, allowing practitioners to connect deeply with each symbol. Many Wiccans craft their own Ogham sets from wood, stones, or even clay, inscribing each symbol by hand. Some choose specific woods for each stave, aligning the material with the tree it represents. This personal creation process infuses the staves with the practitioner's energy, creating a unique bond with the symbols. For those who prefer a simpler approach, Ogham symbols can also be drawn on cards, allowing for easy handling and reading. Each crafted set becomes a magical tool, a conduit for the energies of the trees and the wisdom they impart.

The **individual meanings of the Ogham symbols** offer layers of insight, each tree representing specific qualities, strengths, and lessons. Some commonly used symbols include:

Beith (Birch): Represents beginnings, rebirth, and cleansing. It symbolizes purity, new ventures, and the courage to start anew.

Luis (Rowan): Linked to protection, intuition, and inspiration. Often called the "Tree of Vision," it is believed to enhance psychic abilities and guard against harm.

Fearn (Alder): A symbol of strength, endurance, and determination, Alder is associated with building bridges between worlds, resilience, and tenacity.

Saille (Willow): Represents intuition, emotion, and the cycles of life and death. Willow encourages flexibility and the flow of emotional energy.

Duir (Oak): Symbolizes strength, stability, and wisdom. Oak is often seen as the gateway to spiritual knowledge, grounding practitioners in inner strength.

Tinne (Holly): A symbol of protection, strength, and combativeness, Holly encourages resilience and the ability to withstand challenges.

Coll (Hazel): Associated with knowledge, inspiration, and wisdom. Hazel embodies the spirit of learning and the quest for inner truth.

These symbols, and many others within the Ogham, represent the diverse qualities of the trees and plants they are named after. By studying these meanings, Wiccans deepen their understanding of each tree's spiritual attributes, gaining insight into the natural energies they can work with.

Working with Ogham for self-reflection and growth allows practitioners to explore their inner landscapes, using each symbol as a mirror of their personal journey. Practitioners may draw a daily Ogham symbol to meditate on, reflecting on its message and how it applies to their life. For example, drawing Saille (Willow) might encourage the practitioner to consider how they are flowing with, or resisting, life's changes. Reflecting on each symbol's lessons fosters a sense of personal awareness and connection to the wisdom of nature, supporting the practitioner's growth and understanding of their own spirit.

In addition to divination, **Ogham symbols are often used as talismans or charms** to invoke the qualities of specific trees. Practitioners may inscribe an Ogham symbol onto a piece of wood, stone, or jewelry, carrying it as a source of strength or guidance. For instance, someone seeking resilience might carry the symbol of Oak (Duir), while someone pursuing wisdom might wear Hazel (Coll). These talismans serve as physical reminders of the qualities each tree embodies, aligning the wearer with the tree's energy and reinforcing the spell's intention.

Connecting with the spirit of the trees is a central aspect of working with the Ogham. Wiccans often visit forests or sacred groves to commune with the trees, meditating among them to absorb their energy and wisdom. Practitioners may approach specific trees as guides or allies, seeking to learn from their presence. By honoring the trees associated with the Ogham symbols, Wiccans foster a relationship of respect and reciprocity, understanding that these beings are living manifestations of wisdom and strength. This connection deepens the practitioner's relationship with the natural world, grounding their magic in a profound respect for life.

Spellwork using the Ogham involves invoking the qualities of specific trees to support intentions. For example, a protection spell might incorporate the symbols of Rowan and Holly, blending intuition with resilience. Practitioners may carve these symbols onto candles, inscribe them onto paper, or trace them in the air during ritual. By invoking the Ogham, practitioners align their magic with the energies of the trees, grounding their intentions in nature's power. This form of spellwork reminds Wiccans of the interconnectedness of all life, each symbol a bridge between the practitioner's will and the wisdom of the forest.

Preserving and honoring the legacy of the Ogham is an integral part of Wiccan practice, as this ancient system carries the voices of both ancestors and nature. Wiccans honor the Ogham by studying its meanings, protecting the natural habitats of the trees it represents, and integrating its wisdom into their daily lives. Some practitioners plant trees in honor of the Ogham, cultivating a living connection to the symbols they work with. This practice of preservation is both a tribute to the past and a commitment to the future, ensuring that the sacred knowledge of the Ogham remains vibrant and respected.

Through the Ogham, Wiccans find a bridge to the ancient wisdom of the trees, a way of connecting deeply with the natural world and the cycles of life. Each symbol offers guidance, strength, and insight, allowing practitioners to draw upon the energies that sustain the earth. Working with the Ogham teaches Wiccans to honor the living world, to respect the spirits of nature, and to listen to the silent wisdom that the trees share.

In the study of the Ogham, Wiccans discover a language of the soul, a system of magic that speaks to the enduring connection between humans and nature. The Ogham is more than an alphabet; it is a guide, a teacher, and a reminder that wisdom is found in the roots, branches, and leaves of life itself. Through the Ogham, practitioners walk a path of reverence, attuning to the sacred energies of the earth, and finding purpose and peace within the embrace of the ancient forest.

Chapter 38
Ancient Runes

Runes are an ancient system of symbols originating from the Norse and Germanic traditions, revered in Wiccan practice as powerful tools for divination, magic, and spiritual connection. Each rune holds a unique meaning, representing a concept, energy, or force found within nature and human experience. Unlike written alphabets used for communication, runes are symbols of power that carry both mystical and practical applications. They are seen as tools for understanding the forces that shape life, providing guidance, wisdom, and clarity. In Wiccan tradition, working with runes is a way to tap into this ancient wisdom, aligning oneself with the cycles of the cosmos and the mysteries of existence.

The **origins of the runic system** trace back to early Norse and Germanic tribes, where runes were used for both practical and sacred purposes. Legend tells that the god Odin discovered the runes after a period of intense self-sacrifice, hanging from Yggdrasil, the World Tree, for nine nights. In doing so, he gained knowledge of these sacred symbols and brought them to humanity. This story highlights the reverence with which the Norse viewed the runes, seeing them as gifts from the divine realm. To this day, runes carry an aura of mystery and magic, a link between the mortal and spiritual worlds.

The most commonly used runic alphabet is the **Elder Futhark**, consisting of 24 symbols. These runes are divided into three groups, or "aettir," each containing eight runes. Each aett has its own unique focus, addressing various aspects of life, from material needs and challenges to personal growth and spiritual evolution. The Elder Futhark is named after its first six runes: Fehu, Uruz, Thurisaz, Ansuz, Raidho, and Kenaz. Each rune has its own set of interpretations, attributes, and associations, allowing practitioners to explore a wide range of themes and energies through divination, meditation, or magical work.

Using runes for divination is one of the most common ways Wiccans work with these symbols, seeking insight, guidance, and a deeper understanding of current situations or future possibilities. In a typical divination practice, practitioners cast or draw runes, interpreting their meanings individually and in relation to one another. Each rune holds multiple layers of meaning—some are direct and practical, like Fehu, which represents wealth and prosperity, while others, like Isa, symbolize stillness and obstacles. By interpreting these runes in context, practitioners gain a broader view of their path, understanding both the influences at play and the potential outcomes.

To perform a runic reading, practitioners often **create a quiet, sacred space**, grounding themselves before casting the runes. They may use a special cloth or surface on which to cast the runes, marking it with symbols that represent different aspects of life—such as past, present, and future, or body, mind, and spirit. As they cast the runes or draw them from a bag, practitioners focus on their question or situation, opening themselves to the guidance the runes will provide. By connecting with the runes, Wiccans enter a space of receptivity and intuition, allowing these symbols to reveal hidden truths.

Making a set of runes is a meaningful and personal experience, allowing practitioners to connect deeply with each symbol. Many Wiccans choose to create their own runes from natural materials such as wood, stone, or clay, carving or painting each symbol by hand. This process infuses the runes with the practitioner's energy, strengthening the bond between the reader and their tool. Some practitioners select specific types of wood or stone based on the energies they wish to emphasize, such as oak for strength or amethyst for spiritual insight. Each handmade set becomes a unique expression of the practitioner's path, a reflection of their intentions and relationship with the runes.

The **meanings of individual runes** provide a guide to the energies, concepts, and life forces they represent. Some of the primary runes of the Elder Futhark include:

Fehu: Represents wealth, abundance, and success. It is a symbol of earned prosperity and the energy of beginnings.

Uruz: Stands for strength, vitality, and physical health. Uruz embodies courage and endurance.

Thurisaz: Represents protection and defense, often seen as a rune of challenges and transformation.

Ansuz: Symbolizes communication, wisdom, and divine inspiration. Associated with Odin, it encourages clarity and expression.

Raidho: Represents journey, movement, and life's cycles. Raidho is a symbol of change, direction, and purposeful travel.

Kenaz: Stands for illumination, creativity, and knowledge. Kenaz is the light that reveals hidden truths and sparks inspiration.

Gebo: Represents partnership, balance, and reciprocity. Gebo embodies the gift of connection and harmony in relationships.

Wunjo: Symbolizes joy, success, and harmony. Wunjo brings a sense of peace and fulfillment, embodying positive outcomes.

These interpretations are foundational, and each rune may take on different shades of meaning depending on the context of the reading and the question asked. By studying these meanings, Wiccans deepen their understanding of the runes' spiritual significance, learning to recognize how these energies influence their lives and paths.

Rune casting techniques vary, with some practitioners preferring single-rune draws for daily guidance and others casting multiple runes for more complex readings. One popular method is the three-rune spread, where the practitioner draws three runes to represent past, present, and future or other triadic concepts such as body, mind, and spirit. Another technique is the nine-rune cast, in which the runes are cast onto a cloth and interpreted based on their positions and relationships to one another. Each method provides a unique view into the dynamics of a situation, offering a roadmap for understanding and navigating life's challenges.

Meditating with runes is a practice that allows practitioners to internalize each symbol's energy, exploring its message on a personal level. By focusing on a single rune, such as Raidho for guidance in a life transition or Thurisaz for inner strength, Wiccans can connect with the rune's essence, allowing it to influence their consciousness. Meditation on a rune involves visualizing the symbol, feeling its energy, and inviting insights or feelings to arise. This meditative work deepens the practitioner's understanding of the rune, creating a bond that enhances future divination and magical work.

In addition to divination, **runic talismans and charms** are commonly created to invoke the qualities of specific runes. Practitioners may carve or inscribe runes onto stones, metal, or wood, crafting amulets that carry the protective, healing, or empowering energy of the chosen rune. A rune such as Algiz, symbolizing protection, might be carved onto a pendant or placed at the entrance of the home. These talismans serve as constant reminders of the rune's energy, supporting the practitioner's intentions and offering a touchstone for strength and focus.

Rune magic and spellwork allow Wiccans to incorporate the runes' energy into rituals and spells, using them to reinforce intentions. A prosperity spell, for instance, might include Fehu to attract wealth, while a love spell could use Gebo to encourage harmonious relationships. Practitioners may draw the rune on a candle, inscribe it on paper, or visualize it while focusing on their intention. By invoking the runes in spellwork, Wiccans align their will with these potent symbols, grounding their intentions in the ancient energies the runes represent.

The **timing and context of rune work** add layers of meaning to each reading or spell. Practitioners may choose specific times to work with the runes, such as during the full moon for clarity or the dark moon for introspection. Some also consider the day of the week or astrological influences, aligning their work with energies that support their goals. By grounding rune work in the natural and cosmic cycles, Wiccans enhance their practice, integrating the runes into a broader context of harmony and flow.

Studying the runes over time fosters a deeper connection to their wisdom, as each rune reveals new layers of meaning with each use. Many Wiccans keep a record of their experiences with the runes in a Book of Shadows, noting interpretations, insights, and outcomes. This practice of documentation allows practitioners to see patterns, refine their skills, and track their personal growth. The runes become a mirror of their journey, reflecting their experiences and teaching valuable lessons about life's cycles, challenges, and opportunities.

Through the runes, Wiccans engage with a system of symbols that is both mystical and practical, a language of the soul that connects them with the energies of the universe. Each rune carries its own voice, a message from the past that resonates with the present, offering guidance, strength, and clarity. In the hands of the practitioner, the runes become allies on the path, tools of insight that reveal the hidden forces at play in life.

In the study and practice of runic magic, Wiccans find a source of ancient wisdom, a bridge between worlds, and a means of understanding their place within the web of existence. The runes are more than symbols; they are guides, teachers, and companions, illuminating the mysteries of the world and the journey of the self. Through the power of the runes, Wiccans walk in harmony with the cycles of life, attuned to the ebb and flow of fate, and empowered by the timeless knowledge these symbols provide.

Chapter 39
Black Mirror

The black mirror, a tool of divination and introspection, holds a unique place in Wiccan practice as a gateway to the unseen and the subconscious. Unlike ordinary mirrors, which reflect light, a black mirror absorbs it, creating a surface of profound depth that invites practitioners to journey inward and beyond. Black mirrors are often used for scrying—gazing into their dark depths to receive visions, guidance, and messages from the spiritual realm. For Wiccans, the black mirror is a powerful instrument of self-discovery, intuition, and connection with otherworldly energies, offering a space where intuition and insight blend to reveal truths hidden from the ordinary eye.

The **nature of the black mirror** makes it ideal for accessing the subconscious and the spirit world, where symbolic and intuitive knowledge resides. Its reflective surface, usually made from darkened glass or obsidian, lacks the clear, straightforward reflection of a regular mirror. Instead, the darkness within the black mirror encourages a trance-like state, allowing practitioners to bypass the conscious mind and connect with deeper, more intuitive levels of awareness. This introspective quality makes black mirror scrying both a spiritual practice and a method of psychic development, encouraging practitioners to cultivate their inner vision and trust their intuitive insights.

Creating or choosing a **black mirror** is a personal and significant step, as each mirror becomes a vessel for the practitioner's intentions, energies, and insights. Many Wiccans craft their own black mirrors by painting the back of a glass surface with a dark, matte paint or by using polished obsidian. This handmade approach infuses the mirror with the practitioner's energy, making it uniquely attuned to their inner work. Others may purchase a black mirror specifically crafted for scrying, focusing on the purity and quality of the surface. Whether handmade or chosen, the black mirror becomes a sacred tool, dedicated solely to introspective and mystical practices.

Before using the black mirror, **consecrating and cleansing** it is essential, as this process prepares the mirror to act as a portal to the unseen. Practitioners may cleanse the mirror with saltwater, sage smoke, or moonlight, removing any lingering energies and charging it with their own intent. Consecrating the mirror can involve a ritual blessing, dedicating it to the purpose of scrying and divination. This act of preparation creates a bond between the practitioner and their mirror, ensuring that the mirror serves as a clear and focused tool for their work.

Scrying with the black mirror is an art of deep focus and inner stillness, a practice that involves gazing softly into the darkness of the mirror without expectation or preconceived notions. In a quiet, dimly lit space, practitioners light candles—usually placed behind the mirror to create a subtle glow around its edges—and sit comfortably before it, focusing on their breath and calming their mind. They then gaze gently into the mirror's surface, allowing their vision to relax. At first, they may only see darkness, but with time, symbols, images, or colors begin to emerge. This practice requires patience and openness, as each session unfolds uniquely, reflecting the practitioner's intentions and state of mind.

The **images and impressions** that appear in the black mirror are often symbolic, requiring interpretation that goes beyond literal meanings. Practitioners may see shapes, faces, animals, or even landscapes, each symbol offering insight into their question or intention. For instance, seeing water in the mirror might symbolize emotions or intuition, while a snake could represent transformation or healing. As with dreams, interpreting these symbols is a highly individual process, relying on the practitioner's intuitive understanding and personal associations. Many Wiccans keep a journal of their black mirror sessions, recording the symbols and insights received and reflecting on how they relate to their lives.

Using the black mirror for spirit communication is a practice undertaken with great respect and caution. In this form of scrying, practitioners may invite messages from guides, ancestors, or other benevolent spirits, seeking wisdom or guidance. This process involves casting a protective circle, grounding oneself, and stating a clear intention to connect only with positive, supportive energies. Practitioners often ask specific questions or simply open themselves to messages, gazing into the mirror and allowing any impressions to arise naturally. This form of communication requires grounding and closing practices to ensure a safe and respectful interaction, allowing practitioners to receive guidance while maintaining boundaries.

The black mirror is also used in **past life exploration**, a form of scrying that allows practitioners to glimpse memories or energies from their previous incarnations. In this type of session, Wiccans set an intention to view a past life that is relevant to their current path or lessons they need to learn. They focus on the mirror, asking to see images or symbols that connect them to a past experience. Practitioners may see fragmented images, scenes, or symbols that feel familiar or resonate deeply. This practice offers insights into karmic patterns, relationships, or abilities carried forward, helping practitioners understand their present experiences in light of their soul's journey.

Meditation with the black mirror is a more introspective practice, focusing not on images but on the practitioner's inner awareness. Instead of seeking specific visions, practitioners sit before the mirror and allow its darkness to act as a backdrop for exploring their own consciousness. This meditation can reveal subconscious thoughts, emotions, or fears that may be hidden in the depths of the psyche. Practitioners may gain a heightened sense of clarity, intuition, or inner peace as they connect with their own inner world. This reflective practice is a form of self-discovery, helping Wiccans to understand their inner motivations and align with their true self.

For those seeking to **remove unwanted influences or attachments**, the black mirror can serve as a tool for release. In this ritual, practitioners visualize the negative energy, influence, or attachment as being reflected in the mirror. They then focus on releasing this energy, seeing it dissolve or be absorbed into the darkness of the mirror. Afterward, the mirror is cleansed, symbolically removing the unwanted energy from the practitioner's life. This practice empowers Wiccans to reclaim their personal power, creating a boundary between themselves and influences that may have weighed them down.

Cleansing and storing the black mirror is crucial after each session, as it absorbs and reflects a variety of energies. After using the mirror, practitioners often cleanse it with saltwater, sage smoke, or moonlight, thanking it for its guidance and resetting it for future use. Storing the mirror properly—perhaps wrapped in a cloth and placed in a quiet, undisturbed space—ensures that it remains a dedicated and protected tool. This care for the mirror reflects the respect practitioners hold for its role as a sacred instrument, preserving its purity and effectiveness.

The **timing of black mirror work** can enhance its potency, with many practitioners choosing to scry during specific phases of the moon or times of day. The new moon, representing beginnings and the hidden, is ideal for scrying and spirit communication, as it aligns with the mystery and introspection of the black mirror. Some Wiccans also scry at night or during twilight, times when the veil between worlds is thought to be thinner, allowing for clearer connections and deeper insights. This alignment with natural rhythms amplifies the connection between the practitioner, the mirror, and the energies they seek to access.

Documenting scrying sessions in a Book of Shadows or personal journal allows practitioners to track their growth, explore recurring symbols, and reflect on the evolution of their insights. By recording each session, Wiccans build a personal library of experiences, interpretations, and lessons. Reviewing these entries over time reveals patterns, guiding them in both their spiritual journey and their personal development. The black mirror thus becomes not only a tool for immediate insight but also a long-term source of wisdom, illuminating the practitioner's path through the cycles of discovery and self-awareness.

Through the practice of black mirror scrying, Wiccans engage with an ancient form of divination that deepens their connection to the unseen realms and to themselves. The black mirror is more than a tool for visions—it is a portal, a space where practitioners confront the unknown, seek inner truths, and connect with the mysteries of life. Each session with the black mirror is a journey, a step toward greater understanding and alignment with the rhythms of spirit and nature.

In working with the black mirror, Wiccans find a way to honor the dark and the unknown, embracing the wisdom that lies beyond the conscious mind. The black mirror teaches the value of stillness, patience, and courage, revealing that insight often arises not from seeking, but from allowing. Through this practice, Wiccans walk a path of mystery and illumination, attuned to the silent language of symbols, reflections, and the sacred depths within.

Chapter 40
Oracular Herbology

In Wiccan practice, herbs serve not only as sources of healing and magic but also as oracles, revealing messages from the earth and offering insight through their properties, forms, and energies. Oracular herbology is the art of using plants for divination, accessing the wisdom and spiritual resonance of herbs to gain clarity, guidance, and connection with the natural world. This practice rests on the belief that each herb carries unique energies, shaped by its growth patterns, traditional uses, and the natural forces it embodies. Through oracular herbology, Wiccans tap into the spirits of plants, listening to the messages they hold and inviting their guidance on personal, spiritual, and magical paths.

Herbs as oracles have long been valued in Wiccan tradition and other earth-centered spiritual paths. Ancient peoples understood plants not only for their medicinal and magical properties but also as beings with wisdom to share. Each plant, whether a fragrant flower, a hardy root, or a humble weed, holds layers of symbolism and energy that connect it to certain qualities or insights. By working with herbs in a mindful and receptive way, practitioners can access this hidden knowledge, using the characteristics of each plant to explore answers, understand relationships, or seek guidance on complex questions.

To begin with oracular herbology, practitioners often **create a sacred space** that invites connection with the plant spirits. This space might be an altar decorated with fresh herbs, dried plant bundles, or representations of nature. Practitioners may call upon the spirits of the plants for guidance, expressing gratitude for the wisdom they hold. A cleansing ritual, such as smudging with sage or cedar, can help set a clear, focused atmosphere, allowing the practitioner to be fully present and receptive. This ritual preparation aligns the practitioner with the energies of the herbs, fostering a sense of harmony and openness.

One of the simplest forms of oracular herbology is the **use of single-herb meditations**, where practitioners focus on the qualities of a particular plant to receive guidance. This practice may involve holding a sprig, leaf, or dried portion of the herb in one's hand, breathing in its scent, or placing it on the altar. Practitioners then close their eyes, visualizing the plant in its natural habitat, imagining its life cycle, and meditating on its qualities. As they open themselves to the plant's essence, impressions, images, or emotions may arise, offering insights related to the question at hand. For instance, meditating with rosemary might bring memories or encourage clarity, while lavender may reveal messages about peace and inner balance.

Drawing random herbs from a collection is another form of herbal divination, similar to drawing cards or runes. Practitioners may have a bag or box containing small sachets of dried herbs, each one representing a specific meaning. They ask a question or focus on an intention, then reach into the container and draw an herb at random. The qualities of the chosen herb offer guidance, its characteristics illuminating aspects of the question. For example, drawing basil could signify blessings and abundance, while yarrow might suggest the need for protection or healing. This form of herb reading encourages spontaneity and trust in the plant spirits, inviting them to reveal insights in a way that is both direct and meaningful.

Burning herbs for divination is another practice that combines herbology with fire scrying. Practitioners place dried herbs on a charcoal disc or in a fire-safe dish, setting them alight while focusing on a question or intention. As the smoke rises, they gaze into it, watching the shapes and patterns that form. Each herb's smoke has unique qualities—some create thick, swirling clouds, while others burn steadily and thinly. These patterns, along with any images that appear in the smoke, are interpreted in relation to the question. Sage smoke might reveal paths of cleansing or release, while bay leaf smoke may suggest visions of victory or protection.

In addition to smoke scrying, **tea leaf readings** with specific herbs offer an intimate form of herbal divination. Practitioners prepare an herbal tea, choosing herbs that resonate with their question, and drink it slowly, focusing on their intention. After finishing the tea, they observe the patterns left by the herbs in the cup, interpreting the shapes, symbols, and clustering of the leaves. A single leaf floating near the edge might signify a message ready to be received, while clusters could indicate areas that need attention. This form of reading is both calming and insightful, as it connects the practitioner to the energy of the plant through taste, scent, and visual imagery.

Herbal talismans and amulets are used in oracular herbology to hold intentions, creating physical representations of guidance received from the plants. Practitioners may create pouches, jars, or sachets filled with herbs chosen for their qualities. Each herb within the talisman embodies a specific message, supporting the wearer with its energy. A pouch containing lavender, chamomile, and rose may be worn for emotional healing and calm, while one with bay, sage, and rosemary could serve as a protective amulet. These talismans are carried close to the body or placed in the home, serving as reminders of the plant's guidance and enhancing the practitioner's connection to the spirit of the herb.

Dream work with herbs is another way to access oracular messages, as many plants are believed to aid in dreaming and visioning. Practitioners may place specific herbs under their pillow, brew them as a tea, or burn them as incense before sleep, asking for guidance to appear in their dreams. Mugwort, for instance, is renowned for enhancing dreams and deepening intuition, while chamomile encourages restful, peaceful sleep. Before sleep, practitioners set an intention to receive messages, trusting that the herb will guide them in the dream realm. Upon waking, they journal their dreams, reflecting on any symbols or feelings that may relate to their question.

Each herb in oracular herbology holds **symbolic meanings** that inform its use in divination. Some common examples include:

Rosemary: Represents clarity, memory, and protection. Rosemary may reveal paths to reclaim personal power or cleanse one's mind of confusion.

Lavender: Symbolizes peace, balance, and healing. Lavender often brings insights on emotional well-being, encouraging relaxation and inner harmony.

Sage: Known for purification, wisdom, and release. Sage's guidance often relates to letting go of what no longer serves and seeking clarity.

Mugwort: Associated with intuition, dreams, and psychic ability. Mugwort deepens one's connection to the subconscious, offering clarity in matters of inner truth.

Basil: Represents prosperity, protection, and blessings. Basil's energy reveals paths of abundance and harmony, encouraging gratitude.

Chamomile: Symbolizes calm, patience, and healing. Chamomile brings messages of peace, encouraging patience and emotional release.

Yarrow: Known for courage, protection, and healing. Yarrow may signify resilience and the power to overcome challenges.

These meanings serve as a foundation, and as practitioners work with each herb, they develop their own interpretations based on personal experiences and intuitive responses. Over time, Wiccans form unique relationships with the herbs, deepening their understanding of each plant's spirit and qualities.

In **creating an herb garden for divination**, practitioners cultivate living relationships with the plants they work with. By growing herbs such as rosemary, sage, thyme, and mugwort, they maintain a direct connection with the plants and their energies.

Tending to the garden becomes an act of devotion, an ongoing relationship that enhances the energy of each herb and strengthens the practitioner's bond with the natural world. The garden itself becomes an oracle, each plant offering guidance and support in a living, growing form.

Documenting herbal insights in a Book of Shadows or herbal journal is essential for those practicing oracular herbology, as it allows them to track the meanings, messages, and guidance each plant provides over time. Practitioners note the herbs used, the methods of divination, and the insights received, building a library of plant wisdom. This documentation becomes a personal guide to oracular herbology, providing a rich resource of knowledge that evolves with the practitioner's experience. By reflecting on these records, Wiccans gain deeper insights into both the herbs' energies and their own spiritual growth.

Through oracular herbology, Wiccans find a path of connection with the earth, a way to listen to the silent wisdom of plants and align with the cycles of nature. Each herb is more than a physical remedy; it is a spirit, a teacher, and an ally. By engaging with herbs as oracles, practitioners honor the intelligence of the natural world, receiving messages that speak to both heart and spirit.

In the practice of oracular herbology, Wiccans discover that plants hold an ancient wisdom, one that is both grounding and transcendent. Each herb offers guidance rooted in the rhythms of the earth, reminding practitioners of their place within the web of life. Through this sacred art, Wiccans walk in harmony with nature, drawing strength, healing, and clarity from the living world around them. Oracular herbology becomes a bridge to the spirit of the earth, a pathway to understanding, and a source of inspiration that illuminates their journey.

Chapter 41
Wiccan Totemism

In Wiccan practice, totemism is the art of connecting with animal spirits, also known as totem animals, who serve as guides, protectors, and sources of wisdom. Each totem animal embodies certain qualities, characteristics, and energies that resonate with human emotions, instincts, and experiences. Through totemism, Wiccans connect with these animal spirits, seeking guidance, learning, and strength. Totem animals help practitioners understand themselves more deeply and connect with the primal, instinctual wisdom that animals possess. They are both companions and teachers on the Wiccan path, helping practitioners align with the rhythms of nature and tap into their inner power.

In Wiccan totemism, **totem animals represent aspects of the self** that are waiting to be developed, balanced, or celebrated. Totems reveal traits that the practitioner already possesses, needs to cultivate, or might encounter as challenges in their lives. For instance, the strength and patience of the bear might support a practitioner facing a period of solitude, while the swift energy of the hawk could help one gain perspective on a difficult situation. Each animal holds specific qualities, and by inviting its energy into their lives, practitioners open themselves to the guidance, teachings, and lessons that the animal spirit brings.

Finding one's **primary totem animal** is a foundational step in Wiccan totemism. Many practitioners feel drawn to a particular animal from a young age, sensing a strong affinity or natural connection. Others may discover their totem through meditation, dreams, or specific life experiences where an animal repeatedly appears or strongly impacts them. This connection is usually intuitive and often confirmed through personal experiences or significant encounters. Wiccans believe that each person has a primary totem animal that reflects their core nature, supporting them throughout life as both guide and protector.

To discover their totem, practitioners often engage in a **totem animal meditation**, a visualization exercise that invites the animal to reveal itself. In this meditation, practitioners journey to a sacred natural space in their mind's eye—a forest, mountain, or meadow—and wait for an animal to approach them. They may ask the animal questions, observe its behavior, or feel its energy. If the animal feels right, they accept it as their totem. However, this process is patient and intentional; practitioners do not force a connection but instead wait for the animal spirit to come forward naturally. The totem's appearance is a gift, a sign of the animal's willingness to guide and teach.

Symbolic traits of common totem animals often align with human characteristics, allowing practitioners to draw from their energies and qualities. Some widely recognized totem animals include:

Wolf: Symbolizes loyalty, intuition, and teamwork. The wolf teaches the importance of community, inner guidance, and balance between independence and unity.

Bear: Represents strength, introspection, and protection. The bear's energy offers resilience and self-reliance, encouraging practitioners to find their power in solitude.

Owl: Known for wisdom, intuition, and insight. The owl helps practitioners connect with their intuition and embrace the unknown, seeing through illusions and uncovering truth.

Hawk: Embodies vision, clarity, and focus. The hawk teaches perspective, adaptability, and the ability to see the bigger picture in challenging situations.

Deer: Represents gentleness, sensitivity, and grace. The deer reminds practitioners of the strength found in kindness, patience, and nurturing.

Fox: Known for cleverness, adaptability, and playfulness. The fox teaches practitioners to trust their instincts, embrace change, and navigate life with curiosity.

Snake: Represents transformation, healing, and renewal. The snake encourages embracing life's cycles, letting go of what no longer serves, and finding strength in rebirth.

These animals, and many others, serve as mirrors for personal qualities or life stages. By understanding their symbolic meanings, practitioners gain insight into which traits to embody or refine, allowing them to learn from the wisdom of their totems.

Invoking the presence of a totem animal is a practice that aligns the practitioner's energy with the qualities of the animal, drawing upon its strength and guidance in times of need. This can be done through visualization, chanting, or creating an altar dedicated to the animal. Practitioners may call upon the eagle for clarity and vision, for instance, when seeking answers or making important decisions. Visualizing the animal's energy surrounding them, they feel its presence and wisdom guiding their thoughts and actions. This invocation creates a sacred connection, a partnership between human and animal spirit that enhances the practitioner's intuition, courage, and insight.

Totem animals for specific rituals can be chosen based on the qualities they represent. For example, a bear might be invoked for grounding rituals, providing stability and strength, while a dolphin could be invited into rituals focusing on joy, community, and emotional healing. By calling upon these animals, practitioners align their rituals with the energy each totem brings, enhancing the focus and intent of the magic. Rituals become enriched by these totemic presences, each animal lending its own spirit and qualities to support the work being done.

For Wiccans who wish to connect with **secondary totem animals**, there is the understanding that, beyond the primary totem, many animals may come and go over time, each appearing when needed. These secondary totems represent qualities or challenges that arise during different stages of life, offering support, wisdom, or lessons for the practitioner to integrate. A fox may appear to help someone navigate sudden change, while a spider may come to teach patience and creativity. Secondary totems are not permanent but are companions on specific parts of the journey, showing up as guides and teachers until their lessons are learned.

One powerful practice in Wiccan totemism is **dreamwork with totem animals**, where practitioners invite their totems into their dreams for guidance or deeper insight. Before sleep, practitioners may place a symbolic object (such as a feather for a bird totem or a small stone for a grounded animal) under their pillow and ask for the animal's presence. They set an intention to meet their totem in the dream realm, where interactions with the animal can bring powerful messages or clarify situations in waking life. Upon waking, practitioners journal their dreams, reflecting on how the totem's presence or actions relate to their question or life circumstance.

Altar work dedicated to a totem animal is a meaningful way to honor and connect with the totem's spirit. Practitioners set up a space on their altar with objects that symbolize the animal—such as feathers, stones, or images. They might place candles or herbs associated with the animal's qualities, dedicating the altar as a space for meditation and connection. By regularly spending time at this altar, practitioners deepen their bond with the totem, strengthening their understanding of its teachings and feeling its presence in daily life.

Another significant aspect of Wiccan totemism is **invoking the totem during personal challenges**. Practitioners may call upon the strength of their totem when facing adversity, visualizing the animal beside them, offering support and guidance. A wolf totem may remind them of resilience and loyalty during times of relationship conflict, while a bear totem may offer courage and protection when navigating solitude or self-discovery. Through visualization, prayer, or meditation, practitioners connect with the animal's strength, feeling empowered by its presence and the qualities it represents.

Creating a totem journey stone or charm is another practice that reinforces the connection between the practitioner and their totem. Stones or small charms with symbols of the animal are carried as reminders of the totem's guidance and protection. A hawk feather may be kept for vision and perspective, or a small stone inscribed with a bear's pawprint for grounding and strength. Carrying these charms serves as a constant connection to the totem's energy, a touchstone that empowers the practitioner to face life's challenges with the animal's wisdom at hand.

Through **nature immersion and encounters** with animals in the wild, Wiccans deepen their relationship with totem spirits. By observing animals in their natural environments, practitioners witness their behavior, movements, and interactions, learning from their presence. A fox crossing one's path might signify the importance of flexibility and adaptability, while an eagle soaring above may remind the practitioner to rise above and gain perspective. These real-world encounters with animals enhance the totem relationship, making it a living, dynamic experience grounded in the natural world.

Recording experiences with totem animals in a Book of Shadows or journal allows practitioners to reflect on their evolving relationship with their totems. Entries might include dream encounters, meditations, rituals, or signs observed in daily life. By documenting these experiences, Wiccans build a record of their totem journey, gaining a deeper understanding of the lessons, messages, and insights that each animal brings. Over time, this record becomes a personal guide to their spiritual growth, showing how the wisdom of the animal spirits has influenced their path.

Wiccan totemism is a practice of profound respect and reverence, recognizing animals not as symbols alone but as spiritual beings with unique energies and personalities. Each totem animal is a guardian, a teacher, and a friend, offering strength, protection, and guidance on the journey through life. Wiccans learn to honor these spirits, listening to their teachings, and integrating their wisdom with a sense of gratitude and humility.

In embracing the practice of totemism, Wiccans find a way to connect with the wild, instinctual, and powerful forces of nature. Totem animals become allies on their journey, guiding them through challenges and celebrating moments of growth. Through this relationship, Wiccans deepen their bond with the natural world, aligning with the rhythms of the earth and the wisdom of the animal spirits that walk alongside them. Totemism becomes a path of unity, courage, and discovery, enriching the Wiccan path with the ancient and sacred connection between human and animal spirit.

Chapter 42
Lunar Magic

In Wiccan practice, the moon is honored as a powerful celestial influence, symbolizing the rhythms of nature, intuition, and the cycles of life. The phases of the moon serve as markers for different types of magic, each phase carrying unique energies that support specific intentions, rituals, and reflections. Lunar magic is a way for Wiccans to align their actions with the moon's natural cycles, deepening their connection to the rhythms of the cosmos and enhancing their magical workings. Through the moon's waxing and waning, Wiccans find a guide, a symbol of sacred transformation, and a mirror of their inner world.

The **four primary phases of the moon**—new, waxing, full, and waning—each represent a distinct energy that practitioners can harness. Each phase symbolizes a point in the cycle of growth, culmination, release, and renewal, guiding the practitioner's intentions and actions. By tuning into the moon's phases, Wiccans honor the cyclical nature of life, finding balance between expansion and contraction, action and introspection. The moon becomes both a guide and a reflection of the practitioner's own journey, offering wisdom through its eternal dance of light and shadow.

The New Moon, or dark moon, marks the beginning of the lunar cycle, a time of introspection, renewal, and setting intentions. This phase is a moment of stillness, representing potential and the mysteries of the unknown. The dark sky invites practitioners to look within, to focus on their desires, and to plant the seeds of future goals. The energy of the new moon supports spells for new beginnings, self-discovery, and personal transformation. Wiccans may meditate on what they wish to bring into their lives, using this time to clarify their intentions, clear away the past, and open themselves to new possibilities.

New moon rituals often involve **journaling, meditation, or quiet intention-setting**, allowing practitioners to focus inwardly. During this phase, Wiccans write down their goals or visualize them, planting them like seeds in the fertile soil of the subconscious mind. Some may create a "new moon wish list," listing the qualities or outcomes they hope to manifest over the coming month. By connecting with the energy of the new moon, practitioners align themselves with the forces of renewal, entering a state of openness and readiness for growth.

The Waxing Moon represents the phase of growth, action, and momentum as the moon increases in light. This period, from the new moon to the full moon, is ideal for spells focused on attraction, expansion, and achievement. The waxing moon's energy supports the nurturing of intentions set at the new moon, encouraging practitioners to take steps toward their goals and to build upon what they wish to manifest. This phase is a time for action, motivation, and forward movement, a period when the energy is ripe for actively creating change.

During the waxing moon, Wiccans may engage in **attraction spells and rituals** to draw in what they desire, whether it be love, prosperity, health, or knowledge. This is a time for spells that build, strengthen, and cultivate. Practitioners often light green or gold candles for prosperity spells, pink candles for love, or blue candles for wisdom, each one symbolizing growth and attraction. By focusing on these energies during the waxing moon, Wiccans align with the moon's growing light, inviting abundance and progress into their lives. Each step taken is a way of nurturing the seeds planted at the new moon, working to bring intentions closer to fruition.

The Full Moon is the peak of the lunar cycle, a time of illumination, power, and culmination. The full moon's light is at its brightest, symbolizing clarity, insight, and the manifestation of intentions set earlier in the cycle. Wiccans believe the full moon holds the highest energy, making it an ideal time for powerful rituals, divination, and spells that require additional strength. This is a time for gratitude, reflection, and celebration, honoring what has been achieved and recognizing the progress made on one's path.

Full moon rituals often involve **celebration and offerings** in gratitude for the blessings received. Practitioners may hold group gatherings, dance, sing, or create moon water by placing a bowl of water under the moon's light to absorb its energy. This charged water is then used for anointing, blessing, or enhancing future spells. Many Wiccans take the opportunity to perform divination under the full moon, using tools like tarot cards, runes, or scrying mirrors to gain insights and guidance. The full moon's light enhances psychic abilities and opens the mind to spiritual wisdom, making it a powerful time for receiving messages from the unseen.

The Waning Moon marks the period when the moon's light begins to diminish, symbolizing release, reflection, and letting go. As the moon wanes, Wiccans turn their focus inward, using this time to banish unwanted influences, release negativity, and clear away anything that no longer serves them. The waning moon's energy supports spells for banishing, protection, and inner healing, encouraging practitioners to shed old habits, cleanse their space, and find closure. This phase is a time of release and rest, a moment to make space for new growth in the next cycle.

Waning moon rituals often involve **purification and release work**, such as cleansing the home, banishing negative energy, or breaking harmful patterns. Practitioners may burn bay leaves or sage, symbolizing the release of negativity, or write down what they wish to let go of and safely burn the paper as an act of release. This phase encourages introspection, allowing Wiccans to confront their shadows and release old emotions or beliefs. The waning moon teaches the importance of letting go, of creating space for renewal by shedding the old and stagnant.

Working with the moon's cycles over time allows Wiccans to develop a rhythm that mirrors the ebb and flow of nature, enhancing their connection to the lunar energy and its influence. By observing the phases of the moon and aligning their intentions with each phase, practitioners cultivate a deeper understanding of their own cycles of growth, action, fulfillment, and release. This continuous practice nurtures a harmonious relationship with the moon, a dance of intention and surrender that mirrors life's natural rhythms.

Many Wiccans choose to **document their lunar rituals** in a lunar journal or Book of Shadows, recording each month's intentions, insights, and outcomes. This documentation becomes a valuable resource, allowing practitioners to reflect on their progress, recognize patterns, and refine their intentions over time. By tracking the cycle's influence on their lives, Wiccans gain a greater awareness of the moon's role in their spiritual journey, deepening their understanding of both themselves and the energies they work with.

In addition to the four primary phases, **specific moon phases hold particular significance** in Wiccan lunar magic:

The Dark Moon, the day before the new moon, is a time for deep rest and shadow work. It is a moment of stillness and introspection, a chance to confront hidden aspects of the self and release deeply rooted fears or doubts.

The Blue Moon, an extra full moon that occurs in a calendar year, is considered highly magical, often used for once-in-a-lifetime intentions or significant spiritual work. The rarity of the blue moon amplifies its energy, making it ideal for powerful manifestations or blessings.

The Blood Moon occurs during a lunar eclipse and is associated with transformation, rebirth, and karmic shifts. This phase is used for major life transitions, allowing practitioners to release old energies and step into new beginnings.

Each of these phases brings a unique energy, inviting Wiccans to deepen their understanding of the moon's influence and to explore its many dimensions in their practice. By working with these special phases, practitioners enhance their relationship with the moon, aligning with its most potent and transformative moments.

Through **lunar magic, Wiccans honor the moon** not only as a celestial body but as a symbol of the divine feminine, representing intuition, mystery, and the cycles of change. The moon's phases offer a way to embrace life's natural rhythms, to flow with the waxing and waning of energy, and to find balance in both light and shadow. For Wiccans, the moon is a constant companion, a source of inspiration and guidance that reminds them of their connection to the universe and the magic that exists in every cycle.

In the practice of lunar magic, Wiccans find a powerful ally and a mirror of their own cycles of growth, rest, and renewal. The moon teaches the beauty of change, the wisdom of letting go, and the strength of intentions set in harmony with the natural world. By embracing the phases of the moon, Wiccans walk a path of alignment, purpose, and magic, finding balance in the rhythms of the cosmos and discovering the sacred dance of life, illuminated by the moon's gentle light.

Chapter 43
Solar Magic

In Wiccan practice, the sun is honored as a source of life, vitality, and dynamic energy, symbolizing the active, generative force in the universe. Solar magic draws upon the power of the sun to bring illumination, strength, and clarity to both the practitioner's inner and outer worlds. While lunar magic is often associated with intuition and introspection, solar magic brings forth action, manifestation, and confidence. Through the cycles of the sun, Wiccans connect with the forces of creation, transformation, and growth, aligning themselves with the sun's energy to enhance their personal power and cultivate positive change.

The **sun's journey throughout the year**, marked by the solstices and equinoxes, shapes the foundation of solar magic in Wicca. These four key solar events divide the year into quarters, each reflecting a different stage in the sun's cycle and, symbolically, the journey of life itself. The winter solstice, spring equinox, summer solstice, and autumn equinox serve as points of transformation, celebration, and reflection, guiding practitioners to align with the sun's energy in seasonal rituals and personal growth practices. Solar magic is thus deeply cyclical, inviting Wiccans to harness the sun's power in a way that respects the natural rhythms of increase, peak, decline, and renewal.

The Winter Solstice (Yule) marks the sun's rebirth after its longest period of darkness, a celebration of the returning light. Wiccans honor this time as a moment of hope and renewal, welcoming the rebirth of the sun with rituals that emphasize new beginnings, inner warmth, and faith in the cycles of nature. Solar magic at Yule often focuses on setting intentions for the coming year, symbolizing the seeds of light that will grow with the lengthening days. Practitioners may light candles, meditate on the return of brightness and vitality, and visualize their own intentions growing alongside the increasing sunlight.

Yule rituals often incorporate **fire and candlelight** as symbols of the returning sun, creating a warm, welcoming space that mirrors the light emerging from darkness. Some Wiccans create a "sun wheel" or wreath adorned with solar symbols, placing candles around it and lighting each one to represent the growing light. By invoking the energy of the reborn sun, practitioners connect with the cycle of renewal, drawing strength and inspiration from this ancient promise of light and life. Solar magic at Yule is gentle and hopeful, an act of faith that the sun's warmth will bring growth and abundance.

The Spring Equinox (Ostara) represents balance, a time when day and night are equal, symbolizing harmony and the potential for growth. At this time, Wiccans celebrate fertility, renewal, and the emergence of life. The equinox marks the beginning of active growth, a time when intentions set at Yule begin to sprout, and practitioners focus on nurturing the dreams and goals that were planted in the dark months. Solar magic at Ostara centers on themes of blossoming, balance, and creativity, drawing upon the sun's strengthening power to fuel personal projects and aspirations.

During Ostara rituals, practitioners often plant seeds, both physically and symbolically, as a gesture of hope and growth. **Sun symbols, flowers, and colored eggs** are used to decorate altars, each representing fertility and new beginnings. Wiccans may also engage in balancing rituals, meditating on their goals and considering how they can bring harmony into their lives. Solar magic at Ostara is vibrant and creative, aligning practitioners with the sun's increasing strength and encouraging them to take inspired action toward their dreams.

The Summer Solstice (Litha) is the peak of the sun's power, the longest day of the year, celebrating the fullness of life and abundance. At Litha, Wiccans honor the sun at its zenith, reveling in the energy of growth, passion, and outward expression. This is a time for celebrating achievements, expressing gratitude for life's blessings, and engaging in spells for empowerment, protection, and prosperity. The energy of the summer solstice is dynamic and transformative, a reminder of the sun's role as a source of vitality and a force that drives both physical and spiritual growth.

Litha rituals are filled with **joyful expressions** such as dancing, singing, and outdoor celebrations. Bonfires are a common practice, symbolizing the sun's heat and inviting participants to connect with its transformative power. Practitioners may jump over the flames or pass sacred objects through the fire as a form of purification and blessing. This is a time for **charging crystals and magical tools** under the sun's peak energy, infusing them with strength and clarity. Solar magic at Litha is celebratory, empowering practitioners to connect with their own passions, confidence, and life force.

The Autumn Equinox (Mabon) marks the sun's gradual descent, another moment of balance when day and night are equal. This equinox celebrates the harvest, a time for gathering the fruits of one's labor, expressing gratitude, and preparing for the coming winter. Solar magic at Mabon is reflective, focusing on abundance, completion, and release. Practitioners honor the sun's gifts, acknowledging the cycle of growth that began in the spring and is now reaching its culmination. Mabon is a time of thanksgiving and acceptance, a reminder of the richness of life and the need to let go as the cycle turns.

Rituals for Mabon often include **harvest offerings** such as fruits, grains, and wine, which are placed on the altar as symbols of gratitude. Practitioners may perform release rituals, letting go of any intentions or patterns that have served their purpose. Some Wiccans meditate on the themes of balance and reciprocity, considering how they can contribute to the well-being of their communities or the natural world. Solar magic at Mabon is one of reflection and closure, celebrating the gifts of the sun and preparing for the quieter, introspective months ahead.

In addition to the seasonal cycles, Wiccans may also work with **solar energy on a daily basis**, drawing upon the sun's position throughout the day to guide their magic. Each part of the day carries a different aspect of solar energy:

Dawn is a time of renewal and new beginnings, ideal for setting intentions, cleansing rituals, and spells for fresh starts.

Noon represents the peak of energy and clarity, a powerful moment for empowerment, healing, and spells that require maximum strength.

Sunset symbolizes transition and release, suitable for letting go of unwanted energies, protection spells, and preparing for restful introspection.

By aligning their magic with the sun's daily rhythms, Wiccans create a dynamic and responsive practice, one that flows with the solar cycle and enhances their awareness of the sun's changing influence.

Symbols and tools associated with solar magic include items that reflect the sun's warmth, light, and power. Gold, yellow, and orange are traditional colors used to represent solar energy, often seen in candles, cloths, or crystals such as citrine, amber, and sunstone. These crystals are placed on altars, worn as jewelry, or carried as talismans, each one radiating the sun's energy and reinforcing intentions. Tools like wands or athames may be charged under the sun's light to absorb its strength, and mirrors or discs of gold may be used in solar rituals to reflect and amplify the sun's influence.

Sun salutations and outdoor practices are also integral to solar magic, as they allow practitioners to absorb the sun's energy directly. Many Wiccans practice sun salutations—ritual movements or yoga sequences—in the morning, welcoming the sun's light and aligning themselves with its vitality. Outdoor rituals, especially at sunrise or sunset, enhance this connection, as practitioners can physically feel the warmth and energy of the sun. Absorbing sunlight mindfully is seen as an act of renewal, a way to fill one's body and spirit with life-giving energy.

Solar magic for personal empowerment is often focused on building confidence, courage, and self-expression. By invoking the sun's energy, practitioners can work to overcome fears, embrace their authentic selves, and take action toward their goals. Visualizations of a radiant sun at one's core, shining outward, are common exercises for cultivating inner strength. This inner sun becomes a symbol of personal power, a source of inspiration and resilience that helps practitioners meet life's challenges with determination and clarity.

Documenting solar magic practices in a Book of Shadows allows practitioners to reflect on how the sun's energy influences their personal and magical growth. They may record rituals, intentions, and experiences related to each solstice and equinox, as well as daily solar meditations or sun rituals. By observing the patterns of their solar work, practitioners gain insights into their cycles of growth, challenges, and achievements, creating a record of their journey aligned with the sun's rhythms.

Through solar magic, Wiccans honor the sun as both a physical and spiritual presence, a source of light, warmth, and life. The sun teaches the value of growth, the beauty of abundance, and the power of renewal. For Wiccans, solar magic is not just about drawing energy from the sun—it is about embodying the sun's qualities, using its guidance to live with purpose, courage, and joy.

In the practice of solar magic, Wiccans find a powerful ally in the sun's cycles, a force that mirrors their own journeys of creation, transformation, and renewal. The sun becomes a symbol of their potential, illuminating their path and guiding them through the seasons of life with strength and grace. Through solar magic, practitioners connect with the universal energy that sustains all things, discovering within themselves a source of boundless light, resilience, and inspiration.

Chapter 44
Ancestral Magic

Ancestral magic in Wiccan practice is a deeply personal and spiritual journey that connects practitioners with the wisdom, strength, and legacy of their ancestors. This practice is rooted in the belief that those who came before us continue to guide, support, and influence our lives. Ancestral magic involves honoring, remembering, and building relationships with these spirits, recognizing them as an integral part of the practitioner's identity and spiritual path. By working with ancestors, Wiccans find guidance, healing, and a sense of belonging, creating a bridge between past and present that enriches their lives with a profound sense of continuity.

Understanding the role of ancestors in Wiccan practice goes beyond remembering one's direct lineage. Ancestral magic acknowledges both the blood relatives who share a familial connection and the spiritual ancestors—those who walked a similar path, shared values, or contributed to the legacy of wisdom within a tradition. This broader view includes cultural ancestors, mentors, and even figures from past lives who have left an imprint on the soul. By connecting with these various kinds of ancestors, practitioners tap into a network of support and knowledge that transcends time and space, gaining access to insights that shape their journey.

The **first step in ancestral magic** is often to establish a connection with the ancestors. This can begin through quiet contemplation, meditative journeys, or intentional dream work where practitioners invite their ancestors to reveal themselves.

Many Wiccans ask for guidance from their ancestors, either to gain clarity on their identity or to learn more about the experiences, values, and lessons passed down through generations. This initial connection lays the foundation for deeper work, allowing practitioners to feel their ancestors' presence as a source of guidance and strength.

Setting up an ancestral altar is a powerful way to honor and connect with the ancestors on a daily basis. This sacred space may include photographs, heirlooms, candles, and other items that symbolize or represent the spirits of those who have passed. Practitioners may place offerings on the altar, such as flowers, food, or incense, as gestures of respect and love. By lighting a candle or saying a prayer at the altar, practitioners invite their ancestors' presence, creating a space for dialogue and connection. This altar becomes a focal point for ancestral magic, a physical reminder of the ongoing relationship between practitioner and ancestor.

Honoring the ancestors with offerings is an ancient practice that shows reverence and gratitude. These offerings can vary widely, often based on what the ancestors may have valued or enjoyed in life. A practitioner might leave a favorite food, a symbolic item, or a glass of water, each gesture showing acknowledgment and appreciation. Regular offerings strengthen the bond with the ancestors, creating a flow of mutual respect and goodwill. This practice reflects the Wiccan value of reciprocity, honoring the spirits who support the practitioner's life journey.

Communicating with the ancestors through ritual and meditation is a key aspect of ancestral magic. Wiccans often call upon their ancestors in rituals, inviting them to join in sacred space and lend their wisdom. In meditative practices, practitioners may visualize meeting with an ancestor, asking for guidance on specific questions or simply listening to whatever messages come through. Some Wiccans also practice automatic writing, a method of intuitive writing in which they allow thoughts or images from their ancestors to flow onto the page. By opening themselves to these messages, practitioners find clarity, healing, and a sense of purpose.

One of the most significant aspects of ancestral magic is **healing ancestral wounds**, a practice focused on addressing patterns of trauma, grief, or dysfunction passed down through generations. Practitioners may recognize patterns that have affected their family—such as fear, poverty, or anger—and consciously work to heal these wounds. Through ritual, meditation, and forgiveness, Wiccans release these inherited burdens, freeing themselves and future generations from the weight of past pain. This healing process is often done in partnership with the ancestors themselves, who may offer insight or support as practitioners break cycles and reclaim their power.

Ancestral dream work is a practice where Wiccans seek to connect with their ancestors during sleep, a time when the veil between worlds is thin and receptive. Before bed, practitioners may set an intention to meet with an ancestor, placing an item connected to them under their pillow or lighting a candle before sleep. In dreams, ancestors may appear as guides, teachers, or symbols, providing messages that relate to the practitioner's current life or spiritual path. Upon waking, Wiccans journal these dreams, reflecting on the insights gained and how they might apply to their waking lives.

In addition to individual practices, **group rituals for ancestor honoring** are common during festivals like Samhain, a time when Wiccans believe the veil between worlds is thinnest. At Samhain, many covens and practitioners hold special rites to honor and remember the dead, inviting the presence of loved ones and ancestors to join the celebration. These group rituals create a powerful communal experience, as practitioners honor not only their own ancestors but also the collective spirits who have shaped their culture, traditions, and values. Through these shared rites, Wiccans strengthen their sense of connection to the ancestral lineage that supports their practice.

Ancestral divination is another way that practitioners seek guidance from the spirits of their lineage. Using tools like tarot, runes, or pendulums, Wiccans ask questions and interpret the messages they receive as coming from their ancestors. Some practitioners use specific cards or symbols that they associate with particular ancestors, creating a form of divination that is deeply personal and directed toward family guidance. This type of divination is often used for questions about family matters, personal growth, or spiritual guidance, allowing practitioners to tap into the wisdom of those who have walked before them.

Symbolic acts to honor ancestral values allow practitioners to carry forward the beliefs, virtues, and traditions held by their ancestors. A Wiccan who has learned of their ancestor's reverence for the land, for instance, may choose to perform rituals for environmental healing or conservation. These symbolic acts extend beyond personal gain, contributing to the legacy of values and practices passed down through generations. By honoring the values their ancestors held dear, practitioners reinforce the bond between themselves and their lineage, ensuring that the wisdom of the past lives on.

Reclaiming ancestral knowledge is another important aspect of Wiccan ancestral magic, particularly for those who may have lost cultural or spiritual traditions over time. Some practitioners research historical practices, study folklore, or learn about traditional crafts, seeking to revive and honor these ancestral skills. By reclaiming knowledge that was once part of their heritage, Wiccans feel a deeper connection to their roots and the practices that may have been lost or forgotten. This reclamation enriches their own spiritual path, connecting them to the sacred traditions that shaped their lineage.

Protection rituals for ancestral support are also common in Wiccan practice. Practitioners may ask their ancestors to watch over them, using symbols, amulets, or protective sigils that represent family or cultural heritage. These protective practices call upon the strength and guardianship of the ancestors, creating a shield of familial support. By invoking their ancestors in protection rituals, Wiccans feel a sense of safety and confidence, trusting that their loved ones are guiding and watching over them from beyond.

In daily life, Wiccans may choose to **live in alignment with ancestral wisdom** by incorporating values, practices, and traditions that honor their heritage. They might cook traditional meals, observe cultural holidays, or tell family stories that keep the memory of their ancestors alive. Each act of remembrance strengthens the connection to the past, weaving ancestral influence into everyday life. For Wiccans, honoring the ancestors is not solely a ritual practice but a way of living in tune with the wisdom and legacy of those who came before.

Recording ancestral connections and insights in a Book of Shadows or journal helps Wiccans track their evolving relationship with their lineage. Practitioners may note messages received, dreams, divination outcomes, or feelings of connection that arise in meditation. This record becomes a family history of sorts, preserving the practitioner's journey and interactions with their ancestors. By reflecting on these entries, Wiccans gain a clearer understanding of how their ancestral connections influence their path, building a map of their spiritual lineage that they may one day pass down to future generations.

Ancestral magic in Wicca teaches practitioners to honor the past, recognize the strength of their roots, and seek the guidance of those who came before. This practice is not only about receiving blessings but also about contributing to a legacy of healing, respect, and continuity. Through ancestral magic, Wiccans find belonging, discovering that they are part of a larger story woven by generations of souls who have shared in the cycles of life, death, and rebirth.

In the sacred practice of ancestral magic, Wiccans cultivate a connection that transcends time, honoring those who walked before and opening their hearts to the wisdom that endures across generations. This connection brings comfort, strength, and clarity, guiding practitioners as they walk their own path and adding depth to the journey of the soul. Through ancestral magic, Wiccans affirm that they are never truly alone;

they walk hand in hand with the spirits of their ancestors, carrying forward the torch of wisdom, resilience, and love into the future.

Chapter 45
Power Rituals

Power rituals in Wiccan practice are intricate ceremonies designed to channel intense spiritual energy toward manifesting significant changes, achieving breakthroughs, and enhancing the practitioner's connection to the divine. Unlike everyday rituals or simple spells, power rituals are often complex, deeply intentional, and highly personalized, crafted to align with specific celestial or seasonal energies. These rituals combine various elements—such as invocations, sacred tools, elemental forces, and symbolic actions—to create a heightened spiritual experience. Power rituals serve as transformative rites, allowing practitioners to align fully with their intentions, amplify their inner power, and bring forth profound shifts in their lives and spiritual journey.

The **purpose of a power ritual** varies, often depending on the practitioner's intentions and goals. Power rituals are commonly used for purposes such as self-empowerment, healing, protection, transformation, and invocation of deities or spirits. Each ritual is tailored to align with the practitioner's specific desires, and the ritual's structure, components, and timing are chosen to enhance its potency. Power rituals are moments of deep spiritual commitment, a blend of intention, action, and alignment with the forces of nature that invites the practitioner into a state of elevated consciousness.

Preparation for a power ritual is an essential step, as the success of the ritual depends on the practitioner's mental, emotional, and physical readiness. Wiccans typically begin by cleansing themselves and the ritual space, using practices such as smudging with sage or bathing with salt and herbs. This cleansing removes any residual energies and creates a fresh, receptive environment for the ritual. Practitioners may also prepare by grounding and centering, focusing their minds and calming their spirits to create a state of inner clarity and focus. By entering the ritual with a clear mind and an open heart, practitioners ensure that they are fully aligned with their intentions and the energies they wish to call upon.

Setting up the ritual space is an art in itself, as each element within the space holds meaning and contributes to the ritual's overall power. Wiccans often create a sacred circle, a boundary that separates the mundane from the sacred, providing protection and containment for the energies raised during the ritual. The circle is cast with either a wand, athame, or by visualizing a ring of light, symbolizing the sacred space in which the ritual unfolds. Within this circle, practitioners may arrange candles, crystals, herbs, and other sacred tools, each representing an aspect of the ritual's intention. By setting up a purposeful space, practitioners create an environment that resonates with their goal, enhancing the ritual's effectiveness.

Choosing the timing of the ritual is another important aspect, as certain lunar phases, days, and even hours hold unique energies that support specific intentions. For example, rituals focused on manifestation and growth are often performed during the waxing moon, while the full moon is ideal for rituals that require maximum energy and clarity. The waning moon, by contrast, supports rituals focused on release, banishing, or protection. Many practitioners align their rituals with planetary influences or seasonal festivals, further connecting their work to the natural cycles and increasing the ritual's potency. By choosing the right time, practitioners attune their actions to the rhythms of the cosmos, allowing these forces to amplify their efforts.

Invocations and calling upon deities are commonly used in power rituals to draw in the presence and blessings of specific gods, goddesses, or spirits who resonate with the ritual's purpose. Invoking deities is a way to establish a sacred relationship, asking for guidance, protection, or empowerment. Practitioners may invoke the energy of a particular deity, such as invoking the goddess Diana for protection or the god Apollo for healing. This invocation is done with respect, often through spoken words, chants, or offerings, inviting the deity to join the ritual and lend their energy to the work at hand. This act of invoking elevates the ritual, linking the practitioner's intentions with divine support and guidance.

Elemental work within power rituals involves invoking and balancing the four classical elements—earth, air, fire, and water—each bringing a unique energy that contributes to the ritual's effectiveness. Earth provides grounding, stability, and protection; air brings clarity, inspiration, and communication; fire fuels transformation, passion, and courage; and water offers healing, intuition, and emotional flow. Practitioners may place symbolic representations of each element—such as salt for earth, incense for air, a candle for fire, and water in a chalice—on their altar. By honoring each element, Wiccans balance the forces within the ritual, creating a harmonious space that allows for powerful, multidimensional work.

Chanting and spoken affirmations are frequently incorporated into power rituals as a way to focus energy and reinforce intentions. The power of spoken word in ritual can be profound, as each word carries vibration and meaning. Practitioners may create personalized chants or affirmations that resonate with their goal, repeating them rhythmically to build energy and deepen concentration. These spoken components serve as both a guide for the mind and an anchor for the spirit, allowing practitioners to align their thoughts, emotions, and intentions with the ritual's purpose. As the words are repeated, they become charged with intent, amplifying the energy of the ritual and solidifying the practitioner's focus.

Use of sacred tools within a power ritual enhances the connection between the practitioner and the energies they are working with. Tools such as the athame, wand, chalice, and pentacle each hold specific meanings and contribute unique energies to the ritual. The athame, a ritual knife, represents the element of air or fire and is used to direct energy. The wand channels intent, symbolizing spiritual authority. The chalice, representing water, embodies emotion, intuition, and the connection to the divine feminine. The pentacle, symbolizing earth, grounds and protects. By working with these tools, practitioners infuse the ritual with layers of symbolism, reinforcing their connection to the sacred and strengthening the ritual's impact.

Offerings and symbolic gestures are often made during power rituals as a sign of respect, gratitude, or dedication to the energies or deities involved. Offerings may include flowers, food, incense, or written affirmations, each one symbolizing the practitioner's commitment to their intention and their reverence for the forces they call upon. Practitioners may burn or bury these offerings as a way to release their energy into the universe, showing their dedication and trust in the ritual's outcome. By making offerings, practitioners honor the sacred nature of the ritual, creating a reciprocal flow of energy between themselves and the forces they are working with.

Visualization and energy work are essential components of power rituals, allowing practitioners to direct their personal energy toward their desired outcome. Visualization involves creating a clear mental image of the intended result, seeing it as if it has already been achieved. This image is held in the mind throughout the ritual, serving as a focal point for the energy raised. Practitioners may also perform energy work by drawing energy up from the earth, down from the heavens, or from within, channeling it through their hands or tools and directing it toward the intention. This focused energy amplifies the ritual's power, bridging the physical and spiritual realms to create real, lasting change.

Raising and releasing energy is the culmination of a power ritual, a moment when all gathered energy is channeled toward the intention. This energy may be built through chanting, drumming, movement, or focused visualization. As the energy reaches its peak, practitioners release it with a clear, focused intention, often accompanied by a phrase or gesture that symbolizes the release. This act of release sends the energy out into the universe, carrying the practitioner's intention toward manifestation. The release is both an act of faith and surrender, trusting that the energy will find its mark and bring about the desired change.

Grounding and closing the ritual are essential steps to ensure that the practitioner returns to a balanced state. After releasing the energy, practitioners ground any remaining energy by touching the earth, eating, or visualizing roots extending from their feet into the ground. This grounding restores equilibrium, bringing the practitioner back to the present moment. The circle is then closed with gratitude and reverence, thanking any deities, spirits, or elemental forces who were called upon. This closing brings the ritual to a respectful end, honoring the sacred space that was created and ensuring that all energies are properly balanced.

Reflecting and documenting the ritual in a Book of Shadows or ritual journal allows practitioners to review their experience, noting any insights, feelings, or results. This record provides a valuable reference for future rituals, showing how the practitioner's methods, intentions, and outcomes evolve over time. By reflecting on each ritual's effects, Wiccans deepen their understanding of their own power, recognizing patterns and refining their techniques. This practice of documentation enriches the practitioner's journey, creating a personal archive of their growth and the power they cultivate through ritual.

Power rituals in Wicca are more than acts of magic—they are transformative experiences that connect practitioners to their deepest intentions and to the forces of the universe. Each ritual is an act of courage, a moment of alignment with the sacred, and a step toward self-mastery. Through these ceremonies, Wiccans find empowerment, clarity, and a profound sense of purpose, bringing them closer to their own divine essence and to the magic that lies within and around them.

In the practice of power rituals, Wiccans discover that true magic is a blend of focus, faith, and the willingness to engage fully with one's intentions. These rituals are moments of spiritual transformation, a way to bridge the gap between desire and reality, aligning with the cycles of the earth, the cosmos, and the self. Power rituals teach practitioners to honor their own strength, trust in the energy they cultivate, and walk their path with clarity, purpose, and unwavering confidence. Through this practice, Wiccans embrace their role as co-creators with the universe, wielding their power in harmony with the forces of life and spirit.

Chapter 46
Inner Circles

In Wiccan tradition, an inner circle is a gathering of individuals who share a commitment to learning, practicing, and growing together on the spiritual path. These groups, often referred to as covens, circles, or groves, provide a foundation of mutual support, wisdom, and shared energy, allowing members to deepen their knowledge and practice within a dedicated, sacred space. Inner circles are based on the principles of trust, respect, and shared purpose, making them places of profound connection, transformative experiences, and spiritual development. Through inner circles, Wiccans find a community in which they can explore and honor the mysteries of life in harmony with others, creating a sanctuary where they feel seen, supported, and empowered.

The purpose of an inner circle varies, often shaped by the goals, interests, and values of its members. Some circles focus on magical practice, ritual work, or study, while others emphasize personal growth, healing, or connection with nature. Many inner circles honor the Wiccan wheel of the year, holding gatherings to celebrate the sabbats and esbats, while others may focus on advancing knowledge in areas like herbalism, divination, or energy work. Each circle creates its own unique culture and focus, grounded in the shared commitment of its members to explore and deepen their Wiccan path.

Forming an inner circle is a deliberate and intentional process, as each member contributes to the group's energy, values, and dynamics. For those considering forming or joining a circle, understanding personal intentions, values, and compatibility is key. Trust and harmony among members are essential for the circle's strength, as the work done together often involves deep emotional and spiritual sharing. Many Wiccans choose their circle members carefully, based on shared goals, similar spiritual perspectives, and a willingness to engage in mutual support and respect. By gathering with like-minded individuals, practitioners create an environment where they feel free to explore, experiment, and grow in a supportive, sacred space.

Before formalizing a group, it's common for prospective members to **spend time getting to know one another** in casual settings, discussing their beliefs, expectations, and individual approaches to Wicca. This initial period allows potential members to gauge compatibility, identify shared interests, and ensure that they feel a genuine connection with each other. Once a sense of mutual trust and harmony is established, the group may then decide to formalize its commitment as an inner circle, creating a shared agreement or set of guidelines to honor each member's voice and define the group's purpose.

Creating a group structure that suits everyone's needs is important in an inner circle, as it sets the tone and focus for all group activities. Some inner circles adopt a hierarchical structure, led by an elder or high priestess/priest who guides and mentors the group. Others prefer a more egalitarian model, where each member has an equal role in leading rituals, suggesting topics, or guiding discussions. In many cases, roles may rotate, allowing each member the chance to lead or organize gatherings. This flexible, inclusive approach ensures that each person contributes to the group's growth, fostering a sense of equality, shared purpose, and collaboration.

Crafting a group agreement or charter is a meaningful step in forming an inner circle, outlining the group's purpose, guidelines, and expectations. This agreement may include shared values, such as respect for all members, confidentiality, regular attendance, and commitment to shared learning. It might also establish practices for handling conflict, supporting each other's growth, and respecting boundaries. By crafting this agreement together, members lay a foundation of mutual understanding and commitment, ensuring that everyone feels valued and respected within the group.

In addition to shared values, many inner circles also establish **codes of confidentiality** to protect the privacy of each member and create a safe space for open sharing. This code allows members to speak freely about personal matters, emotions, and spiritual experiences, knowing that what is shared within the circle remains there. This practice of confidentiality is essential for building trust, allowing members to be vulnerable and authentic without fear of judgment or exposure. By honoring each other's privacy, members create a sanctuary of respect, deepening the bonds of trust that hold the circle together.

Establishing group rituals and practices is a central aspect of inner circles, as these shared ceremonies become the spiritual heart of the group. Many circles perform regular rituals for protection, energy-raising, and intention-setting, often aligning these practices with the cycles of the moon or the changing seasons. Each member may contribute to planning and leading these rituals, bringing their own insights, creativity, and knowledge to the circle. These shared rituals reinforce the group's bond, allowing members to experience a collective flow of energy, purpose, and focus that amplifies their individual power.

Celebrating the Wiccan sabbats and esbats is common within inner circles, as these gatherings offer a way to mark the rhythms of the year and honor the phases of the moon. Sabbats are often celebrated with seasonal rites, reflecting the energy of each festival, from the rebirth of the sun at Yule to the harvest celebrations of Lughnasadh and Mabon. Esbats, typically held on the full moon, are moments for personal reflection, divination, and spellwork. These gatherings serve as sacred times when the circle comes together to honor nature's cycles, connecting with the earth, the cosmos, and each other in meaningful ways.

Group meditation and energy work are often integrated into inner circle practices, fostering a shared experience of focus, grounding, and connection. Meditation helps each member attune to the group's collective energy, harmonizing their individual vibrations with the circle as a whole. Through energy work, such as group visualizations or Reiki, practitioners support one another in healing, protection, and spiritual growth. This energy-sharing creates a field of collective power, a tangible force that enhances each member's experience, allowing them to connect with energies that are greater than their own.

Teaching and knowledge-sharing are vital aspects of inner circles, as members often have diverse skills, insights, and areas of expertise. Each person brings their unique knowledge to the group, whether in herbalism, tarot, ritual crafting, or other areas of Wiccan practice. Members may take turns leading workshops, guiding discussions, or teaching new techniques, creating a shared learning environment where everyone has the opportunity to expand their understanding. This culture of mutual learning strengthens the circle, allowing each member to feel valued and enriched by the collective wisdom of the group.

Inner circles often include **rites of passage and personal ceremonies** that honor significant milestones in each member's life. These rites can mark life transitions such as birth, marriage, initiation, or even a change in spiritual focus. By creating and performing these rituals together, the circle acknowledges and supports each member's personal journey, providing a sense of belonging and affirmation. Such rites are sacred moments that reflect the depth of connection within the circle, a shared recognition of each individual's growth and transformation.

Dealing with conflicts within an inner circle is a necessary and often sensitive aspect of group dynamics. In any gathering of individuals, differing opinions, personalities, or misunderstandings may arise. Many inner circles establish guidelines for addressing conflicts, encouraging open communication, respect, and active listening. Some groups use practices such as speaking circles, where each person has an uninterrupted chance to voice their perspective, allowing everyone to feel heard and understood. By handling conflicts with care, the group fosters resilience and respect, strengthening the bonds that hold the circle together.

Commitment to regular meetings is essential for maintaining the energy and connection within an inner circle. Many groups meet weekly, biweekly, or monthly, with each gathering serving as a time to reconnect, share experiences, and perform rituals. Regular meetings provide a structure that supports the group's intentions, allowing members to engage deeply with their practice and to continue building trust and camaraderie. Each meeting becomes a touchstone for the group's collective journey, an opportunity to renew their shared purpose and commitment.

Documenting group experiences and insights in a shared Book of Shadows or group journal allows the inner circle to reflect on its journey, tracking rituals, insights, and collective growth. Members may contribute to this record, noting rituals performed, symbols used, and any messages or outcomes. Over time, this collective Book of Shadows becomes a sacred archive of the group's experiences, a testament to their shared journey and the knowledge they have built together. Reviewing this record deepens the circle's sense of continuity, reminding each member of their contribution and connection to the group's legacy.

Closing and honoring the group's journey is an important ritual if the circle reaches a natural end. Some inner circles form for specific purposes or periods and may decide to dissolve once their work is complete. This process is often honored with a closing ritual, celebrating the time shared and offering blessings for each member's path forward. Such ceremonies acknowledge the sacred bond that was created, allowing each person to depart with a sense of fulfillment, gratitude, and closure.

In the formation and development of inner circles, Wiccans find both a community and a shared spiritual experience, a place where each person's strengths, insights, and spirit are valued. These circles are not just gatherings—they are sacred containers that hold the transformative power of shared energy, intention, and wisdom. Through the collective practice of Wicca, inner circles become vessels of growth, healing, and profound connection, guiding each member on a journey that is enriched by the presence of others.

In joining an inner circle, Wiccans discover that they are part of a greater spiritual family, a community that honors the individual journey within the collective. These circles embody the spirit of Wicca itself—unity, respect, reverence for the cycles of life, and a commitment to learning and growing together. Through inner circles, Wiccans embrace a path of shared strength, wisdom, and transformation, walking side by side as they explore the mysteries of magic and spirit together.

Chapter 47
Personal Initiation

Personal initiation is a profound rite of passage in Wiccan practice, marking an individual's conscious and dedicated commitment to the Wiccan path. Unlike formal initiations performed within a coven, personal initiation is a private and deeply personal experience, an intentional act through which practitioners declare themselves to the path, the divine, and the mysteries of Wicca. It is a spiritual milestone, a moment of self-dedication where the practitioner steps fully into their role as a seeker of wisdom, an embodiment of Wiccan values, and a steward of sacred knowledge. This chapter explores the meaning, process, and power of personal initiation, guiding practitioners through the preparation, ritual, and symbolism that make this ceremony transformative and enduring.

In Wicca, **personal initiation holds profound meaning** as it symbolizes a conscious choice to walk a path of reverence, learning, and self-discovery. This initiation is not merely a ritual but a commitment to align one's life with the principles and practices of Wicca, such as respect for nature, pursuit of wisdom, and honoring of the divine. The act of initiating oneself is a declaration of intent, a way of saying "yes" to the journey ahead, with all its joys, challenges, and mysteries. It is a way to honor the sacred calling within, embracing Wicca not as an external set of practices but as an intrinsic part of one's being.

Preparing for personal initiation involves reflection, introspection, and clear intention. This phase is a time to examine one's motivations, beliefs, and goals, ensuring that the decision to initiate is grounded in authenticity and readiness. Practitioners may spend weeks, months, or even years exploring their spirituality, studying Wiccan teachings, and practicing rituals before feeling prepared for initiation. Journaling, meditation, and self-reflective questions are common practices during this time, allowing the practitioner to deepen their understanding of Wicca and clarify their intentions. This preparation is an act of dedication in itself, a way to honor the sacredness of the commitment they are about to make.

One powerful preparatory practice is the **creation of a personal vow or dedication statement**, in which practitioners articulate their commitment to the Wiccan path. This statement may include intentions to live in harmony with nature, seek wisdom, practice compassion, or honor the divine. The vow can be written in a journal, on parchment, or spoken aloud during the initiation ritual. By crafting this vow, practitioners crystallize their commitment, creating a personal charter that will guide them on their path. This statement serves as an anchor, a reminder of the promises made during the initiation that can be revisited in moments of challenge or reflection.

Choosing the time and place for initiation is a sacred act, as both the environment and timing contribute to the ritual's power and significance. Many practitioners feel drawn to perform their initiation at a place in nature that resonates with them—a forest, beach, meadow, or mountain—where they feel a sense of connection and belonging. The timing of the initiation can align with natural cycles, such as a full moon for illumination, a new moon for new beginnings, or a seasonal sabbat that reflects their personal journey. These choices bring layers of meaning to the ritual, allowing the practitioner to feel aligned with the forces of nature as they step onto their path.

Creating a sacred space for the initiation ritual is essential, as this space will hold the energy of the dedication and commitment. Practitioners may cast a circle to protect and contain the energy, symbolizing a sacred boundary between the mundane and spiritual realms. The circle may be marked with stones, candles, flowers, or other items that hold personal meaning. An altar is often set up within the circle, adorned with symbols of the elements—earth, air, fire, and water—and items that resonate with the practitioner's intentions, such as crystals, herbs, or representations of the goddess and god. This sacred space becomes a vessel for transformation, holding the practitioner in a field of protection, focus, and reverence.

The **components of the initiation ritual** are often personalized, allowing each practitioner to create a ceremony that resonates deeply with their spirit. Common elements include cleansing, invoking the elements, calling upon the divine, making a vow, and performing a symbolic act to mark the transition. Cleansing may involve a ritual bath with herbs or salt, symbolizing purification and readiness. Invoking the elements brings balance and harmony, calling upon the earth for grounding, air for clarity, fire for courage, and water for emotional flow. This invocation connects the practitioner with the natural world, reinforcing their commitment to live in harmony with the elements.

Calling upon the divine is a central part of many personal initiation rituals, as practitioners invite the presence of the goddess, god, or other deities they feel aligned with. This invocation may be done through prayer, meditation, or visualization, asking for blessings, guidance, and support on their journey. Some practitioners feel called to work with a particular deity who resonates with their spirit and values, while others may invoke the divine as a more universal, archetypal presence. This connection to the divine reinforces the practitioner's sense of purpose and belonging, grounding their initiation in a relationship with the sacred.

Making a vow of dedication is a powerful moment in the ritual, a verbal or silent affirmation of the practitioner's commitment to the Wiccan path. This vow may be spoken aloud, written, or held in the heart, depending on the practitioner's preference. It often includes promises to uphold Wiccan values, seek truth, respect all life, and honor the sacred. This vow is an intimate exchange between the practitioner and their own soul, a way of solidifying the dedication they feel within. By speaking or affirming their commitment, practitioners give voice to their intentions, infusing their words with energy, focus, and conviction.

Symbolic acts to mark the transition are often included in personal initiation rituals, representing the transformation from seeker to dedicated practitioner. This act might be as simple as lighting a candle, tying a ribbon, or holding a special object that represents the path ahead. Some practitioners may choose to anoint themselves with oil, symbolic of blessing and consecration, or to touch the earth, grounding themselves in the support of the natural world. This symbolic action makes the commitment tangible, anchoring the spiritual promise in the physical realm.

Grounding and closing the ritual brings the initiation to a respectful and intentional end, allowing the practitioner to return to everyday consciousness. After the vow and symbolic act, practitioners may take a moment to feel the energy of their dedication settle within them, visualizing it as a flame or light within the heart. The circle is then closed with gratitude, thanking the elements, spirits, or deities who were called upon. By closing the ritual, practitioners honor the sacred space they created, allowing the energies to be released and balanced as they step forward into their new role.

Commemorating the initiation is an act of respect for the commitment made. Practitioners may keep a token or object as a reminder of their initiation, such as a piece of jewelry, a candle, or a crystal. They may also record the experience in their Book of Shadows, noting the date, time, place, and any significant insights, emotions, or visions that arose during the ritual. This record becomes a personal artifact, a point of reference they can look back on as they journey further on their path. By commemorating the initiation, practitioners honor the sacredness of the moment and affirm the promises they made.

Integrating the initiation into daily life is the ongoing journey that follows the ritual, as each day presents an opportunity to live in alignment with the vows made. Practitioners may create daily or weekly practices that reflect their commitment, such as meditation, journaling, ritual, or honoring the cycles of nature. These practices keep the energy of the initiation alive, reinforcing the bond between the practitioner and their spiritual path. Each small act becomes an extension of the initiation, a way of embodying the sacred in everyday life and deepening their connection to Wiccan values and wisdom.

Reflecting on the initiation over time allows practitioners to revisit their vows, understanding how their intentions have grown or evolved. This reflection might take place at significant moments, such as an anniversary of the initiation or during key seasonal festivals. By revisiting their vows, practitioners reconnect with their original intent, gaining insight into their personal and spiritual growth. This reflection is a celebration of the journey, a recognition of the transformations that have unfolded since that first commitment.

In the sacred act of personal initiation, Wiccans find a profound connection to their inner self, the divine, and the mysteries of the path. This rite of passage is both a beginning and a deepening, a threshold crossed with courage, commitment, and clarity. Through personal initiation, Wiccans embrace their journey with intention, stepping forward with the knowledge that they are dedicated, empowered, and aligned with the sacred forces that shape life.

The journey of personal initiation is one of transformation, as practitioners claim their identity as seekers of truth, guardians of wisdom, and practitioners of Wiccan tradition. This initiation is not an end but a beginning, a door that opens onto a lifelong path of discovery, learning, and growth. Through this rite of dedication, Wiccans honor the sacred calling within, becoming bearers of light, stewards of nature, and voices for the divine, walking their path with grace, strength, and unwavering purpose.

Chapter 48
Wiccan Priesthood

The Wiccan priesthood represents a profound level of commitment and responsibility within the Wiccan path, embodying both spiritual leadership and service to the divine and community. Unlike many hierarchical religious traditions, Wicca sees the priesthood as accessible to all practitioners who choose to dedicate themselves to this deeper role. Becoming a Wiccan priest or priestess is an act of devotion that requires a comprehensive understanding of Wiccan practices, rituals, ethics, and the ability to guide others on their spiritual journeys. This chapter explores the roles, responsibilities, and sacred duties of the Wiccan priesthood, guiding those who feel called to serve in this capacity and providing insights into the path of spiritual dedication, community, and mastery.

In Wicca, **the role of a priest or priestess** is to serve as a bridge between the divine and the earthly, guiding others in rituals, teaching the wisdom of the Craft, and fostering a sense of community and sacred connection. Wiccan priests and priestesses act as facilitators for the spiritual growth of others, creating spaces where magic, learning, and transformation can occur. This role is not about power or authority; rather, it is about humility, dedication, and the willingness to serve the needs of both individuals and the larger community. Those who take on this role embody the ideals of Wicca, living by its values and serving as examples for others to follow.

The calling to priesthood often begins with a personal, internal prompting—a sense of responsibility, purpose, or deep connection with the divine that inspires practitioners to dedicate themselves to a path of service. This calling is typically experienced as a gradual realization, often emerging after years of personal practice, study, and introspection. Wiccans who feel drawn to the priesthood are often motivated by a desire to support others, guide rituals, and cultivate a life that honors the divine through acts of compassion, teaching, and dedication. Responding to this calling involves not only understanding one's purpose but also embracing the spiritual growth and discipline needed to fulfill the role.

Training for the priesthood is essential, as the responsibilities of a Wiccan priest or priestess require a strong foundation of knowledge, practice, and self-discipline. This training often includes advanced study of Wiccan philosophy, ethics, ritual design, and the skills necessary for spiritual guidance and counseling. Some practitioners pursue this training within a coven under the mentorship of an elder or high priestess/priest, while others embark on a solitary path of study. Training also includes mastery of various magical techniques, such as energy work, divination, healing, and protection, as well as the ability to lead others through these practices with confidence and respect.

For those training in covens, **the mentorship process** plays a crucial role, allowing future priests and priestesses to learn through direct experience, observation, and feedback from experienced elders. Mentors guide trainees through the intricacies of ritual leadership, ethical considerations, and the spiritual demands of the role. This relationship provides a safe and supportive environment where trainees can develop their skills, reflect on their growth, and receive guidance on challenges. The mentorship process often includes regular check-ins, opportunities to lead rituals under supervision, and constructive feedback, all of which help aspiring priests and priestesses mature in their path.

Self-initiation and solitary study are also valid paths to the priesthood in Wicca, allowing practitioners to develop their skills independently through rigorous study and practice. Solitary practitioners often follow a structured curriculum that includes extensive reading, self-reflection, ritual work, and mastery of Wiccan techniques. Many create a personal Book of Shadows to document their learning, insights, and ritual experiences, building a record of their journey. Solitary Wiccans on the path to priesthood must develop strong self-discipline, patience, and integrity, trusting in their inner guidance and the divine as they progress.

Ethics and integrity are cornerstones of the Wiccan priesthood, as those who serve in this role are expected to uphold the highest standards of honesty, compassion, and responsibility. Wiccan priests and priestesses are bound by the Wiccan Rede—"An it harm none, do what ye will"—and are called to live by this principle in all aspects of their lives. This ethical code extends to their work with others, requiring respect for each individual's autonomy, privacy, and spiritual beliefs. Practicing ethics in priesthood includes being mindful of the influence one holds, using it only to uplift, empower, and guide others in ways that are supportive and non-intrusive.

Leading rituals and ceremonies is a significant responsibility of the Wiccan priesthood. Priests and priestesses are often called upon to design, organize, and lead rituals that honor the cycles of the moon, the seasons, and other spiritual milestones. Ritual leadership involves understanding the structure, flow, and energy of a ceremony, from casting the circle to raising energy, performing invocations, and conducting the closing. Leading rituals also requires sensitivity to the group's needs, flexibility, and the ability to adapt rituals for diverse settings and individuals. A skilled priest or priestess creates a safe and sacred space, guiding participants through an experience that allows for spiritual connection, healing, and transformation.

Celebrating life passages is another sacred duty of Wiccan priests and priestesses, as they often officiate rites of passage such as handfastings (marriages), blessings, initiations, and funerals. These ceremonies mark significant transitions in life, providing support, recognition, and meaning. In these rites, the priest or priestess acts as a facilitator, honoring the personal journey of the individuals involved and offering blessings for their path ahead. These ceremonies are crafted with care, honoring the uniqueness of each person's journey while drawing upon Wiccan symbolism and tradition. By officiating these passages, Wiccan priests and priestesses provide comfort, guidance, and a sense of continuity, strengthening the bonds between individuals, community, and the sacred.

Providing spiritual guidance and support is a core aspect of the Wiccan priesthood, requiring both empathy and wisdom. Wiccan priests and priestesses may serve as mentors, counselors, or confidants for those seeking guidance, helping them navigate personal challenges, spiritual questions, or moments of doubt. This role requires active listening, an open heart, and the ability to offer guidance without imposing personal beliefs or judgments. Spiritual guidance may also include teaching meditation, visualization, and other tools for self-discovery, empowering individuals to connect with their inner wisdom and the divine.

Community building and outreach are also significant aspects of the Wiccan priesthood, as priests and priestesses often work to foster a supportive and inclusive community. This might involve organizing gatherings, hosting study groups, or facilitating open rituals where newcomers can learn about Wicca in a welcoming environment. Community-building also includes outreach, providing information and resources to dispel misconceptions about Wicca and fostering a sense of unity and understanding within the larger society. Wiccan priests and priestesses are often called upon to represent Wicca in interfaith settings, advocating for respect, tolerance, and understanding across spiritual traditions.

Personal development and continual learning are essential for those who choose the path of the priesthood, as this role requires a lifelong commitment to growth, self-reflection, and learning. Wiccan priests and priestesses continually expand their knowledge, studying various aspects of Wicca, magic, healing, divination, and spiritual philosophy. Many also seek to understand other spiritual paths, broadening their perspective and deepening their empathy. Personal development may include meditation, journaling, shadow work, or other practices that foster self-awareness, allowing the priest or priestess to serve from a place of clarity, compassion, and groundedness.

Building a personal relationship with the divine is central to the Wiccan priesthood, as priests and priestesses are seen as channels for divine energy and wisdom. This relationship is cultivated through regular meditation, prayer, ritual, and communion with the natural world. Many Wiccan priests and priestesses feel a connection to specific deities, archetypes, or spirits, building a relationship that supports and guides their work. This bond with the divine provides strength, inspiration, and clarity, grounding the priest or priestess in a sense of purpose and reinforcing their commitment to their spiritual path.

Protecting sacred spaces and resources is another duty of the Wiccan priesthood, as priests and priestesses are stewards of both physical and energetic spaces. This includes maintaining altars, ritual tools, and sacred objects with care and respect. It also involves cleansing, protecting, and consecrating spaces for rituals and gatherings, ensuring that these environments remain safe, supportive, and conducive to spiritual work. Through this stewardship, Wiccan priests and priestesses honor the sanctity of the spaces they inhabit, creating environments that support healing, connection, and transformation.

Documenting one's journey in the priesthood through a personal Book of Shadows or journal allows priests and priestesses to reflect on their growth, challenges, and insights over time. This record becomes a source of wisdom and inspiration, a personal archive of rituals led, insights gained, and lessons learned. Many priests and priestesses view their documentation as a legacy they may one day pass down to future practitioners, preserving the knowledge and experiences gained over a lifetime of spiritual service. This act of documentation honors the sacredness of the path, providing a source of inspiration for future generations.

Balancing service with self-care is crucial for Wiccan priests and priestesses, as the demands of spiritual service can be emotionally and energetically intense. Maintaining personal boundaries, grounding, and regular self-care practices ensures that they remain balanced, healthy, and centered. Self-care might include daily meditation, spending time in nature, or engaging in practices that restore their energy. By prioritizing their well-being, priests and priestesses are better able to serve others with integrity and compassion, maintaining a sustainable path of spiritual service.

The path of the Wiccan priesthood is a journey of dedication, transformation, and deep connection with the divine. Through this role, Wiccan priests and priestesses become vessels of wisdom, compassion, and healing, offering guidance to those who seek the mysteries of Wicca. This path is both a privilege and a responsibility, a way of embodying the principles of Wicca and serving as a beacon of light, inspiration, and guidance.

In choosing the path of the priesthood, Wiccans embrace a life of service, devotion, and continued growth, walking a path that honors the cycles of nature, the wisdom of the divine, and the sacredness of all beings. Through the Wiccan priesthood, they become keepers of ancient knowledge, protectors of the sacred, and mentors to those who walk the path. This journey is one of profound beauty, purpose, and transformation, a testament to the enduring spirit of Wicca and the divine calling that guides all who embrace this sacred role.

Chapter 49
Spiritual Legacy

The concept of spiritual legacy in Wiccan practice extends beyond personal experience, connecting practitioners to the lineage of Wicca, the ancestors who laid the foundations of the Craft, and the future generations who will carry it forward. Spiritual legacy is the act of preserving, teaching, and passing on the knowledge, practices, and values that define the Wiccan path. Through the creation of a spiritual legacy, practitioners ensure that the wisdom they have gained on their journey remains a beacon for others, nurturing a lineage of seekers, teachers, and guardians of sacred knowledge. This chapter explores the meaning and methods of creating a Wiccan spiritual legacy, offering guidance on how to preserve one's teachings, support the growth of others, and honor the enduring spirit of Wicca.

In Wicca, **spiritual legacy is both a personal and communal responsibility**, a way of honoring the path that has guided countless practitioners over centuries and leaving a foundation for those yet to come. This legacy includes the preservation of rituals, philosophies, spells, and teachings, but it also embodies the essence of the Wiccan values of respect, harmony, and reverence for life. Creating a spiritual legacy allows practitioners to contribute to the larger tapestry of Wicca, building a bridge between past, present, and future. It is an act of devotion to the path and a recognition of the interconnectedness of all who walk it.

Documenting personal experiences, insights, and rituals is a central aspect of creating a Wiccan legacy, allowing practitioners to record their journey, practices, and revelations in a way that others can access and learn from. Many Wiccans keep a Book of Shadows or a spiritual journal where they document spells, rituals, correspondences, and personal reflections. This record becomes not only a guide for the practitioner's own path but also a resource that can be shared with students, coven members, or family. By preserving their journey in written form, practitioners create a lasting testament to their dedication and wisdom, providing future generations with a window into their experiences and insights.

Teaching and mentoring others is another powerful way to create a spiritual legacy, as sharing knowledge with others perpetuates the values and practices of Wicca. Mentoring can occur formally within a coven or study group or informally through discussions, guidance, and support. Those who choose to teach or mentor others offer their skills and knowledge, empowering new practitioners to walk their path with confidence and integrity. Mentoring involves both sharing practical skills—such as casting circles, crafting spells, and working with elements—and imparting the ethical and philosophical foundations of Wicca. By guiding others, Wiccans create a ripple effect, ensuring that the teachings continue to thrive and evolve within the community.

Passing down sacred tools and artifacts is a cherished tradition in Wicca, where ritual tools, books, and symbols hold energy and history. Practitioners may choose to gift or bequeath these items to students, family members, or other practitioners, believing that the energy infused within them will support the next generation. A wand, chalice, or athame passed down from a mentor carries a sense of continuity, a tangible link to those who have walked the path before. This act of gifting sacred items creates a chain of connection that honors both the tools and the practices they represent, ensuring that the spirit of Wicca lives on through these objects of power.

Writing about Wicca for a wider audience allows practitioners to reach those who may not have access to a coven or teacher, sharing their insights with the broader Wiccan and spiritual community. Many Wiccans write books, articles, or blogs, contributing to the body of literature available to seekers around the world. By sharing their knowledge, practitioners make Wicca accessible, breaking down misconceptions and opening doors for others to explore the Craft. These writings serve as a form of legacy, a way to preserve the author's unique understanding of Wicca while also guiding others on their path.

Creating or contributing to communal spaces dedicated to Wiccan practice, such as coven temples, sacred groves, or community altars, is another way to establish a legacy. These spaces become gathering places for rituals, seasonal celebrations, and study, providing a physical location where practitioners can connect, learn, and honor the divine. By establishing or supporting such spaces, Wiccans leave a lasting contribution to the community, ensuring that future practitioners have a place to experience and grow in their spiritual journey. These sacred spaces are tangible embodiments of the Wiccan values of connection and reverence for nature, providing a sanctuary for generations to come.

Participating in environmental preservation is also seen as part of a Wiccan legacy, as reverence for nature is a cornerstone of Wiccan practice. Many Wiccans engage in environmental work, such as conservation, reforestation, or ecological education, as a way to honor and protect the earth. By supporting these efforts, practitioners contribute to the health and vitality of the natural world, ensuring that future generations inherit a planet that is vibrant, diverse, and sacred. Environmental work embodies the Wiccan ethic of "harm none" and extends the legacy of Wicca beyond individuals and communities to encompass the earth itself.

Fostering inclusivity and acceptance within the Wiccan community is another vital aspect of creating a legacy that reflects Wiccan values. Those who create welcoming spaces, encourage diversity, and support practitioners of all backgrounds contribute to a culture of respect and inclusivity. By actively working to make Wicca accessible and open to all, practitioners foster a legacy of compassion and unity, creating a community that values each person's unique journey. This inclusive spirit reflects the Wiccan belief in the sacredness of all beings and ensures that future practitioners feel welcome, valued, and respected.

Sharing traditional wisdom while encouraging evolution is an essential balance in creating a Wiccan legacy. Practitioners who preserve traditional rituals, beliefs, and symbols also recognize the importance of adaptability, encouraging future generations to refine, question, and expand upon these foundations. This balance allows Wicca to remain a living, evolving tradition that respects its roots while growing to meet the needs of each generation. By fostering both preservation and innovation, Wiccans create a legacy that is dynamic, resilient, and true to the spirit of the Craft.

Connecting with and honoring ancestral knowledge is another way to build a Wiccan legacy, as practitioners draw strength and wisdom from those who walked the path before. Many Wiccans feel a strong connection to the ancestors of the Craft—those who practiced witchcraft, preserved folk knowledge, or honored the old ways. This connection is honored through ancestor rituals, historical research, and the preservation of folklore and traditions. By acknowledging and learning from these ancestors, practitioners ensure that their legacy is rooted in a lineage of resilience, wisdom, and devotion.

Encouraging self-discovery and individual empowerment is a hallmark of the Wiccan path, and those who inspire others to trust their own intuition contribute to a legacy of independence and self-respect. Wiccan teachers, mentors, and writers often emphasize the importance of personal connection with the divine and individual exploration of the path. By encouraging self-discovery, Wiccans foster a legacy of empowerment, inspiring future generations to honor their own truths and to walk their spiritual path with confidence, courage, and authenticity.

Creating a personal Book of Shadows for future generations is a powerful way to preserve one's spiritual journey, wisdom, and practices. This sacred text may contain spells, rituals, meditations, and reflections that hold personal meaning, capturing the unique insights and experiences of the practitioner. Some Wiccans choose to pass down their Book of Shadows to a trusted student, family member, or fellow practitioner, ensuring that their knowledge and legacy are preserved. This book becomes a living artifact, a source of guidance and inspiration that carries forward the essence of the practitioner's journey and dedication to the Craft.

Inspiring future generations through example is perhaps the most profound form of spiritual legacy, as actions often speak louder than words. By living in alignment with Wiccan values—honoring nature, practicing kindness, seeking wisdom, and living with integrity—practitioners serve as role models for others. The legacy they leave is not only in the rituals, writings, or teachings they produce but in the way they live their lives. Those who walk the path with humility, reverence, and dedication become a source of inspiration, lighting the way for others to follow and embodying the heart of Wicca.

Celebrating and reflecting on the legacy created can be a sacred practice in itself, as practitioners look back on their journey, their contributions, and the lives they have touched. This reflection may occur in solitude or as part of a ritual, honoring the dedication, learning, and experiences that have shaped their path. Practitioners may offer gratitude to the mentors, guides, and divine forces that have supported them, recognizing that their legacy is part of a larger tapestry woven by many hands and spirits.

Through the creation of a spiritual legacy, Wiccans contribute to the enduring presence of the Craft, ensuring that its wisdom, magic, and beauty continue to flourish. This legacy is not limited to tangible artifacts or teachings but includes the values, intentions, and energy that practitioners infuse into the world. Wicca lives on through each generation, shaped by the contributions of those who came before and enriched by the spirits of those yet to come.

In honoring the past, guiding the present, and inspiring the future, Wiccans embody the essence of the Craft—a tradition that is both timeless and evolving, rooted in the cycles of nature and the mysteries of the divine. Through their legacy, they affirm the sacredness of life, the power of the earth, and the wisdom of the unseen, leaving a mark on the world that is as enduring as it is beautiful. As each practitioner walks their path, they become part of a living lineage, a testament to the resilience, magic, and spirit of Wicca—a legacy that will continue to light the way for generations yet to come.

Epilogue

You have reached the end of this work, yet the journey it inspires is only beginning. Through these pages, you have been guided to look beyond the obvious, to explore the unknown, and to recognize the ancient wisdom inhabiting every aspect of existence. Now, as you close this book, you carry with you more than words or concepts; you carry a new perception of the world and of yourself. The energies that flow through all that lives and breathes, the forces of the elements, the eternal cycles, and the sacred balance between masculine and feminine—all of this has found a place in your heart and soul.

The knowledge you have found here is not an ending but an invitation to continue seeking and discovering. The practice of Wicca is like a mirror, reflecting what you offer the universe and revealing that true wisdom lies in living in harmony with the whole. You have been called to respect the energies around you, and in doing so, you have learned to respect yourself. This is a journey of continuous growth, where each step reveals a bit more of life's mystery.

The understanding of natural cycles and the energies that move the universe leads you to see existence with reverence and gratitude. You now understand that life is not a straight line but an eternally turning wheel. This knowledge allows you to face change with wisdom and serenity, knowing that each end brings within it a new beginning. And thus, the story of your life intertwines with the story of the Earth, as part of a greater, sacred whole.

What you have learned and experienced throughout this book prepares you to live consciously and fully. The Wiccan journey is one of self-discovery, an awakening that unfolds a little more each day. No matter how far you go, the sacred is always around you, in the trees, in the waters, and in the stars, waiting for you to look and see the reflection of the divine. The practices and teachings shared in this book are not merely rituals; they are reminders that you are part of a cosmic dance and that the balance between opposing forces within you is the key to peace.

So, as you close this book, carry with you the certainty that magic exists in every moment of life. It is in the simple act of breathing, in the silence of nature, and in communion with others. And remember: you carry within you the spark of the divine, the same energy that moves the cosmos and gives life to all. Honor that spark, care for what is sacred, and share that light with the world around you.

This is not the end of your spiritual journey; it is only a step among many to come. May you continue to explore, to learn, and to grow, carrying with you the knowledge that each act of love, respect, and harmony is an act of magic. May the journey back to your roots, to your essence, and to unity with the whole guide you to a life that is full and meaningful. May you always find, in the universe's reflection, the wisdom and strength to live in peace and balance.